The Road to West 43rd Street

Also by Nash K. Burger

Confederate Spy: Rose O'Neale Greenhow
South of Appomattox with John K. Bettersworth

The

ROAD

to

WEST
43rd
STREET

Nash K. Burger
with
Pearl A. McHaney

Afterword by
EUDORA WELTY

University Press of Mississippi
Jackson

Eudora Welty's address "Nash K. Burger Jr. of Jackson, Miss." is printed here with permission.

Excerpts from Nash K. Burger's essays "Eudora Welty's Monsieur Boule and Other Friends: A Memoir of Good Times," *Southern Quarterly* 32, no. 1 (Fall 1993), "Eudora Welty's Jackson," *Shenandoah* 20, no. 3 (Spring 1969), and "Truth or Consequence: Books and Book Reviewing," *South Atlantic Quarterly* 68, no. 2 (Spring 1969) are reprinted with permission.

Photographs from the Eudora Welty Collection at the Mississippi Department of Archives and History, the general collection of the Mississippi Department of Archives and History, the Alumni Office of Millsaps College, Louis Lyell, Lorna Stark, Maggie Berkvist, and NYT Pictures are reprinted with permission.

The paper in this book meets the guidelines for permanence and durability of the Committee on Production Guidelines for Book Longevity of the Council on Library Resources.

Library of Congress Cataloging-in-Publication Data

Burger, Nash K. (Nash Kerr)
    The road to West 43rd Street / Nash K. Burger with Pearl A. McHaney.
      p.   cm.
    Includes index.
    ISBN 0-87805-793-5 (alk. paper)
      1. Burger, Nash K. (Nash Kerr)   2. Journalists—United States—Biography.
    3. Book reviewing.   I. McHaney, Pearl Amelia.   II. Title.
    PN4874.B834A3   1995
    070 '.92—dc20
    [B]   95-11739
                                                                              CIP

British Library Cataloging-in-Publication data available

To my father and mother

Nash Kerr Burger, Sr.
1868—1936

Clara Isabel Eddy Burger
1880—1973

We think our fathers fools, so wise we grow,
Our wiser sons, no doubt, will think us so.

Alexander Pope
"An Essay on Criticism"

Contents

Acknowledgments

The writing of this book was suggested to me by Noel Polk, professor of English at the University of Southern Mississippi, at our first meeting in the Rare Book Room of the University of Virginia's Alderman Library. My initial response was, "That sounds like work." It was.

Seetha Srinivasan of the University Press of Mississippi issued the formal invitation to proceed and on my acceptance began the long months of advice and encouragement that proved helpful.

Completion of the task was only made possible by the tireless and intelligent cooperation of Pearl Amelia McHaney, who researched and rounded up documents, discovered and cross-examined witnesses, transcribed, photocopied and kept mail and phone communications between Georgia, Mississippi and Virginia humming. She wrote, edited, cajoled, and when necessary she acquiesced.

Robert James Landis, longtime Jackson friend and fellow teacher at Central High, supplied useful recollections and documents of olden times and, best of all, was ever encouraging.

Louis Lyell, whose Jackson family and mine have been friends since the century began, furnished helpful suggestions and information from family papers, especially as relating to his elder brother Frank, one of Eudora's closest friends.

Also generously giving help and encouragement in numerous ways were Hank Holmes and his staff at the Mississippi Department of Archives and History; the librarians of the Eudora Welty Library in Jackson, the Alderman Library at the University of Virginia, and the Pullen Library at Georgia State University; the Galloway School in Atlanta, Georgia; and LeAnne Benfield and Tom McHaney.

And as always the first reader of the manuscript as it processed from the typewriter was my wife Marjorie Williams Burger, ever vigilant for typos, misspellings, gaucheries, non sequiturs and errors of fact. No matter the final quality, she manages to find words of cheer. Woe betide the critic who thinks otherwise.

And to Eudora Alice Welty, whose grace and favor are so evident in these pages, two words much favored by Miss Lotte Eckhart of the story "June Recital": *Danke schoen.*

The Road to West 43rd Street

ONE

Early Years in
Jackson-on-the-Pearl

My parents, Nash Kerr Burger, a thirty-four-year-old native of Botetourt County, Virginia, and Clara Isabel Eddy, a twenty-two-year-old native of Somerville, Massachusetts, were married in Boston on July 16, 1902, by the pastor of the Ruggles St. Baptist Church in Boston's Roxbury. The marriage took place "at the residence of the bride's father, Mr. Frederick Eddy," as the groom's hometown paper in Fincastle, Virginia, dutifully reported a few days later, adding that "Mr. Burger is a genial and popular young man, a traveling salesman for a large boot and shoe house of Boston."

Six years later, on the eighth of September, in Jackson, Mississippi, I was born in a house on the southwest corner of North and Mississippi Streets.

How did this North-South romance and marriage come about? Probably as a result of that event to which so many events in our history have been ascribed—the War Between the States.

Henry Burger, born in Germany, settled in Botetourt County in 1793 just south of the James River. He married Anne Warner in 1795. On the family's two-hundred-acre farm, my father, Henry's great-grandson, was born in 1868.

My mother's immigrant ancestor, John Eddy, son of the vicar of St. Dunstan's Church, Cranbrook, Kent, had come from England to the Massachusetts Bay Colony in 1630. He settled in Watertown, his descendants spreading and prospering in the region, my Eddy grandfather being born in New Hampshire.

A near relative married a certain Mary Baker, henceforth better known as Mary Baker Eddy, founder of Christian Science. Another Eddy relation married a Stearns, descendant of that Isaak Stearns who, like John Eddy, came to Watertown from England in the 1630s, making me a kinsman of poet Thomas Stearns Eliot, whose mother was a Stearns. Other notable New England connections are of record, but by the time my mother was born in Somerville in 1880, things were modest enough.

My mother's father, Frederick Eddy, was a bookkeeper who commuted to a Boston job, found a wife, Clara Emily Kelley, in that city's Roxbury section (Edgar Allan Poe had been born just around the corner) and struggled, not always successfully, to support himself and family while indulging in the distractions of city life. Fortunately there was at hand a benevolent aunt, an indomitable Unitarian spinster right out of the pages of Henry James's *The Bostonians.*

Aunt Nell saw to it that my mother was clothed, fed, kept in school ("such a pretty, little thing," her teacher wrote Aunt Nell) and instilled with the proper New England virtues. Aunt Nell's oversight proved effective, and by the turn of the century my mother was living in Boston with her sister Mae and working as a secretary in a Boston department store when my father, the young traveling salesman from Virginia, turned up.

Hard times in the Reconstruction South had forced my father to leave the family home and seek work in nearby Roanoke, where he was a reporter for the *Roanoke Herald* ("The work is interesting, but the pay is small," he wrote his father), then a traveling salesman based in Richmond, then Boston. His father, Henry Rinehart Burger (grandson of that first Henry), had conducted a small saw-making project in antebellum Richmond, which converted to the fabrication of Confederate swords and small arms during the war and was destroyed in the burning of the city at war's end.

He returned to Botetourt County, became a county official and married the former Mary Anne Switzer, widow of Jabez Leftwich, mother of George J. Leftwich. The existence of George Leftwich was responsible for my being born in Mississippi. George moved to that state, became a successful lawyer and state senator, and, after marrying in Boston, my father followed his admired elder half-brother to the Magnolia State.

Following a honeymoon trip to New York, Nash and Clara Burger spent a few weeks in Boston preparing for the move to Mississippi. The selection of Jackson as their future home was a logical one. It was the capital of the state and in a central location where several railroads met, both important factors for a traveling salesman.

Jackson, however, at the turn of the century was one of the smallest of the southern capitals, far from the metropolis it was to become. Frederick Sullens, a young newspaperman from St. Louis, who arrived in 1897 to become city editor of the *Clarion-Ledger*, found the capital "only a dusty little town of about 5,000 population with no paved streets and a handful of flimsy buildings" and decided to take the next train back to St. Louis. But he missed the train and remained to become, as editor of the Jackson *Daily News*, one of the town's biggest boosters—and a good friend of my parents.

Also at this time another young man arrived in Jackson: Christian Welty, a native of Ohio, sometime teacher and bookkeeper. He came to accept a position with the newly organized Lamar Life Insurance Company, became secretary and director, and guided the company to a quarter century of growth and prosperity. More important for me was the fact that Christian Welty's decision to settle in Jackson meant, in one of those inexplicable turns of events, that forty years later I would move to New York and spend the rest of my working years at 229 W. 43rd Street with the *New York Times Book Review*.

When Christian Welty came to Jackson, he was already engaged to Chestina Andrews, a West Virginia teacher, and their marriage followed soon after. At the Welty home on North Congress Street, Eudora Welty was born in 1909, a few months after I was born on nearby North Street. Descendants of German and English forbears, children of North-South romances, Eudora and I were in a few years to become friends at Jefferson Davis School, almost across the street from the Welty home.

And it was Eudora, who, working at the *Book Review*, suggested to *Book Review* editor Robert van Gelder in 1944 that he send me some books to review. This he did, and a few months later (somewhat to my surprise) I was living in New York, reviewing and editing at the *Book Review*, and Eudora was back in Mississippi. But all this was far in the future.

Jackson in the early 1900s was not only small but subject in the summers to almost annual outbreaks of yellow fever, from which many died and others fled the city to escape. Editor Sullens recalled: "I remember standing by the old State Capitol and watching them go, first by the hundreds, then by the thousands, fleeing into the countryside. They were on foot, in buggies, surreys, wagons, on horseback and on mules. Finally the city was empty of everyone except me and a few stray dogs."

There had been an outbreak of the fever in the summer of 1902, but this had subsided by fall, when my parents set out for their first trip to the Deep South together. They stopped for a visit with my father's family in Fincastle, then went on to Mississippi, where they stayed with "Brother George" and "Sister Elgie" Leftwich at Aberdeen. (For some reason, when I came along, I always spoke to and of my aunt as "Sister Elgie," as my parents did, but it was always "Uncle George." No trifling with that large, dignified gentleman, though he was always kind to me; and when he laughed, he came forth with the heartiest guffaw I have ever heard.)

My mother, probably the only Bostonian in Jackson, was saved in these early years from possible homesickness and too much culture shock by traveling with my father on many of his business trips and making her first acquaintance with such pleasure spots as the Gulf Coast and New Orleans. In Jackson they stayed in one or another of the several houses near the State Capitol at State and Capitol Streets where rooms and board were available to businessmen, lawyers, legislators or couples situated as my parents were.

And there were the journeys once or twice a year back to Boston with a chance to visit friends and relatives and for my father to familiarize himself with Tedcastle's upcoming season's new styles in footwear. In January 1904, before one such trip to Boston, my mother wrote her mother-in-law in Virginia a letter that showed her still bemused with local customs:

> One would hardly recognize the Sunny South just now as everything is covered with snow. Night before last we had about fourteen inches, the most they have ever had here, and people seem to think they are snowbound. Everyone acts crazy. Even grown men seem to have nothing to do but stay in the street and pelt everyone that comes along. Nobody thinks of shoveling off their sidewalks, so of course the walking is fierce. I had to wade to my knees to get over to breakfast.

On returning to Jackson from Boston in March of the same year, my mother wrote again to Virginia:

> When we first got here it was so hot I nearly collapsed, and then it got awful cold and today it's hot again. It's hard to know when it's safe to take off one's flannels in such changeable weather. We intended to stop at Aberdeen on our way down, but the very last minute Nash changed his plans and we went right through to Gulfport, which is on the Coast.

We were there three days, and from Gulfport made two other towns, and then back to Jackson.

We came down from Boston a different route this time, by way of Chicago and spent one night there, arriving in a regular blizzard and then going straight to the theatre with no supper as the train was five-hours late and we had no time to eat until afterwards. When we landed in Mississippi, we found everything green and quite a change from where we came from. We are all settled now in the same room we had before.

Nash left a week ago for his long trip of five or six weeks, and of course I hate that. It's so hard to get used to having him away after being together so long. He told me I could stay in Boston while he made this long trip, but somehow or other I couldn't do it.

Advice and encouragement and bits of local news from Virginia were not lacking. Grandmother Burger was living in the family's Fincastle home (my grandfather had died a few years before), aided by assistance from her widely scattered sons and two unmarried daughters living with her or nearby.

She wrote frequently to "My Dear Little Girl" or "My Dear Daughter," especially while my father was away on his trips. Thus: "I was glad to hear that you are pleasantly situated and so well satisfied and contented. That is right. You know the Good Book says, 'Godliness with contentment is great gain.' And if you would join a Sunday School and go to Church regularly, your Sabbaths would be profitably spent and not seem nearly so long, but likely you do that, but you've never spoken of it."

Sicknesses were reported, along with the treatments (will ours today sound as strange to future generations?): "My sister Lucretia and husband at Hollins came near dying a week ago from eating beef gotten from Roanoke off of cold storage. The Dr. did not allow them a drop of water nor anything to eat for several days but a little piece of cracker and 2 or 3 tablespoons of milk. I am glad to say they are recovered and have ravenous appetites."

Though nearly seventy years old, she kept busy on garden and household chores: "I have been working over a kettle of soap and pulling a few weeds and sowing a few turnips and all together it nearly broke me down, but I will rest up in a few days."

She never lost her devotion to the rural church near Switzer's Mountain, where her Switzer forbears had worshipped for generations, and happily wrote her daughter-in-law: "Last Sunday a friend drove me out in the country to Mt. Pleasant [Methodist] Church for a service, and the chance to worship in the dear old church of my childhood made it a very enjoyable time to me."

In November 1905 she commented,

> I am so glad you are again back in the South, for where your business is, there one is happiest . . . I think the fever in the South has helped to build up the trade. I think Nash has not made such large sales before. I hope he'll keep well, so he can travel and make up for lost time. I guess on account of the quarantine the people get pretty well out of goods. Now that it is raised they will buy liberally.
>
> Tell Nash I am having a hard old time trying to pay the taxes before the penalty is added, which is the 1st of Dec. I've been borrowing from [daughter] Anna for some time to buy wood and Geo. [Leftwich] sent me $5 to buy more of Dr. Green's tonic. That will help a good deal and I can wait for the tonic till the tax is paid. I do hate to be bothering Nash so much, but he tells me to and I can't help it.

My father's business must have been good in those early Jackson days, for his checks acknowledged in his mother's letters to him were usually the largest of those she mentions receiving from her children.

Then on 2 December 1905, she wrote to "My Dear Nash":

> I thank you for the check, which came in *so good*. I needed it. I had been on the borrow away up in the *teens* and it came just in time for the taxes, too. Wish you and Claribel could come home for Xmas, but, of course, if you are buying little tiny wardrobes for a little stranger, there is no hope of seeing you soon. I hope all will be right and she may have as good time as she possibly can have and a dear, healthy little responsibility to cheer your lives and give you something to live for. Tell Claribel to be careful and take good care of herself in every respect so she may come through all right . . . Be good and take care of the *dear, little girl*, give her much love and a large share for yourself and accept hearty thanks for your kindness and write soon again.

But this first birth did not go well. The child did not survive, and my mother scarcely did. Today the earliest marker in the family plot of Jackson's Cedarlawn Cemetery is for Lois Randolph Burger. My parents had already begun to attend St. Andrew's Episcopal Church, had come to know the saintly and revered Bishop Theodore Bratton and his wife, Lucy Randolph Bratton. I have always believed the name chosen for my parents' firstborn reflected their affection for the Brattons.

There is a significant break at this time in the collection of letters my mother preserved over the years, as though the period was too painful to be remembered. I know she seldom spoke of it to me.

When my parents first came to Jackson, they were able to observe the largest construction project ever carried out, up to that time, in the city: the building of the state's New Capitol, on an expansive four-block site at the head of Congress Street, previously occupied by the state penitentiary. Built at a cost of a million dollars (a huge sum in those days) and in use by 1903, it remains one of the nation's finest, most handsome capitol buildings.

The legislature had authorized bonds to pay for the construction; but prudent and careful management enabled the state to complete the building on a pay-as-you-go basis, and no bonds were issued. Today, state legislatures and the United States Congress should take notice that borrowing and deficits are not inevitable.

There is no doubt that the building of the New Capitol did much to spur a period of growth and prosperity in Jackson from which my father's business benefited. State Archivist Dunbar Rowland proudly announced in his 1907 volume, *Mississippi*, that "In four years Jackson has more than doubled its population . . . is a railroad center, with railroads in seven directions, several state institutions, five grade schools, several colleges, industries relating to timber and cotton, several miles of well-paved streets . . . an electric street-railway system [my parents often recalled the mule-drawn street car that greeted them on their arrival only a few years before] . . . hotels, banks, churches."

Both the historic Old Capitol and the grander New Capitol were easily visible from the house at North and Mississippi Streets where I was born in 1908. That the site of my birth is now the location of the city's Eudora Welty Library is a turn of events that I can only approve.

However, in a few months my family removed to "the Crafts'," a three-house establishment offering fine board and comfortable lodging at Amite and President Streets, just a block down the hill from the Old Capitol grounds. Here we lived for thirteen happy years.

The owners of this well-known and popular property were Sidney Craft, an official of the Jackson State National Bank, and his wife, Gulie McLean Craft, who lived in one of the houses, facing President Street, but where lodgings were also available. The two other houses faced Amite: a two-story structure with some Victorian embellishments, at the corner of President and numbered 511 Amite, where we lived on the upper floor; and a rambling, antebellum-appearing story-and-a-half house next door, containing lodgings, a large dining room with three long tables and two fireplaces, and, across an entrance hall from the dining room, an ample parlor with fireplace, piano, paintings, and an elaborate, floor-to-ceiling gilded mirror.

Miss Mary Craft, sister of Mr. Craft, lived in the latter house and managed the establishment. The meals, planned by Miss Mary and prepared by her cook Charity and assistants, were famous in Jackson. Many visitors to town and local citizens who were not lodgers came to dine. The broiled steak, baked red snapper and shrimp creole, the beaten biscuits, fig ice cream and all manner of pies and pastries were especially renowned.

None of these delights were of concern to me when I arrived at 511 Amite at the age of one or two, but the cheerfulness and liveliness of the scene must have been apparent even to a toddler. My mother, long after we had departed the Crafts', would speak nostalgically of the good years there. For there she became a Jacksonian (though never ceasing to pronounce "Alabama" with a Bostonian's broad "a"), and when, of necessity, she left the town, she did so with sadness and regret.

My earliest memories of these years are of my mother's nighttime visits to my bedside, first to teach me the prayer "Now I Lay Me Down to Sleep" and then to hear me repeat it nightly, and of the early, often when it was yet dark, morning kiss from my father before he departed to take the train for a business trip of a day, a week, perhaps a month. His freshly shaved face would smell slightly of peppermint, from the lotion he concocted from a dilution of Dr. Tichenor's Antiseptic, our all-purpose, household medication. Then I would snuggle down into my bed and go back to sleep.

"Tichenor's," as we referred to this product, was, in various dilutions, recommended for cuts, stings, rash, sore throat, as an emetic, for aches and pains of every description. It was made in New Orleans, and we were never without a bottle at home or abroad. I have read that it was the first product issued a patent by the Confederate government, and the label bore the picture of an embattled southern soldier holding high the Confederate battle flag. In my own adult years we continued to seek out and purchase Tichenor's wherever we were, and dubious New York druggists, among others, were induced to stock it for our use. Today, the Confederate flag having been removed from the label, Tichenor's has lost its charm, and we and the good Dr. Tichenor have parted company.

I was certainly a loved, well cared for, closely watched over only child, surrounded by friendly adults and with parents who had themselves known no little adversity and deprivation and were determined that I should fare better. I don't know just when my parents employed a nurse to help care for me. I expect it was soon after my arrival, since my mother only slowly regained her health after a difficult birth. I was fortunate in their choice, a loyal and intelligent young black woman originally from Rankin County, across the Pearl River from Jackson. Strangely enough, her given name was Eddy, my mother's family name and one not often encountered in Mississippi (which, as I have been told, was why she was chosen), and she was married to Will Harper, a Jackson carpenter.

Eddy would roll me in my carriage or, when I was older, walk with me around the neighborhood, mainly to State Street (with its handsome residences and better sidewalks) and along State for several blocks. We would stop for ladies or couples to inspect me and ask my name or greet me by name if already known. Other nurses might also be out with their charges. Nurses and children became well acquainted, and many of my earliest Jackson friends, young and old, were met in this way.

Some of the State Street houses had back yards extending through the block to North Street on the east or President on the west, and Eddy, who had friends among the cooks, gardeners or other servants there, would often steer our outings down those back streets, where she could have some talk with these friends.

I remember many pauses at the North Street back fence of the Presbyterian manse for Eddy's conversation, while Pastor Hutton's dog raised a great clamor within. And often Eddy and I, and another nurse or two, would meet for a visit on the walk at State and High Streets, beside the magnolia-shaded yard of the impressive Harley Shands home, a columned residence worthy of a role in *Gone with the Wind*, now long vanished from the Jackson scene. (In later years, Dr. Shands was to tell me that when my parents first came to town, my mother was beyond doubt "the prettiest little thing" he had ever seen.)

On the porch at 511 Amite, Eddy would entertain me with talk or simple games or observe my playing in the yard. There were seldom other children at the Crafts', though next door Maynard, one of the Craft sons, and across the street Jane, one of the pretty daughters of George Power (a state official), and up the hill at State, Selah, daughter of the Dr. Hunter who brought me into the world, were my own age, and in time I played with them.

I remember a bright red wagon I had, and sometimes Eddy or an older neighborhood or visiting youth could be induced to take me for a ride. Otherwise I rolled myself down the Amite Street hill (no automobile traffic in those far-off years). Much later, when I spoke to my mother about a writer at Oxford named William Faulkner, who was writing some good books and stories, she said, "Oh, I know Willie Faulkner. He used to visit Jackson with some of his family. They would stay or eat at the Crafts', and sometimes he pulled you around in that wagon you had." It was the only time I ever saw the Nobel Prize winner.

Eddy performed another notable service. When we were not visiting or taking the air on State Street or in our own yard, we were apt to be upstairs at our house, by a hall window, where she would read to me. When her voice grew tired from this and she sought to pause for a while (as she later told me), I would demand more. "Yead, Eddy, yead!" I would cry, not yet being able to handle the "r" sound. I don't remember now what she read, except for the Peter Rabbit stories of Beatrix Potter, my favorites, but there was much else.

More important, when I was older but not yet in school, Eddy taught me to read some of the stories for myself; so when I did start to school, I was ready. It was our own Head Start Program, upstairs there at 511 Amite.

In time Eddy and her husband had children and a home of their own. I kept in touch with her over the years, stopped by on my bicycle as a teen-ager (there were good figs on a tree in Eddy's backyard), and drove my mother there still later. Our handsome Victrola, the only one at the Crafts' when my father bought it before World War I, had been given to Eddy (with records from Caruso to vintage Louis Armstrong) and was ever in her living room.

A few momentous incidents from earliest times are impressed in my memory: a heavy iron cap from the fireplug at President and Capitol Streets falling on my foot, breaking a toe or two and putting me out of circulation for days; my father's alarm when, tossing me in the air in the Hunter-McGee Drug Store at State and Capitol, my head was grazed by the blades of the circulating overhead fan (I remember his alarm more than the grazing); and falling from bed and cutting my left arm on the hinge of my toy box, making a wound from which I bled profusely and from which a lengthy scar remains to this day ("You might have bled to death!" my mother lamented for years, wrongly accusing herself for letting it happen).

But most of my memories are of harmless or pleasant incidents. My father's outgoing nature early gained him many friends, and to walk down Capitol Street with him was to make slow progress as he stopped to greet shopkeepers at their doors or talk with one acquaintance after the other. When friends died, my father was so often asked to serve as pallbearer that once when a lady newcomer, seated at our table at the Crafts', asked me what my father did (he was away on a trip), I announced to a startled table, "He's a pallbearer!" Even my mother smiled.

My mother was probably not amused (though I am sure our fellow diners were) on an occasion when my Uncle George was down from Aberdeen for a state supreme court case and was eating with us at the Crafts' as he often did. My mother had always impressed me with the importance of removing one's spoon from the cup, for reasons of safety and good manners, after stirring a drink. My eagle eyes spotted Uncle George's spoon left in his coffee cup as he was eating. "Uncle George," I exclaimed, "take your spoon out of your cup!" Whether I was an amusing or impossible child, I can't say. I know that within my career, naiveté and precocity have ever contended for mastery.

At the time of the spoon-in-the-teacup incident, Uncle George had already served a distinguished term in the state senate. When the New Capitol was completed, there was talk of demolishing the historic but run-down Old Capitol, which would have been a tragedy. But the 1908 senate session "at the instance of George J. Leftwich," as one account states, "went on record as favoring preservation of the old State House as a hall of records, a State Museum and Confederate memorial." As a result, the restored Old Capitol stands today in all its original glory.

Uncle George also played a major role in one of the most bizarre events in the state's political history. In 1909, one of Mississippi's United States senators having died, the vacancy was to be filled by a vote in the state senate. There ensued the historic and hectic campaign between supporters of LeRoy Percy and James K. Vardaman. Intense pressure was put on the state's senators by supporters of each candidate. Percy won by a close vote. Then Theodore G. Bilbo, one of the state senators, announced he had taken a $645 bribe to vote for Percy. Emotion intensified; charges and countercharges were tossed about.

A senate committee, appointed to investigate the matter, condemned Bilbo and suggested he resign. Bilbo declined. The chairman of the committee, chosen for his known integrity and freedom from factional bias, was George J. Leftwich.

Uncle George, however, did not care for political life, and did not seek a second term. My mother had typed many of his letters while he was in Jackson for the legislative session, and as compensation (she declined any monetary payment) he bestowed on her a copy of *Webster's Unabridged*

Dictionary, which bulky volume we hauled around for many years and which I, in time, made great use of.

As I grew older and the time for entering school grew near, it was decided that I should visit a doctor and dentist for a good check over. Actually the doctor, John F. Hunter, son of the Reverend John H. Hunter, longtime pastor of Jackson's First Presbyterian Church, visited me. He lived just up the hill at Amite and State Streets, as I have mentioned, and occasionally walked down to diagnose or prescribe when we were ill. (I remember my first acquaintance with aspirin presented by Dr. Hunter in powdered form from a folded paper, which I vigorously sought to reject, with no success.) Dr. Hunter found me fit for school and the smallpox vaccination that was to be administered there.

So to the dentist. Sitting next to me at the end of the dining-room table at the Crafts' each day were two unmarried brothers, both dentists. It was decided that I should visit one of them, E. A. May, with whom I had become good friends. I went at the appointed time, though with some misgivings, to his office in the Century Theater Building, just around the corner on Capitol Street.

Dr. May sat me down in his treatment chair and after some pleasantries, which did not allay my concern, turned to his instruments and apparatus. I saw all these unfamiliar objects of curious shape and gleaming metal. It was too much. I had heard too many jokes and tales of dentists and their ministrations. I bounded from the chair and out of the office, raced down the stairs, not waiting for the elevator, and home.

Some days later I was induced to return, escorted by my mother. My teeth were attended to with no great discomfort and were pronounced sound. My friendship and trust for Dr. May were not impaired, and he remained my dentist for many years. I once invited him to one of my high school classes to speak and answer questions concerning dentistry as a profession. However, he did not refer to our first professional encounter.

It was about the time of my first dental visit that readers of the Jackson *Daily News* were treated to a large picture of me, seated, in a baseball suit and cap with glove and baseball at my feet. There was an accompanying laudatory text. (I have been told that, no baseball being available, Daniel, "the artist photographer of children," substituted a billiard ball, but no matter.) This appeared in a regular Sunday feature, "Future Belles and Beaux of Jackson."

"Why on earth should there ever be a question as to the leadership of the baseball team in Jackson, or any anxiety as to the efficiency of this leader cannot be understood in view of the face which smiles out [I was not smiling] from this page over the name 'Nash Burger, Jr.' this morning," begins the enthusiastic text, somewhat incoherently.

However, the next sentence is clear and accurate (except for the "sturdy"— I was never sturdy, but somewhat skinny): "The little son and only child of Mr. and Mrs. Nash Burger, the little lad combines in his sturdy frame the pride of his Virginia ancestors with that of his Massachusetts forbears, his father being a Virginian and his mother a Bostonian." And continues, "Nash, however, is 'pure Jackson,' as he would not acknowledge any other home nor would his devoted friends yield him to the most persistent claimant.

"Born in Jackson, about six years ago, the little lad soon made a place for himself in many hearts other than his parents' and as the years have gone on this list of friends has grown, and their friendship has deepened, since he is a manly lad and richly repays his grown-up friends, as he does those of his own age, for the love they give him." And so on.

It seems that "one of Nash's devoted admirers gathered him up without warning and had his picture made in his beloved baseball suit, as a surprise for his parents. If the manager of the Giants or Red Sox could see him when he is thus arrayed, they would steal him for a mascot, dead sure."

So much and such uncritical praise I had not known before or since, and it may have helped turn my thoughts to journalism and the wonders of the printed word. The author of the effusive prose was perhaps Miss Annabel Power, Amite Street neighbor and relative of the George Powers across the street. Miss Annabel for many years chronicled in the local press the goings on of Jacksonians and incidents from the city's passing scene.

The "devoted admirer" who gathered me up and had my picture made was probably Albert ("Bert") Eyrich described in a later Annabel Power column as "a popular bachelor and successful business man." He and his sister Gladys were also (with Episcopal Bishop William M. Green II) my godparents and among my and my parents' earliest and longest friends.

The father of Bert and Gladys was George C. Eyrich, who came as a teenager with his parents from Germany to New Orleans in antebellum times, moved to Jackson soon after the Civil War with a wife and family and opened a bookstore, Eyrich's, on Capitol Street, half a block from the (not yet "Old") Capitol. He purchased one of Jackson's few surviving antebellum homes on North State Street at the corner of Boyd and lived there until his death, which occurred about the time we arrived in Jackson. (In 1915 my father bought the Eyrich home, which had been moved back and turned around to become 715 Boyd Street, and we lived there from about 1920 to 1935.)

After their father's death both Bert and Gladys were taking their meals at the Crafts'. Gladys had a room there as well and for some years taught physical education in the Jackson schools. (You can meet her in that role in Eudora Welty's *One Writer's Beginnings*.) Bert was managing Eyrich's and living nearby, for many years over the store, in the European fashion.

Neither ever married and had time and inclination to assist my parents' adaptation to their new home and keep a kindly eye on my progress, most notably by seeing to it that I was early supplied, to my great pleasure and benefit, with books, books, books from Eyrich's.

They were also responsible for our early attendance at St. Andrew's Episcopal Church (now Cathedral), where they were members and where Gladys was ever active in church affairs; their father had for many years been vestryman and warden. Sunday by Sunday we sat with Bert and Gladys in the pew they had occupied since the church was built, now nearly a century ago.

TWO

"Wake Up, Little Schoolboy"

Then came the day (I well remember it) in September 1914, when I was to enter Jefferson Davis School. My mother came to my bedside and, seeing me still asleep, gave my shoulder a nudge and instead of a conventional morning greeting, announced: "Wake up, little schoolboy." A new day had begun for both of us.

Davis School, only a half-dozen short blocks from our Amite Street home, was a buff-colored brick building on Congress Street. It faced west, toward the town's Greenwood Cemetery a block away, with its Confederate dead and its monument to the Episcopal rector from New York who died ministering to yellow-fever victims in antebellum times. A short distance up a low hill to the north was Fortification Street, where fortifications had indeed been erected in 1863 and Joseph E. Johnston's hard-pressed Confederates had lobbed shells at Grant's Yankees approaching from Raymond and Port Gibson.

Atop another small hill to the south sat the large, gleaming New Capitol, not unlike the nation's Capitol in Washington, and less than a dozen years old on my first school day. On the New Capitol grounds, when not chased off, I would soon be playing baseball and football after school and on Saturdays, and roller-skating and bicycling on the vast stretches of concrete walks and esplanades.

17

My mother walked to school with me that first day. She wanted to be sure I found the right classroom and teacher. The teacher proved to be Miss Florence Granberry, and I believe she taught my class for two or three years; but I cannot be sure, as I remember not a single thing about this lady or our classroom activities except her name and, vaguely, her appearance.

Perhaps this lack of recollection suggests a calm and orderly school experience. I have, indeed, no clear recollection of what went on in Davis School until about the third or fourth grade when I was in the class of Mrs. McWillie, a motherly widow of antebellum Governor William McWillie's family. The McWillies lived on North State Street, and I had known Frances McWillie, who was in my Davis School classes, since my earlier perambulations with my nurse Eddy. My mother and I had often visited this family, which is probably why my memory of Mrs. McWillie as teacher is so distinct.

Mrs. McWillie, like any good mother, could be stern. She clamped down early on my ingenious mischievousness. I remember dismembering an old front-door bell and bringing to school the clapper and metal shell it struck to make its sounds. In class I repeatedly and surreptitiously tapped clapper and shell together to make a tinkle-tinkle that entertained the class and for some time bewildered our teacher as to its origin. All too soon for me, she discovered the source, and I spent my recess, not playing games as usual, but standing by Mrs. McWillie and making my tinkle-tinkle for half an hour until I wished I had never seen that bell.

Eudora Welty has told in her *One Writer's Beginnings* how Mrs. McWillie on dark and rainy days at Davis School would stand by a classroom window, the better to see—since for reasons of economy, there had been no lights installed when the school was built—and read to her class stories such as John Ruskin's *The King of the Golden River*. I recall that story and also remember hearing George Macdonald's *The Princess and the Goblins* and *The Princess and Curdy* and being fascinated by them, adding all three later to my own library. Other cloudy-day activities included the reciting of multiplication tables, spelling contests and various oral exercises that required no special lighting.

Eudora lived in a comfortable, two-story, white frame house almost across the street from Davis School. Like most Jackson homes of that time, the Welty house was neither new nor old. Antebellum Jackson had been pretty well destroyed during the Yankee occupation, and the area around the school was made up of postwar houses set in the midst of ample yards. I remember Mrs. Welty often at the door or on the porch, smiling and speaking as I went to and from school and Eudora emerging on some mornings to share pomegranates or persimmons before school. Whether these fruits were purchased or grew in the yard, I don't know; they are remembered because they were not everyday fare.

Around the corner from the Weltys was a little grocery store where, before school, Eudora and the rest of us bought Red Bird tablets, penny Tootsie-Rolls, little chocolate-flavored candies and other essential items. Our textbooks were bought at a store downtown. This was before the days of "free" textbooks, and the books were, I would say, the more appreciated and used, the money to buy them having come directly from the family purse.

Before school and at recess, boys and girls played in carefully separated parts of the school yard until time to line up, boys on one side of the building, girls on the other. Boys and girls were considered different orders of beings in those days. We marched to our rooms while one of our classmates (for years it was the same pretty girl with long, brown hair) played "The National Emblem March," "Dixie," and other lively airs on a piano in the main hall. I don't recall too much about what went on in those classrooms except that we were exposed to what would be called today a traditional curriculum: the old math, spelling as old as Webster, geography full of capitals, and history full of patriotism.

Dominating Davis School for many years (before and after my appearance) was its principal, Miss Lorena Duling, an intelligent and dedicated lady who had come down from Kentucky when the school was new and who guided several generations of young Jacksonians into the ways of learning and righteousness. She guided the teachers, too, keeping a close eye on their work and methods, even overseeing their examination questions. Davis had its own standardized tests, the Duling tests. They were austere but fair, and they brought results.

Miss Duling had encyclopedias and reference books in her office, and any student or teacher could send her a request for information on a complex or recondite subject and expect an answer. Encountering in my geography class several towns named Aberdeen other than the Mississippi one my Uncle George lived in, I sent a note asking Miss Duling how many Aberdeens there were and where. The next day I had from her a list of a dozen or so towns by that name and their locations. Miss Duling was a hands-on principal, no doubt about that.

First aid was not beyond Miss Duling's expertise. One day after perhaps too much reading at home and school, a too-hasty lunch, too vigorous play thereafter, I had a sick headache (not my first). I was sent to Miss Duling, who prepared a concoction tasting of Dr. Tichenor's Antiseptic and I don't know what else. I swallowed it and immediately threw up on the polished hall floor.

I became more alarmed at this misadventure to Miss Duling's floor than at my illness. She calmed me, called for the janitor to mop up, and had me lie down on a couch in her office. Soon I was feeling better, and Miss Duling sent me home, accompanied by an older boy who lived nearby and had, as she knew, a little wagon in which to pull me.

One other incident remains in my memory: Miss Duling as coach. There was no big hullabaloo over school athletics in those days to divert attention from our primary objectives, but in the spring the several grammar schools would play a few baseball games with each other to establish a city champion. One year Davis School seemed about to be the winner, but something went wrong. It seemed several of our best players would not be eligible. I do not remember if this was because of scholastic or behavioral difficulties, but Miss Duling called the remaining team members and a few others who would be replacements (including, incredibly, me) into her office. She gave us a fine pep talk, telling us we would be representing Davis School and must do our best; if we did, we would surely win.

I believe we were to play Galloway School on Bailey Avenue in west Jackson (or was it George School?). Anyway, we journeyed one afternoon by streetcar with Miss Duling and a teacher or two to the playground of the other school—and won the game. On that historic occasion I played in right field, where I could do the least damage. I don't remember what I did at bat, but I do remember fielding at least one ball and making a mighty throw to our second baseman that resulted in a third out, thus retiring the opposition for that inning. For this Miss Duling and our pitcher (my hero) later gave me high praise. You may be sure I delivered a rosy account of all this to anyone who would listen when I got home to Amite Street.

One final word on Miss Duling. She never married. She was wedded to Davis School and to her ideals for its students. Years later I learned she had once been engaged to a Jackson bank president, one of the town's wealthiest men. But she called it off. Davis School won out.

Ours was an education that emphasized the basics, the three R's: reading, 'riting and 'rithmetic—and a bit of the fourth R, religion. There were few distractions and entertainments of today's ilk. We did have a music teacher who came in one day a week and an art teacher and a physical education teacher who did the same.

The physical education teacher who took us outside for some organized group activities, wand drills, and so on, was my godmother, Gladys Eyrich. Always brisk and energetic, she was especially so in her professional role. She gave me no special consideration—quite the opposite. Once I complained I had a sore knee and could not perform some of the calisthenics she favored. She examined the knee and told me to continue. I reported this at home, and my mother expostulated with Gladys. The result was that I was kept at my desk for some weeks and not permitted to go outside with the others for the games I enjoyed. Worse, I was teased by some of my classmates, including the pretty girl I was fond of and had been walking home with for some time. Life seemed harsh.

One year Gladys directed a performance of her students from the town's grammar schools at the annual Mississippi State Fair. This included all manner of drills, marches, exercises and so on. A festive and well-publicized occasion. At Davis School we practiced our part for weeks. At home our mothers prepared our costumes, which, as I recall, were of a piratical nature, with similar shirts and trousers, a bandana head piece and earrings made of curtain rings attached to the ears by thread.

However, as often happened, I had not been paying attention during the preparations, and on the afternoon of the performance I reported in my pirate ensemble to the wrong place, an empty Davis schoolyard, while my classmates were displaying their skills at the Fairgrounds a mile away. I don't recall how my failure to turn up at the Fairgrounds proceedings was received by Gladys and my mother, but there must have been some negative repercussions.

Although Davis School had no library, I never lacked books for reading. At first (my nurse Eddy being now engaged in raising her own family) my mother read to me. I remember the fairy tales of the brothers Grimm, *Little Black Sambo*, Thomas Nelson Page's *Two Little Confederates* and Frances Calhoun's *Miss Minerva and William Green Hill*, the latter a particular favorite.

I read several of the sequels (eleven in all, I believe) to the Calhoun book for myself when they appeared years later, without realizing they were by a different author, Emma Sampson—a remarkable and successful example of auctorial substitution. It seems that Mrs. Calhoun, a Tennesseean, died before her best-seller appeared in 1909, and it was not until 1918 that Mrs.

Sampson, a Kentuckian transplanted to Virginia, was induced to continue the story with *Billy and the Major* and other popular volumes.

While the Carnegie Public Library in Jackson, facing the New Capitol at North Congress and Mississippi Streets, was built about the time I was beginning to read and be read to, most of these early books came from Eyrich's and were returned to Eyrich's. Bert would make an extra book jacket of wrapping paper to protect the original, turn the book over to my mother to be carefully read to me at home or read by me ("Wash your hands before you begin to read," she always said). Once read, the book was returned to Bert.

Often my mother or father bought one of these borrowed books so generously provided by Bert, or had him order a book thought to be especially good. My mother enjoyed Frances Hodgson Burnett's *The Secret Garden* so much that she purchased a copy and, at my request, read it to me several times. Later I read it for myself.

She also bought, and we both enjoyed her reading of the *Uncle Remus* stories. Her attempts to handle the dialect of Uncle Remus and the other characters as spelled out by Joel Chandler Harris caused no little amusement for us both. The same was true of her efforts with the dialect poems of Mississippi's Irwin Russell—"Christmas Night in the Quarters," "Nebuchadnezzar" and others.

Bert's pleasure in entertaining me manifested itself in ingenious ways. A book called *Stories of Dixie,* published in 1915, was by James W. Nicholson, a noted southern educator of the time and teacher at Louisiana State University. The stories, as I recall, were woven together into an anecdotal narrative of the antebellum and Civil War South and center on a boy named Nick (the author, no doubt), who grows up, serves in the war, and returns home safely. Bert not only gave me a copy of the book but also carefully pasted under almost every mention of the name "Nick," beginning with the youthful, frontispiece portrait, the printed word "Nash," which he must have clipped from a local newspaper article about me or my father. No small labor was involved in that clipping and pasting. I enjoyed the book (now long gone from my possession) and its pen-and-ink illustrations. But I chiefly remembered it for Bert's enrichment.

I had not thought of the book for years, when, browsing in the endless stacks of the University of Virginia Alderman Library recently, a well-worn volume with a cover that seemed familiar caught my eye. It was *Stories of Dixie.* Inside the cover I found the bookplate of Edwin Anderson Alderman, first president of the university, for whom the library is named. I was flabbergasted. I took the volume from the shelf, sat down in some graduate student's unoccupied carrel and read it through without stopping. It is a fine book, much better than I was able to appreciate those long years ago. Written mainly for young people, the stories tell of the settling of the lower South, of the clearing of the wilderness and the life of farm and village, of secession and war, all in a lively and humorous style. ("One has a lopsided knowledge of the people of Dixie who knows nothing of their jokes and sports," the author says, and writes accordingly.) Adult as well as young readers can find pleasure and profit in these tales, set down as they are with charm and wisdom. I am sure Edwin Anderson Alderman found this to be so, as I now have. (My investigations disclose that *Stories of Dixie* is still in print, as it should be.)

My father, who had no little input into my early reading, usually had an eye to practical, collateral benefits. He purchased for me at Eyrich's a copy of *Robert E. Lee and the Southern Confederacy*, by Henry A. White, a teacher of history at Washington and Lee University. This volume gives the story of Lee's family background, boyhood and prewar career, as well as of the years of North-South conflict. My father was interested in Lee as a model Virginian, a man of honor, courage, religious faith and morality.

To be sure I gave the book a careful reading; he suggested I copy Lee's letters and words quoted in the book and send my copies to him on his trips. For each letter or quotation I was to receive five cents, payable by my mother in his absence. These copies (and here appears my father's astuteness) were to be made on the family's old-fashioned Oliver typewriter, on which I had already begun a hunt-and-peck apprenticeship. Thus, over some weeks and months, I developed my typing skill, as well as an acquaintanceship with Robert Edward Lee.

I was ever reading, scores of books. They expanded my knowledge, opened my eyes and stimulated my imagination. Sometimes the title is remembered, sometimes the author. Conventionally moral, these books emphasized courage, kindness, respect for others, ingenuity and persistence in overcoming difficulties. The violence was not excessive. Good conquered evil. If this is not always the way of the world, it should be. And books can point the way.

There were Horatio Alger, Zane Grey, the Tom Swift and Rover Boy series, Jack London's *The Call of the Wild* and *The Sea Wolf*, Ernest Thompson Seton's *Two Little Savages*, O. Henry, James Oliver Curwood, Stevenson's

Treasure Island and *Kidnapped*, Sax Rohmer's Dr. Fu Manchu, Rafael Sabatini's historical swashbucklers, Kipling's *Wee Willie Winkie* and other tales. (My mother especially enjoyed Kipling, an author she had actually seen—he was a reclusive, mysterious figure observed during her childhood days in Brattleboro.)

But above all, in my Davis School years, there was Edgar Rice Burroughs, prolific author of the Tarzan books, fascinating portrayer of an Africa he had never seen. I not only read these books, I acquired them (by gift or purchase) as fast as they appeared, and they appeared frequently. My enthusiasm for this author expanded to include his other books, the Martian series, such volumes as *At the Earth's Core* and that little-known and frenetic novel, *The Mucker*.

I learned my first French word from the opening sentence of *The Return of Tarzan*. " '*Magnifique!*' ejaculated the Countess de Coude, beneath her breath." The Countess, it seems, is on a ship and is referring to the handsome man she has just seen. She asks a steward who he is. " 'He is booked, madam, as Monsieur Tarzan of Africa,' replies the steward." And the narrative is off and running.

My propensity for organizing knowledge impelled me to compile a glossary of the words used by Tarzan and his great ape friends in communicating: Numa, the lion; Horta, the boar; Manu, the monkey; Tantor, the elephant; Buto, the rhinoceros; and so on. Then there must be a club, True Followers of Tarzan, entrance to which required a familiarity with these words.

I remember sitting in a tree in the backyard of the Garner Green home on North State Street with my best friends from Davis School, George and Charles Stephenson, as we quizzed another good friend, Marcellus Green, a candidate for T.F.O.T. membership, on his knowledge of the Tarzan vocabulary. All T.F.O.T. activities naturally took place in trees and involved much climbing about and some minor injuries, cheerfully borne. Marcellus, in later years a University of Virginia graduate and a Jackson attorney, passed his T.F.O.T. test and was proclaimed a full-fledged member.

Well, as one sober literary critic has declared, "Probably few literate adults could read a Tarzan story with pleasure—but probably few of them failed to devour Tarzan stories in their earlier years."

And I remember my father's unpacking a set of *The Book of Knowledge*, just arrived in a great wooden box, and the monthly appearance of the eagerly read *American Boy*, *Boys Life*, and *National Geographic* magazines—the latter accumulating in stacks over the months and years, but carefully preserved and frequently referred to.

At the Crafts' after supper each day, the men would linger talking, standing around, or sitting on the steps outside the dining room, while the wives would gather on the porch at 511 next door to exchange news and gossip. One of the men, C. D. Brinkley, a salesman for one of the tobacco companies, I believe, on those spring and summer days it was yet light enough, was apt to have me bring out a ball and two of my baseball gloves and let me practice my pitching skills by throwing to him. He urged me on, gave me advice, called for this pitch or that, declared I would become a Walter Johnson or Grover Alexander (two greats of the time). I believed him.

There was a United Cigar Store on Capitol Street, which at that time gave coupons with tobacco purchases to be accumulated and exchanged for baseball equipment (balls, gloves, bats, etc.) temptingly displayed in a store window. In addition, each Camel cigarette pack for a while contained a small, foreign flag of one country or another as an inducement to buy that brand.

I badgered the men at the Crafts' so insistently to step up their tobacco purchases and save the coupons and flags for me that I may well have had a deleterious effect on the health and longevity of a number of Jackson males. Women, of course, were not smoking in those days, and I certainly wasn't. At any event, I obtained some handsome sports equipment at no cost and increased my knowledge of the flags of many nations.

Books naturally played a part in my pursuit of baseball excellence. There were paperbacks at Eyrich's with such titles as *How to Pitch*, *How to Play First Base*, and so on. These I purchased and studied assiduously. There was also a series of books about a sterling character called "Baseball Joe," and these George, Charles, and I found so fascinating that we undertook to compose a volume in the series. I believe this got no further than our narrating the plots to each other, but it was my first attempt at literary composition.

In the summer there was the Cotton States League. The Jackson Senators played their home games at the Fairgrounds, just over the Amite Street hill. I was there early for every game, hoping to be one of those selected to recover practice balls in the outfield and then allowed to stay for the game. One could also slip into the games without too much trouble. Sometimes my father or one of his friends would take me to the game, and one happy summer my father talked the team owner into giving me a season's pass, citing my dedication to the national sport.

Anything I did by choice, I did wholeheartedly, sometimes to excess, and not always successfully. I was dedicated to baseball, as to football, when it came time for that, though I was too frail to make the teams or the headlines.

I played tennis enthusiastically for years, along with George, Charles, and Marcellus, where I did better. I was serious about stamp collecting and coin collecting (my collection of silver dollars and the dollar-sized coins of other nations is still impressive). Chemistry experiments, homemade radios, photography, all had their day. But books and reading and the putting of words on paper have ever been my greatest pleasure. To these pursuits above all, I am addicted.

Although George and Charles Stephenson were my best and longest friends in the Jackson of those days, I did not encounter them at Davis School until about the third grade, having met them earlier at St. Andrew's Sunday school. Their mother, Mrs. Ruth McDowell Stephenson, kept George (my age) at home until Charles, his younger brother, was old enough to enter Davis. They and their mother lived with their grandfather McDowell in a large house facing the New Capitol at North President and College Streets, where the First Baptist Church was later built when it moved from Capitol and North President.

George had received some home instruction before entering Davis in the third grade, and he and Charles immediately became top scholars at Davis— as they both were in every school they ever attended. Mrs. Stephenson was a niece of the Mississippi writer Sherwood Bonner; and Charles, whose middle name was Bonner, eventually dropped the Stephenson from his name and became Charles Bonner (the name of Sherwood Bonner's father and Charles's great-grandfather).

Only a year or two after George and Charles entered Davis School, a tragic accident involving them shocked the school and community. They came across an army .45-caliber pistol (left at their home, as I recall, by a McDowell relative who had served in World War I). Handling it, they caused the pistol to fire, and the bullet went entirely through George's upper body from left to right, barely missing the heart. Doctors were surprised that he survived, though he missed the rest of the school year.

As it happened, our Sunday school teacher of many years, Flora B. Walthall, annually gave a book to the student with the best record for the year (performance, decorum, attendance, etc.), the book to be chosen by the winner. George would easily have won this prize but for his absences resulting from the accident. I came next and was declared the winner. That disturbed me, and I told Miss Flora I wanted the prize awarded to George, since his absences were unavoidable. She agreed to my offer, and the book was to be given to George. Hearing what I had done, my mother told me she would buy me the book I might have chosen, since my action itself deserved a reward. So George and I both won a prize. And we each chose a book by—Edgar Rice Burroughs.

Returning to Davis School in the fall, George easily caught up with the work he had missed and was again a class leader. Then Miss Duling announced a full day's holiday from school for any student who would learn the names of all eighty-two of Mississippi's counties and how to spell them. I remember only two students who qualified (though there may have been more), George and Eudora. I earned only half a day, because I misspelled Oktibbeha. Years later I reviewed a fine Civil War novel on page one of *The New York Times Book Review*. I detected only one error in the book (though I did not mention it): the author misspelled Oktibbeha.

Other memorizing of names, dates and literary passages (an educational tool and discipline more popular then than now) that I recall from Davis School days was of Psalms from the King James Bible. We would read a Psalm aloud together every morning for several days until it became fixed in the memory, then move on to another. The students would usually decide which one. I am sure there was much benefit—spiritual, moral, rhetorical— in getting those splendid phrases and concepts into our growing minds and psyches.

That, of course, was a time when education, according to the Tenth Amendment, was one of those powers reserved to the states, and the state of Mississippi in its wisdom considered prayer and Scripture essential elements of a sound and civilized education. The state also thought racially separate schools beneficial to whites and blacks, and so decreed (at that time Jackson was about half white and half black). Perhaps the education at Davis and other Jackson schools became better when it was no longer racially separate. But it was already good, it seemed to me.

In 1921, the same year that our class left all-white Davis School to go to all-white Central High School, a black student our own age entered Jackson's all-black Jim Hill School and went on to graduate from all-black Smith-Robertson School four years later, the same year we graduated from Central High. He was Richard Wright, and he has told us he wrote his first story at that time. You can read his account of Jackson in those days in his *Black Boy*. I wonder if the school system of any small, provincial town has ever nourished at the same time two such remarkable talents as Eudora Welty and Richard Wright.

As for the Psalms, most of us were already familiar with them. In my case, I heard and read them at St. Andrew's Church Sunday by Sunday from the Book of Common Prayer, and it was a rare Jackson boy or girl in those days who, at least some of the time, did not attend Sunday school or church services and have some exposure to the morality and spirituality not only of the Psalms but of all the biblical books.

I have said that there were seldom other children living at the Crafts' (though some of my friends gathered almost daily in the side yard of the Crafts' home next door for games and frolic). But for several years Wiley P. Harris, his wife Grace and daughter, also named Grace (younger than I), occupied the room next to ours—and, on summer nights, the other end of the adjoining sleeping porch, the two families separated only by a canvas partition. I believe that my father and Wiley (as I always called him, though not to his face) actually paid for the construction of the porch atop an already existing lower porch.

Both Wiley and his wife were of prominent and well-to-do Mississippi families, Wiley's father being a state supreme court justice, and Wiley was just getting established as proprietor of Harris Store for Men on Capitol Street. Years later he was to become station manager of Jackson's first radio station, WJDX, established by the Lamar Life Insurance Company (under the direction of C. W. Welty and for which Eudora wrote publicity and program notes, as she has recalled in *One Writer's Beginnings* and in numerous interviews).

Wiley was a tall, slender, dignified man, and, I believe, had been a baseball pitcher in his years at Ole Miss. One day he decided to demonstrate and refurbish his pitching skills by practicing with me, as Mr. Brinkley did—but Wiley would pitch to me, not the reverse. We went to the Crafts' side yard next door where there was more room, and Wiley began to hurl the ball at me with more speed and impact than I was accustomed to. I handled this as well as I could until one mighty pitch, poorly caught by me, knocked a finger of my glove hand out of joint. This ended Wiley's warm-up and required a doctor's visit. It was also the occasion for some negative comment to Wiley by my mother. That finger is still a bit crooked.

On another day, a beautiful Sunday morning, Wiley took me over the Amite Street hill to the Pearl River bottomlands for some target shooting with his .22-caliber rifle. Wiley and I were both supposed to be at St. Andrew's Church at that time. Once again my mother, always protective of her only child, spoke firmly to Wiley about the matter. Ever the gentleman, he apologized, pleading ignorance of my Sunday school commitment.

One year, St. Andrew's longtime rector, Walter B. Capers, prevailed on Wiley to assume the task of teaching our Sunday school class, replacing Miss Flora Walthall, of whom we were quite fond. Dr. Capers probably felt that a younger person, free of Anglo-Catholic and ritualistic tendencies, might be a more appropriate teacher for growing boys than an aging high-church spinster.

The change did not last long. Wiley appeared several Sundays with a carefully prepared lesson plan and did his best, but we were not cooperative. We wanted Miss Flora. Several other young men were tried but soon gave up. Dr. Capers saw the light. Miss Flora returned. Our Saturday night gatherings at her house—where refreshments and much talk of books and ideas, secular as well as religious, were dispersed and word games and other entertainments were enjoyed—had meanwhile never been interrupted.

Miss Flora was a remarkable lady, a secretary by profession, the daughter of Major W. T. Walthall, C. S. A., who had been a friend and neighbor of Jefferson Davis after the war, both men active in the affairs of St. Mark's Church on the Gulf Coast. She worked five days a week and half a day on Saturday, then spent the afternoon preparing for the arrival that night of half a dozen or more boys for whom she would provide material and intellectual sustenance, as well as instruction in the centuries-old traditions of Anglicanism as promulgated by the Episcopal Church, most especially its Anglo-Catholic wing.

The attendees at Miss Flora's soirees (which continued into our college years) varied over time, but the core group consisted of George and Charles Stephenson, the brothers Marcellus and Garner Green, Frank Lyell and the present writer. Miss Flora had a sister, Miss Maud, who helped with the preparations and attended our gatherings.

Miss Maud worked with the Old Ladies Home on West Capitol Street, her assignment being to travel over the state soliciting contributions from public bodies and private citizens to maintain the home, whose inmates came from all over Mississippi. Miss Maud, with her impeccable southern credentials and no little southern charm, was very good at her job. The home, indeed, was a model of its kind, though it failed to impress a youthful Eudora Welty, as readers of "A Visit of Charity" will recall.

Following some hours with their tireless, loquacious guests, the Walthall sisters would tidy up their house and retire, only to arise early Sunday morning and walk (without breakfast, no food before the Sacrament) the half mile, winter or summer, to St. Andrew's Church for the 7:30 A.M. celebration of Holy Communion (Mass, as Miss Flora would call it; Miss Maud was not quite so "high").

During our Saturday evenings, a brother, Arthur Walthall, a quiet, pleasant man, would often be glimpsed, coming or going, but he did not participate. He was, however, an active churchman, who sometimes read the service at St. Mark's Church in west Jackson, when that black congregation was without a priest. An admirable and most unusual family.

The Walthall home was on President Street, near Davis School and the intersection with George, President, and North State a block to the east. The street rose to a hilltop near the middle of the block, and atop the hill and facing east on North State was the large home of Marcellus Green, Sr., patriarch of the Green family in my day.

The hill was known as Green Hill, and the entire block on both North State and President was largely occupied by Green family members and might well have been called Green Block. The elderly Marcellus Green, with his goatee and dignity, was the very model of a southern gentleman. He had been senior warden at St. Andrew's for as long as I could remember; the entire Green clan were pillars of that church. (My friends Marcellus Green and Garner Green, Jr., were grandsons of the patriarch.)

My father encouraged me always to save a little of whatever money I might earn or be given, wisely pointing out that one never knew when needs might increase or income decline. To spend beyond one's income can only result in eventual unhappiness and disaster, he assured me. To start me on the way to implementing this obvious truth, he took me to a nearby Amite Street savings and loan office and had me open an account with a five-dollar bill so that I could begin to experience the wonders of compound interest. He supplied other funds from time to time, and I made such small additions as I was able.

My first attempt to make a little money to spend and also to add to my account involved gathering up old magazines and newspapers, silver foil, scrap iron, old bottles and other items and hauling them to a junk dealer on South State Street. This did not produce much cash but perhaps helped to clean up the neighborhood. Finding on one occasion quite a cache of old iron under the side porch of an Amite Street house, I loaded it into my wagon and laboriously hauled it to the junk yard (no short trip, perhaps half a mile), where I received some meager sum. But then the lady who lived in the house called the police to help locate the dismantled stove taken from under her porch. I was forced to acknowledge my mistake, return the money and haul back the missing stove.

More remunerative was selling the *Saturday Evening Post*, which I did for several years. Once a week I picked up from the dealer as many copies of the *Post* as I thought I could sell, paid two or three cents for each one and set out to sell them at five cents a copy in stores and offices on Capitol Street, nearby homes and anywhere I might find a likely customer.

The Merchants Bank Building just across from the Old Capitol was a place where several regular customers were found. A major drawback was that the dealer (or the Curtis Publishing Co.) required that I take a certain number of the *Post*'s sister publication, *Country Gentleman* (which sold for ten cents and was less popular), to obtain the number of *Posts* I knew I could sell. Dr. R. L. Price, an osteopath and old family friend, was about the only customer who would buy a *Country Gentleman* without considerable cajoling. Even so I learned a few things about business dealings and human nature and earned enough to buy a book now and then, or a ball or bat, and to deposit an occasional dollar in my account.

Mrs. Wiley Harris set me forth on another career, that of golf caddy. She played at the newly opened country club west of town and paid me twenty-five cents to caddy the nine-hole course for her. Other golfing wives also used my services, picking me up at home after school or on weekends and taking me out to the club.

Here again my understanding of economics and adult psychology was enriched (especially when the ladies missed the putt or even the ball). At the end of a round my employers would usually have a Coke or Lake's Celery (a Jackson specialty), and I would stand around looking thirsty until they offered me a drink, too. From such small things one lives and learns.

In the summertime during my Davis School years my parents and I were often in New England to escape the Mississippi heat. My mother's sister (Aunt Mae) had married Albert Reaves, an employee of Boston's well-known jewelry store, A. Stowell; with their son, Paul, and daughter, Dorothy (my age), they lived in Malden. My father and Uncle Albert would stay in town (coming out for weekends), and my mother, Aunt Mae, her children and I would occupy a cottage on some lake, usually Forest Lake, near Winchester, New Hampshire, where we had relatives. (Winchester, of course, is where Aunt Mae had spent several years as a child and is near Brattleboro, Vermont, where my mother had stayed.)

These summers were very fine I thought, as we learned to swim, rowed out to catch turtles dozing on logs near the shore, fished for pickerel (and sometimes caught one) and hiked and gathered blueberries on the meadows and slopes of a nearby mountain. I know my mother and Aunt Mae relished the chance to be together again and talk over old times. They were both very merry during these months.

There were days in Malden going and coming and visits to Boston, where I was able to expand my coin and stamp collections and to wander in such great stores as Filene's and Jordan Marsh and inspect the dazzling and expensive displays in A. Stowell along with the many-storied head offices of A. W. Tedcastle & Company at Lincoln and Beach Streets. There were meals at the Parker House, attendance at theatre matinees and even an occasional Red Sox game (a real thrill). And at the Reaves home in Malden, I discovered and read not only *Peck's Bad Boy* but a book called *Uncle Tom's Cabin*, a volume not often seen in Mississippi.

Then, in Jackson, about the end of our seventh and last year at Davis School, in the spring of 1921, a photographer came up and took a picture of our grade. There we stand, twenty-three boys, fourteen girls. One of the boys is barefooted—it was that far south and that long ago. George Stephenson, Marcellus Green, other of my friends. Eudora, in a middy blouse, is in the second row, one of three girls with hair ribbons, her hair in braids around her head, large-eyed, smiling, then as now. I am in the first row, my new Boy Scout belt clearly visible. Scouting was to be one of my major enthusiasms for years.

I had forgotten the class was so large, but I remember it was orderly—a little corporal punishment now and then in the cloakroom took care of that. And besides it was a time when all were agreed that teachers knew more than students and that young people should adapt themselves to the adult world rather than the other way around.

Next year it was to be Central High, where there would be many more students and different teachers, but a principal, John Luther Roberts, as durable and dedicated as Lorena Duling.

THREE

Of Central High School
and Related Matters

Central High School was just a short walk along Amite Street and through
Smith Park from my home. When our class enrolled there in 1921, it was
an undistinguished brick structure facing east on North West Street, with
the New Capitol grounds easily visible almost across the way. When we
graduated from Central four years later, it was in the process of being noisily
enlarged into the handsome, red-brick, collegiate-Tudor building with oriel
window, twin towers and wide central entrance that it is today—though it
is no longer a school.

About the time I entered Central High, my parents decided we would
move from the Crafts' to the former Eyrich home, now facing Boyd Street,
that my father had purchased some years before. Miss Mary Craft had died,
and the popular Craft establishment had been run for several years by others
(and not so well run, my mother thought).

It was quite a change for me, leaving the busy downtown block (Capitol,
State, Amite, President), with businesses on two sides and residences on
the others, where I knew everyone, where I was in and out of the stores
(front door and back), humored by the proprietors and their employees. No
more climbing the sycamore and chinaberry trees in Dr. Hunter's backyard,
disturbing his cow, eluding his angry dog, making popguns for the china-
berries from his trees. I would race with my friends through the alley that

led from Amite Street to the delivery area for the businesses on North State and Capitol, climb the fire escapes on the backs of the Medical Building and Century Theater and enter the buildings through a hall or even office window to the alarm of the inhabitants (the fire escape on the Medical Building alarmed me, too; it was straight up for several stories). I spent much time in Eyrich's, of course, looking at books and sporting goods, and also in Kress's next door, where I bought penny candies and endlessly examined other items, while wearying the sales girls with chatter.

There was some real mischief, I fear: ringing the bell for the elevator from the top floor of the Century Theater, hiding when the operator came up to find no one, then ringing again when he had gone and bringing him up once more; shining the sunlight with a mirror from my window on Amite Street to the windows of the business school beyond the Crafts' yard to annoy the students trying to learn typing and shorthand (the school eventually complained to my mother, and that was the end of that). With a companion I threw firecrackers one evening on the Amite Street porch across the way where Erskine Helm lived with his friend Charles Pierce; and when one or the other came to the door, fired Roman candles to force them back inside. They summoned the police, and when we heard Jackson's one mounted policeman, Officer McGee, clopping up President Street, we skeedaddled. No real crime, no real violence in all these antics, but imaginative pranks that amused us and annoyed others. We should have known better.

As a matter of fact, I was very friendly with Erskine and his aged, well-to-do father and often visited them in their attractive Swiss-chalet-style home. I played checkers and a smattering of chess with the father, who spent much of his time on the Helm front porch and encouraged my visits. Charles Pierce, who moved in when the father died, was always somewhat cool, perhaps considering me, with some reason, a nuisance. Charles sold silks, satins and other cloths and designed dresses for the ladies of Jackson at a Capitol Street department store. He traveled to New York and other cities on business for his store, often accompanied by Erskine. Jacksonians who glimpsed "this well-traveled pair" (as Eudora has called them) in New York have reported that even there they made an impression.

During World War I, I read such patriotic best-sellers as Arthur Guy Empey's *Over the Top* and played Enrico Caruso's recording of "Over There" endlessly on our Victrola. And it was early on the day the war ended that I scampered up the Amite Street hill to the Old Capitol grounds and banged away on the firebell hanging there in connection with Liberty Bond sales, thereby alerting the citizenry. This patriotic act was reported in the local press, but the credit was given to others, an error that early taught me not to believe everything I read.

The Jackson city fathers had decreed that, beginning in 1925, an additional and twelfth grade should be added to the eleven that heretofore had sufficed for the town's public-school scholars. This would have meant that the year we were to complete the 11th grade, there would be no graduating class, no senior pictures in the yearbook, no commencement oratory, no awarding of diplomas—unthinkable. So a sizable proportion of the graduates from the town's several grammar schools were selected to take a little extra work each year at Central, the town's one high school, and accomplish five years' work in four. I somehow was included.

Things were quieter on Boyd Street than on Amite, and Central High was farther away, but I had friends in the Boyd neighborhood, too, and life went on. About the time we moved, the First Baptist Church bought the property where George and Charles Stephenson lived as the site for their new church, and George and Charles moved with their mother to a North Street house just a block from me. And they and I saw more now of Marcellus and Garner Green, who were nearby on North State.

We spent much time at the large, handsome Green home. The parents were always hospitable. Memorable meals were taken at their long dining-room table and lighter repasts consumed in an adjoining breakfast room, where half a dozen of us might also be found studying of an evening. Studying and homework were high on our student agendas.

Mr. Green himself would invariably be sitting in a library-living room to the left of the entrance hall, reading the *Wall Street Journal*, when I arrived for an evening visit or study session. A large radio with an impressive Magnavox speaker (at a time when most people with a radio at all had only headphones) would perhaps be giving forth with news. We students studying at the back of the house, if unable to handle a Latin construction or a math problem, never hesitated to take our difficulties to him. Unperturbed, he would put down his paper, lower the radio sound and proceed to answer our questions, usually adding a few explications on related matters for future reference.

On a Sunday afternoon Mr. Green would often take some of his several children and a friend or two for a tramp over the hill to the Pearl River lowlands, expounding on flora and fauna and generally proving himself an entertaining companion. It was his idiosyncrasy that on these excursions and at other times he never wore an overcoat, though Jackson could sometimes have chilly weather and, rarely, even snow. You would see him walking briskly down State Street on a cold day, his hands drawn up into coat sleeves a bit, but no overcoat. A remarkable and amiable man and the source of many unheralded philanthropies to Jackson individuals and institutions.

From the four years at Central High I remember especially our Latin classes—Caesar, Cicero, Vergil, because they baffled me—and the English classes, especially the literature and composition, because I liked them. The Latin, indeed, proved so difficult that my mother enlisted the help of Annie Virden, a college-graduate neighbor to tutor me in Cicero. The neighbor, being both patient and attractive, lifted my grades and spirits, and I moved on to Vergil in better shape. I was cheered, too, when our teacher let me take up class time each day by telling a chapter from some book relating to Roman history. I managed to take up more time and extract more melodrama and even comedy from William Stearns Davis's fine story, *The Victor of Salamis*, than our teacher or the author could have foreseen.

In English we made book reports, some on assigned books—"classics," considered needful for young readers—others on books of our choice. Once when a teacher complained of my unvarying selection of Zane Grey and Edgar Rice Burroughs, I reported on an entirely imaginary book and author. This nonexistent author (we had just been reading "L'Allegro" and "Il Penseroso") was named Milton C. Milton. The title and subject of his book escape me, but the report (which I read aloud), complete with plot summary, characters, setting, etc., was enthusiastically received, especially by those students who knew the true identity of Milton C. Milton. Eudora, who was aware of the hoax, raised her hand and said she would like to read that book if I would bring it to school. I promised to do so. For several days she repeated her request in class, but I always pleaded forgetfulness. So the matter has rested for more than three score years.

I wrote assiduously for our school paper, *Jackson Hi-Life*, edited by my longtime friend (dating from the days Eddy walked me around the neighborhood), William Calvin Wells, Jr. I remember an editorial on Loyalty (or was it Duty?) in which I invoked Pickett's Charge at Gettysburg. A friend and I were listed as "Joke Editors." And for the school annual, *Quadruplane*, I composed various items over the years, including a short, comic tale of Western derring-do titled "Dead-Eye Dick."

Most of our teachers at Central were unmarried and female. (I had only one male teacher, in science, and he didn't stay long.) They worked hard, knew their subjects, were unburdened by educational theory and were firm but patient with the recalcitrant. If they were not already veterans, they soon were, because there was little turnover. They were, of course, underpaid; but if they knew it, they never said so in letters to the editor, sick-outs or marches on City Hall. As a matter of fact, most Mississippians at that time were underpaid. Mississippi, like the rest of the South, was not a rich state.

John Luther Roberts, Central's principal, expected order and decorum in the halls and classrooms, and he had them. The curriculum stressed the basics, and the basics took root in our minds. As at Davis School some hymn singing and Psalm reading were considered normal, and Boy's Hi-Y and Girl's Hi-Y clubs met weekly, where the Bible was read and prayers were said. Members of the clergy spoke at our assemblies. Morality was not unmentioned.

No one questioned that at least some Latin should also take root in our minds, as an aid to clear thinking and correct English usage and spelling. I wondered about the need for Latin in my student days; but years later, when I had returned to teach at Central, my little Latin once proved an embarrassment. After a visit to my English classroom, Mr. Roberts pointed out (when the students had left) that I had misspelled a word on the blackboard. He reminded me, with a smile, that if I had remembered the Latin origin of that English word, I would not have made that error.

Mr. Roberts had been an athlete at Mississippi College and had for years been coach as well as principal at Central. Early every morning before school, he could be seen running through his neighborhood to keep in shape (jogging had not yet been invented). *Mens sana in corpore sano* was a phrase he liked to quote.

Somehow another uplifting phrase from my high-school Latin days has stuck in my mind all these years. Whether it was encountered in class, was used as a club or school motto or what, I don't recall. But I expect that Mr. Roberts, who had once taught the language and sometimes still did when our Latin teacher failed to appear, was somehow involved: *Esse quam videri*. That phrase, too, is worth heeding. Thus, bits and pieces of that ancient language did take root. (I hope I have those phrases right—or John Luther Roberts will surely come to haunt me.)

Eventually a full-time coach relieved Mr. Roberts of his coaching duties. The coach also introduced a physical-education program to which male students reported once or twice a week. This was held across the street in Smith Park and often consisted of an abbreviated softball game. One of these games was the occasion of the only fight I ever remember being involved in.

Although I was easily aroused to anger, I usually kept my emotions under control, since I was not the hefty type and felt that discretion was indeed the better part of valor.

However, I loved baseball and eagerly sought my chance at bat during our brief softball games. One fellow student had on several occasions shoved ahead to bat in my turn. He did it once too often. I grabbed the bat from him with one hand and poked him in the nose with the other. We exchanged a few blows until the coach broke it up. My opponent was Theodore G. Bilbo, Jr., son of the famed Mississippi governor and senator. Our relationship had previously been and subsequently remained cordial enough. Bilbo, Jr., went on to attend West Point and became in time, I believe, a United States Army general.

Smith Park had swings, tennis courts, gymnastic bars and a bandstand. After school and on holidays and weekends, George, Charles, Marcellus and I often played tennis. Charles and Marcellus went on to do well in state tennis tournaments, and I continued to play throughout my college years and even later, with much pleasure and some proficiency but no prizes.

As I recall, the bandstand in Smith Park was used more for political and religious speeches than for music. It was also used by a happy, somewhat fey character named Wiley Cooper, a friend to all, who loved to emulate the politicos and ascend the bandstand to make speeches of his own on subjects not altogether clear. He would also watch our tennis matches and cheerfully comment on our performance. Sometimes he would offer a piece of gum or candy, even a small coin or two on a hot day to purchase a soft drink (an inadequate sum even in those low-cost days). We would decline with thanks. I never knew where Wiley lived or how he subsisted, but I often encountered him in the neighborhood; we would shake hands and have a bit of talk. He loved to be around people and to talk and could be seen at the circus in the spring and the state fair in October.

Once or twice on a late Sunday afternoon or evening in summer, I saw Wiley enter the side door of the Baptist Church (located at that time on Capitol and President Streets) to attend a service or organizational meeting and, the door being open for coolness, could observe him singing lustily or even speaking ("testifying?") at some length. Years later, when I read Eudora's *The Ponder Heart*, about Daniel Ponder and his outgoing adventures and misadventures in the town of Beulah, his being taken needlessly to the state asylum at Jackson, his visits to the fair and so on, I said to myself (but never yet to Eudora), "Wiley Cooper!" Spruced up, made prosperous, transferred from Jackson to Beulah and transformed by the rich imagination of a master storyteller, Uncle Daniel will ever be Wiley Cooper to me.

The Jackson Public Library was only a block from Central High, and I began to use it increasingly, dropping by after school and on weekends to read the magazines and check out books. I discovered *Lorna Doone*, *The Cloister and the Hearth*, *Quentin Durward* and *The White Company*, among other favorite books at this time. The latter, a fine historical novel, was an unexpected pleasure, coming as it did from the creator of Sherlock Holmes, a longtime favorite. I remember trying Wilkie Collins, too, but found myself not yet ready.

My mother, a great reader, was also a regular patron, and we became friends with the librarian, Mrs. Annie Parker, a somewhat formidable lady, who sternly enforced the library's No Talking and Silence rules on everyone except herself. She would laugh and talk with my mother, whom she amiably called "a little damn Yankee" (when I was alone to check out recommended books for her). Eudora has immortalized Mrs. Parker and the Jackson Public Library of those days in a number of essays and interviews.

Other of my Central High friends who were frequent visitors to the library with me were Ralph Hilton and Buford Yerger. Ralph turned up at Central in about the tenth grade when his lawyer father moved his family to Jackson from Mendenhall, a small county seat south of Jackson. Ralph was a gregarious, unflappable sort, who shared my interest in books and dreamed of writing short stories and editing his own newspaper. Together we analyzed the stories in popular magazines and the winning stories in the annual best-short-story collections. We became lifelong friends; and when he did eventually publish books after a long career in the State Department, I had the pleasure of reviewing them in *The New York Times Book Review* and also of reading the newspaper he founded at Hilton Head, South Carolina.

Buford was a native Jacksonian of a family prominent in business and Episcopal Church affairs in Mississippi since antebellum times. His father was a newspaperman, and Buford talked of a journalistic career. He made a beginning with a newspaper route (which included the Welty home on Congress Street), and I often accompanied him, tossing the Jackson *Daily News* from the Yerger Ford coupe, as Buford drove briskly.

After delivering our papers, some of which, I regret to say, landed on porch roofs, we frequently ended up at the Yerger home on Fortification Street, where Buford and I were planning a novel concerned with pirates and a Caribbean treasure. The novel, needless to say, required more time and ingenuity than we had at our disposal, though a good many pages were, in fact, typed out.

It was at this period, as I recall, that I wrote a letter to Harris Dickson in Vicksburg, whose novels, stories and articles in popular magazines had caught my attention and admiration. A real author only forty-odd miles away! I naively asked his advice on how to go about becoming a writer. Strangely enough he replied, cryptically but not unkindly: "Before you set out to write a story," he advised, "be sure you have a story to write."

Because of the similarity of our family names and (it was said) our appearance, Buford and I were sometimes confused by those who did not know us well. This amused us and served to strengthen our friendship. But our paths diverged. He became a state official, bank president and treasurer of the Episcopal Diocese of Mississippi—all areas in which his family had long been active.

Even before entering Central High and as soon as I had reached my twelfth birthday, I hastened down to the offices of the Jackson Council, Boy Scouts of America, to purchase a Boy Scout handbook and discover how to go about joining that organization. Most of my friends who were old enough were members or soon became so. The offices were located on the upper floor of a two-story Capitol Street building facing the post office. Here, Scout executive Thomas B. Abernathy, a short, wiry, red-haired Scotsman, presided, assisted by an attractive secretary, Grace Davidson.

Awed by the khaki-clad Mr. Ab (as he was called) and charmed by the ever-cheery Grace (on whom more than one Scout had a bit of a crush), I obtained a handbook and departed with the information I needed. The Scout motto, "Be Prepared," was somewhat expansive, but I proposed to meet it.

I had been a subscriber to the Scout magazine, *Boy's Life*, for some time, had been attracted by the Scouting program of camping, nature study, athletics, healthy living and good deeds. With World War I only recently over, the Scout uniform and semi-military practices were more than usually appealing. I don't know how long Scouting had been active in Jackson, by 1920 a city of some twenty thousand persons; but it must have been for several years. There were already a dozen or so troops, sponsored by the various churches of the town.

I became a member of Troop 1, based at St. Andrew's Church, with N. Pugh Lightcap, the local Buick dealer and faithful member of the parish, as Scoutmaster. Wearing my Tenderfoot badge (symbol of fledgling membership) and khaki uniform, I was soon busy demonstrating that (as the Scout laws have it) a Scout is Trustworthy, Loyal, Helpful, Friendly, Courteous, Kind, Obedient, Cheerful, Thrifty, Brave, Clean and Reverent. I was busy, too, in mastering the skills and requirements for advancing through the various rankings of the organization. As usual, I was whole-heartedly involved.

Troop 1 was small in numbers, as the St. Andrew's congregation was small in numbers compared to the Baptist and Methodist churches. The result was that we in Troop 1 had greater opportunity to hold titles in the troop's organization. I became zealous in office seeking. I was soon patrol leader of Troop 1's Wolf Patrol. The troop assembled Friday nights at the church to attend to official business, followed by fun and games. A secretary or scribe kept a record of all this. I became scribe and reported on our activities in the weekly Scout page of the Jackson *Daily News*, my first words to see print.

The troop could have a bugler. I ordered a bugle from an army surplus store, bought a Victor record with bugle calls on it, played the record endlessly, learned the calls and taught myself to bugle. I became bugler. A drummer was possible. As it happened, the troop had a drum. I practiced a bit and became drummer. Scoutmaster Lightcap and my fellow Scouts were indulgent, intrigued by my enthusiasm. Each office entitled me to wear a distinctive insignia on my uniform, which my mother carefully sewed on. All very grand, I thought.

On the way to achieving the rank of Eagle Scout one earned "merit badges" in various practical subjects. I set busily to work earning as many badges as I could (astronomy, forestry, electricity, carpentry, masonry, poultry raising, etc.) and eventually acquired thirty-two. More sewing. Earning the badges involved some learning activity, initiative and meeting of people and was certainly worthwhile.

My parents naturally encouraged me in my Scouting zeal, my mother not only sewing on my insignia and keeping my uniform in repair but supplying refreshments for our afternoon patrol meetings, helping round up equipment for our troop and so on. My father became a troop com-mitteeman (faithfully wearing on his lapel the miniature pin of this office), contributed and helped collect funds for various expenses, attended some troop meetings and the occasional films on Scouting (one or two along the lines of what-every-boy-should-know, mild by present-day standards but something of an innovation at that time and not universally approved by all parents).

My father's interest in good causes led him to assume the presidency of Jackson's Community Welfare Association, which he helped organize, and to raise funds so that Robert Barber, an ailing and popular newsboy, could go to New York City's Memorial Hospital for "treatment under the direction of Dr. William B. Coley, cancer specialist," as reported in the Jackson *Daily News*.

The *Daily News* ran several of Robert's letters from New York to my father, thanking him for his help, which continued with financing and the sending of clothing, games, a camera and other items. And once Robert wrote, "Mr. Burger, I sure did enjoy reading the books your son gave me. I am letting some of my friends in the hospital read them also." I don't remember the books, but I do remember visiting Robert with my parents on a trip to Boston, stopping off for a day or two and watching from a hospital window the snow (the first real snow I had seen) falling on a park across the way.

Though my father was often away during the week, from my earliest years he gave me much attention when home. He would walk me down Capitol Street, stopping in one store or another to greet the owner and give me a chance to do the same. No doubt a bit of business was included in my father's remarks as well. In the shoe stores or shoe departments of the larger stores, I would note the rows of shoe boxes on the shelves, many with the logo of A. W. Tedcastle & Co., a logo designed by my father and suggested to Mr. Tedcastle, who adopted it for all the firm's boxes and advertising over the country.

At the far end of Capitol Street's business district was the railroad station and the Edwards House, Jackson's major hostelry (not yet rebuilt into the much larger Edwards Hotel, which in turn became the King Edward, only to die a slow death with the decline of passenger rail service and the decay of the neighborhood). The Edwards in its prime was a gathering place for tourists, politicians and local citizens. Many a business and political deal was shaped in its lobby and restaurants.

At the Edwards, too, were the storage rooms for my father's several sample trunks, large trunks as tall as I was, and the sample rooms with their long tables where the hundred or so latest samples were displayed so that Jackson and nearby merchants could inspect them and place their orders. There was a great deal of time and labor involved in packing and unpacking these samples, having them hauled over to the train station for shipping to other towns, and then repeating the process for the return.

I often accompanied my father as he prepared his samples at the hotel and even remained as he greeted the buyers, many of whom I knew. Other salesmen with their own wares on display were encountered as well. I remember especially Ellis Engel, who represented a large shirt company, because when he received new samples, he let me have any of the boy-size discontinued samples I wanted. For some years my parents never needed to buy me a shirt. I did not benefit from my father's samples, since all of these were for the same foot.

It was at the Edwards sample rooms that I met Mr. Engel's son, Lehman Engel, a year or two younger than I. I did not know Lehman at Davis School, because he attended Robert E. Lee School on South State near where he lived—the South's two most admired leaders of the time giving their names to Jackson's earliest grammar schools. Lehman grew up to become the famous New York music teacher, composer and conductor of Broadway and other musical shows. But before that happened he was a member of our Boy Scout Troop 1 and as a student at Central High the composer of the school's alma mater. He has recalled all of this, his friendship with Eudora, Frank Lyell, Hubert Creekmore and others of our Jackson group and much else in his very readable 1974 autobiographical volume, *This Bright Day*.

Near the Edwards Hotel for several years was a popular cafeteria, the source of the first money I ever made in using the English language. Before the cafeteria opened, it announced a twenty-five-dollar award for a name. Without too much cogitation, I wrote in with a somewhat anachronistic suggestion—"Old Southern Cafeteria"—and won the prize. Since I won out over a number of my older and wiser adult friends, I felt unusually pleased with myself. And at $8.35 a word that is still the best pay I have ever received for my use of English.

Every summer the Boy Scouts conducted a summer camp for a few weeks at what was called the Old Country Club Lake, a few miles east of Jackson across the Pearl River on an old road to Brandon. I never knew why the lake was so called; there was nothing there except piney woods and red-clay hills. The name of the lake, however, once caused me to make an error in my weekly Boy Scout report in the Jackson *Daily News*—and taught me the importance of getting my facts straight.

Our troop had invited the venerable Marcellus Green, Sr., to attend a troop meeting and tell us of his boyhood memories of the Civil War Battle of Jackson. He obliged and recalled how the approaching Federal troops precipitated a skirmish with Confederate defenders "out by the Country Club" and how the battle developed. Well, the newly developed Jackson Country Club west of town had not yet penetrated my consciousness, and

I reported the skirmish as occurring miles east of town in the opposite direction at the Boy Scouts' Old Country Club Lake campsite. This location would have given added interest to my report if true, but, of course, it wasn't. I was embarrassed and more careful thereafter.

Anyway, I eagerly attended the camp for several years, equipped with all sorts of camping gear, including a pup tent. Several of us in Troop 1 had purchased pup tents and proposed to set these up on the hill above the large, room-size army tents set up for the camp. We thought thus to experience more rugged field conditions. Mr. Ab agreed to this but resisted our plan to call ourselves Bear Cat Company, the name of an expensive sports car of the time, instead of choosing the name of a real animal as the other groups did.

However, we prevailed. And at morning formation and flag raising (with bugle call) and Pledge of Allegiance, I lustily called out, "Bear Cat Company, all present or accounted for." And did the same at the evening flag lowering.

These weeks of camp were great fun, though there were chores to perform. For the hearty meals taken in a mess tent, water for drinking and cooking had to be brought in pails from a nearby spring, and there were daily inspections of each tent for order and neatness. But there was much swimming and many games, contests and opportunities to earn merit badges and advance in Scout ranking. I always brought a fishing rod and was up before reveille to catch a fish, which I would clean, and which Van, our agreeable black cook, would fry and add to my already ample breakfast.

Several summers I followed Scout camp with a visit to my Uncle George's family in Aberdeen. The several Leftwich children were now grown and had moved to other towns, except for the youngest, Frank, a little older than I, so there was plenty of room in the Leftwiches' big house. I helped in the garden and in caring for Sister Elgie's large flock of chickens, gathered the eggs, fed the pigs and felt that I was being useful. There was a cow (milked faithfully but unwillingly by Frank), and from the milk Sister Elgie churned the family butter. My efforts to assist in the milking were not successful.

I slept in a room with several pictures of my cousins, George, Jr., in Ole Miss baseball uniform and William Groom, in Sewanee football regalia. I gazed at these pictures with awe and admiration and wished I could follow in their steps, but knew this was unlikely. Both George and Groom were powerful athlete-sized men as most of the Leftwiches were. Frank, my summer companion and still in high school, while sturdy, was not so large, though he played football at Ole Miss in his time and was always admired by me.

On one memorable occasion Frank and a friend took me on an overnight camping trip on the Tombigbee River. We paddled a few miles, set up camp on a sand bar, swam, had a good supper, set out trot lines to catch fish for breakfast and got up before dawn to check the lines.

Sister Elgie had been somewhat concerned about my going along on such an adventure, but Frank and I had reassured her. Her forebodings were justified. I sat half awake in our skiff as Frank and his friend paddled, but I finally dozed off, slumped to the side and fell into the Tombigbee. The water waked me up. Frank grabbed me as the boat moved along, and we made it to shore. But for swallowing and inhaling some muddy water and strangling a bit, there was no damage. It was agreed, however, that it would be better not to report this episode at home.

On rainy days and other times I read in the many-volumed Stoddard Lectures, novels by Scott, Thomas Nelson Page, Mary Johnson, Charles Egbert Craddock and less familiar authors found in the family's library, and law books, Methodist journals and historical quarterlies. Uncle George, who had an interest in the history of his adopted state, served on the board of the Mississippi Historical Society and occasionally wrote for its journal.

On Sunday mornings Frank would polish his father's shoes (for which he was awarded twenty-five cents), and we all set out for church. I disembarked at St. John's Episcopal Church, an impressive brick, antebellum edifice erected during the rectorate of Massachusetts-born Joseph Holt Ingraham, who was later Mississippi writer Sherwood Bonner's pastor at Holly Springs, himself an author who shot himself fatally there on the eve of the Civil War (an accident it was said). At St. John's I would encounter my friend, Andrew Jackson Gillespie ("Boo") Bumpass and his family, who lived next door to the Leftwiches, another neighborhood friend, Arthur Dugan and family, and a few other acquaintances less well remembered. Arthur went on to become a Rhodes scholar and longtime Sewanee teacher and benefactor.

Sister Elgie and Frank attended the Baptist Church; Uncle George, a lifelong Methodist like his Virginia mother, was a mainstay of that denomination. If any of the other Leftwich children were in town, the sons would accompany their father to the Methodist Church, and the girls would go with their mother to the Baptist. That had always been the arrangement: sons, Methodists; daughters, Baptists. Frank, for some reason, had not conformed and had become a Baptist. There was no friction but mutual respect and harmony all around.

Once I attended the Methodist service and found it easy to follow and not unlike the Episcopal ritual. (When my father was confirmed in the Episcopal Church in Jackson, Uncle George wrote him a letter of congratulation, saying it was a step he had often contemplated himself.) A visit with Sister Elgie and Frank to the Baptist Church kept me on edge. I was ever about to hop up for the hymns and kneel for prayers. Sitting for the sermon was no problem, except that the pastor's remarks were longer and more fervent than I was accustomed to.

Visits to Aberdeen and Scout camps became less frequent as I began to explore the local job market in order to earn a few dollars for my hobbies and savings account (looking forward to college). Eyrich's was first to use my services, on weekends and holidays. I enjoyed this work in familiar surroundings, with the opportunity to browse in the books and magazines during quiet moments. I remember discovering *The Meditations of Marcus Aurelius*, Oscar Wilde's *Salome*, *Letters of Brother Lawrence* and *The Rubaiyat of Omar Khayyam* (a mixed bag, indeed) in handsome, leather-bound gift editions, along with the usual Zane Grey, Sax Rohmer and Edgar Rice Burroughs. I usually bought the Burroughs volumes to enjoy at leisure.

However, one last summer camp itself produced a bit of income and a novel experience. The Jackson Y.W.C.A. sponsored a camp for girls at the same site used by our Boy Scout camp. Cynthia Virden, the director, a neighbor and friend (indeed, she was sister to Annie Virden, who had tutored me in Latin and smoothed my path through Cicero), asked me to serve the camp as bugler and lifeguard. I believe I was paid one dollar per day for this service. One or two other Scouts from Troop 1 were sometimes on hand to perform odd jobs or bring out supplies from town, and there were several older girl staffers or counselors.

I bivouacked on the hillside in my Bear Cat pup tent and emerged to blow reveille every morning and sound taps at night. There were flag raisings and lowerings at which I bugled and campfires as on the Scout camps. And I monitored the swimming periods with no fatalities.

Then on a weekend between camp periods when few campers were on hand, one of the older girls, a counselor (and an attractive one, as I recall), with a professed interest in astronomy, asked me to point out for her that evening several constellations she had not been able to locate. I agreed. She arrived on my hillside in due time, and the Pleiades, Cassiopeia or whatever, appeared on schedule. (On the strength of my Scout merit badge in astronomy, I had expounded on the constellations at a recent campfire.)

But my inquirer lingered, and it soon became apparent that her interest lay also in what might broadly be termed sociability; the evening continued for some time, as the constellations wheeled in their courses. I eventually asked if the camp director was aware of her late night astronomy study. She thought not; anyway she hadn't mentioned it. Finally, Judy (which might have been her name but wasn't) prepared to depart but said she would return the next night for more star gazing. That was all right with me. A Scout is helpful.

George and Charles Stephenson were coming out the next day to stay overnight, as they did several times. That evening Judy, George, Charles and I talked and studied the heavens for some time, until it was suggested we go for a dip in the lake. We knew this would certainly not be approved, so we went quietly to a remote area, entered the water noiselessly (we thought), swam over to the raft by the swimming area and began to clamber aboard.

But sound travels easily over water, and in no time at all a light from shore fell upon us and an alarmed camp director demanded to know who we were and what was going on. George, Charles and I identified ourselves and were admonished to get out of the lake and go to bed. Judy remained in the water, concealed by the raft, until all was quiet, then made her way to shore and her tent.

So ended my most pleasant and surprising experience as a Scout camper. I recounted this adventure many times over the years as the Adventure of a Boy Scout Bugler at a Girl Scout Camp. It wasn't a Girl Scout camp, but it sounded better that way.

Years later Eudora wrote one of her best-known stories, "Moon Lake," which tells a somewhat similar tale (without Judy or the astronomy). She moved the action to Moon Lake in the Delta, as one of her Morgana stories. And she has said that it describes her own experience as a little girl camper at the Old Country Club Lake site (sometimes called Camp McLaurin) and that the lifeguard is based on her brother Edward (whom I well recall as a member of the Methodist Church's Troop 5). So be it. A Scout is courteous. I am willing to share the role of lifeguard-bugler (but not Judy) with Edward.

As for Moon Lake, strangely enough there is a bit more. A year or two after the events narrated above, I went with my friend Ralph Hilton and his lawyer father on an overnight trip to a Delta county seat. We stayed with Hilton relatives, who always seemed to be available statewide. This happened to be near the town from which Judy had come to be counselor at the Y.W.C.A. camp. It was also near Moon Lake.

That evening while the Hilton family talked, Ralph and I drove over to Judy's town, made inquiries, and found Judy, now a Mississippi State College for Women student, at home. Once again Judy and I (plus Ralph and a friend of Judy's) went swimming in a lake, Moon Lake this time. And once again it was late, the lake was deserted and the constellations were in their appointed places. Happily Judy's interest in astronomy and sociability had not diminished. It was a fine evening. And twenty-odd years before "Moon Lake."

FOUR

Hard Times Comes
A-Knocking at the Door

The prosperity that had marked the affairs of A. W. Tedcastle & Co. during my father's association with that firm (and to which prosperity my father's own abilities and efforts had contributed more than a little) began to decline after World War I. I was too young to understand just what was going on; but from what I remember and have picked up over the years, I gather that Tedcastle's ambitious expansion in connection with the wartime boom, followed by a postwar recession, had placed the firm's affairs in jeopardy.

Struggling to meet payments on loans taken out to finance wartime contracts, Tedcastle lacked the funds to keep up with the annual fashion changes in their shoe-manufacturing business. I remember my father's comments on receiving some new samples that the shoes were not up-to-date and would sell poorly.

He had been with Tedcastle for many years and in his own affairs had always followed his advice to me of waste not, want not and regular saving and investment. He was close to Mr. Tedcastle, loyal to the firm and decided to stick it out, using his own savings to get by, hoping that Tedcastle's situation would improve.

A letter to his lawyer-brother George Leftwich from my father at this time regarding the handling of his estate reveals that his savings and investments were indeed in good shape. The letter also reveals something of his warm attention for his family (all of his brothers and sisters were to receive legacies and "collection of the indebtedness of [brother] John W. Burger for which you hold note should not be pressed unless he is able to pay without embarrassment") and is couched in a dignified, lapidary style more often met with in those times than our own. Most income was to be paid to my mother as collected, though funds were also "to be used for the development and advancement of Nash K. Burger, Jr." And "I would have him understand his duty and the great obligation he owes his good mother, who has so studiously endeavored to do for him as only a faithful, loving mother can."

The two-page letter concludes, "Lastly I want to express gratification that a cherished hope and constant aim on my part to encourage Nash to be at all times and in all things absolutely truthful and honest has been most fruitful of results. This evidence of his love, affection and obedience more than repays me for all my efforts in his behalf. I thank our most merciful Heavenly Father who has always been good and kind to me for the blessed privilege of providing Nash with sufficient funds for a good start in early life, and which I hope he may invest wisely, always avoiding useless and extravagant expenditures."

My father was to live a score or more years after this letter was written, but the decline of A. W. Tedcastle & Co. and the subsequent Great Depression were to upset the carefully laid plans set forth. By 1926 the letters between my father and Mr. Tedcastle, friendly as always, showed both men increasingly in a financial bind (many of Mr. Tedcastle's letters, written personally in longhand, asked that the contents be kept private). Thus he writes, "We have practically been through in a large way what you have been through in a small way for the past five years. We have been liquidating a stock of $1,500,000 that we had on hand or contracted for in 1920, so the writer has been living on capital also and like yourself is not using a car or chauffeur. . . . I would not like what I am writing you to go outside yourself."

My father eventually gave up his expensive effort to help the firm sell off its out-of-date overstock and made a change of employment. Through the help and encouragement of an old friend from the days at the Crafts', a salesman in Mississippi for the Miller-Smith Hosiery Company of Chattanooga, my father took a position with that company. His territory was the entire state of Texas.

Thus, at sixty years of age, he began a new job in an unfamiliar territory, doing so with his usual determination, confidence and no little success. His new territory was larger than his old, and his product no longer involved the boots and shoes he knew so well. There was at least one advantage, he pointed out: the packing and transporting of his hosiery samples was much easier than coping with several trunkloads of shoes.

Mr. Tedcastle, though not his company, seemingly emerged in better shape from the crisis than did my father. Their correspondence continued intermittently, and in a 1934 letter Mr. Tedcastle wrote (after my father had mentioned his age and health might cause him to seek a nontraveling position):

> I was very glad indeed to hear from you, and from your steady hand-writing you evidently have not taken to drink. If or when we have any inquiries about you, there is no salesman that we had during the many years of our business career that we would more cheerfully recommend for honesty, integrity and diligence than your good self, so do not hesitate to call on us for that kind of assistance.
>
> As to the old business, years ago we gave up the local and United States portion and gave our time and attention to foreign trade and sold to practically every country in the world, built up a business of several million dollars and had it gradually wiped off the slate by the mistaken ideas of the Republican party on the tariff question. Our friends became our enemies apparently, and we are now liquidating the business.

I had sometimes wondered about my father's close and familiar relations with Mr. Tedcastle, which seemed something more than merely those of a salesman with the president of his company. On our trips to Boston Mr. Tedcastle would take us all to lunch, and my parents would visit him and his family at their suburban estate. My father was treated almost like a company official himself. Then a few years ago I happened on the answer.

Running through the index to the many-volumed *New England Historical and Genealogical Society Register* at the University of Virginia library (looking in the T's for Tibbetts, my great-grandmother's family name), I was surprised to see the name "Tedcastle, Arthur White." Pulling out the 1940 volume referred to, I found the article, which turned out to be an obituary of Mr. Tedcastle, and discovered, as I often have, that seemingly casual events are more often than not related.

It seems that our old friend Mr. Tedcastle, born in London of a Scottish family, grew up in New Jersey and worked in Wall Street and in a New York private bank. When his employer bought a bank in Rome, Georgia, in 1875, and moved there, twenty-year-old Tedcastle tagged along and took a job as bookkeeper in a small, wholesale shoe and drygoods business. By 1890 he owned the company, now much expanded and renamed A. W. Tedcastle & Co., was married to a lady of some distinction (both she and Tedcastle fortunately became members of the NEHGS, hence the obituary), and was active in a number of local enterprises, including the removal to the area of a Lowell, Massachusetts, textile mill.

Having done his part in the creation of Henry W. Grady's New South, this canny Scot (who might, I suppose, be termed a carpetbagger, though a benevolent one) returned to the East in 1898, with his A. W. Tedcastle & Co., Manufacturer and Jobber of Boots and Shoes, now located in Boston. Among the first hired of the salesmen for the expanded and newly located business was my father, whom he had known for some time in Rome, through my father's role as salesman in Georgia for the New England Shoe Company and United States Leather Company. This latter fact I discovered after reading the obituary.

So my father was headquartered in Boston before Arthur Tedcastle and may well have played some part in his removal there. Certainly both men prospered for years in their Boston location and relationship.

A quarter of a century later as our family fortunes declined along with those of A. W. Tedcastle & Co., I was aware of my parents' concern, but our life on Boyd Street continued for a time very much as it had. Our summer trips to the East or to the North Carolina mountains near Asheville, where we had sometimes gone (as did the Garner Green family with my friend Marcellus), came to an end. And, during the rest of the year, my father's business trips to his more distant Texas territory kept him away from home for longer periods. Yet like most young people I was more aware of my own aims and ambitions than those of the adult world.

For several summers in the mid-1920s I worked at Jackson's Merchants Bank, across from the Old Capitol, mostly as a bank runner, taking checks, drafts and financial documents to other banks and various businesses around town for payment or whatever was required. Among acquaintances made in my job was Theodore G. Bilbo, Sr., whose son I had poked in the nose at Smith Park. Bilbo, Sr., was always running for some office, and when I came to know him he was issuing a newspaper called *The Free Lance* from a Capitol Street office. It seemed that every few days I presented him with a draft from the Mergenthaler Linotype Co. for payment due on some of his equipment.

Sometimes Bilbo paid, sometimes not. In any case, he was politician enough to be pleasant to a future voter and would engage me in conversation about the weather, my job or some equally important topic. I did not tell him of my encounter with his son or that my Uncle George had once headed a committee that suggested he resign from the Mississippi legislature.

Being a bank runner in a Mississippi summer was hot work, outside and inside, there being no air conditioning in those days. Sometimes to the more distant businesses—which ranged from an oil company at the city's eastern edge near the banks of the Pearl River, where LeFleur's trading post had once stood, to a grocery wholesaler several miles away on the western edge of the business district—I rode my bicycle.

Yet I was used to the heat and did not mind the work, especially since I was able to save most of my sixty-dollar-per-month salary to apply on my upcoming college expenses. Millsaps College, which I entered in September 1925, was not my first choice, but it was the least expensive option, a prime consideration at that time. I had long wanted to attend the University of the South in Sewanee, Tennessee, where the medieval atmosphere (as it seemed to me) of that school's stone, Gothic buildings on the ten-thousand-acre domain was more appealing, but I knew we could not afford that.

Then there was the University of Mississippi at Oxford, where Billy Wells and so many of my Central High friends were going and my cousin Frank Leftwich was playing football. But Millsaps was only a few blocks away, and I could live at home. In retrospect I believe Millsaps was the best place for me at that time. It was and is a very good school.

I profited from my summer work at the Merchants Bank in more ways than just my small salary. I learned the workings of the banking system (a very useful thing to know) and became aware of the power that money exerts in large things and small, public and private. When some years later I read of F. Scott Fitzgerald's remark to Ernest Hemingway that "the rich are different from you and me," and of Hemingway's reply, "Yes, they have more money," I knew they were both right.

I also learned, especially when the Great Depression arrived and the Merchants Bank collapsed along with many other banks, businesses and personal fortunes, that the world could indeed be, as the poet has it, "too much with us," that in "[g]etting and spending, we lay waste our powers." And another line from my reading at that time (the English writer James

Elroy Flecker's *Hassan*, I believe) has stuck in my mind with good effect: "Let not ambition's tiger devour contentment's sheep."

Such bits of wisdom mostly came later, and for a few summers I worked away well content with my lot. My bank employers were not too strict. I found time on my rounds to sample records at a music store on Capitol Street and occasionally buy one, to check out the new books at Eyrich's, and to talk with Aunt Nancy, the old, pipe-smoking black woman who lived in a cabin near the oil wholesaler and who would tell my fortune (she shrewdly foresaw both good things and bad in my future).

I sometimes found time, too, to sit on a Mill Street bench across from the wholesale grocer, have a Delaware Punch, and compose a few lines in the manner of what I conceived to be the style of Sherwood Anderson or Mark Twain. Or, carrying in each hand down Capitol Street a bag of currency to the express office for shipment to an out-of-town bank, I might spend some time talking with a friend parked at the curb (how did she so often happen to be there?), oblivious to any danger of being robbed.

Not infrequently I stopped in to speak with Pat Buckley, a teller at another bank, who helped me expand my silver-dollar collection. He would hold on to any silver dollars that passed through his hands (normally these went into the vault, because there was little demand for them), and I would exchange rolls of pennies saved from my pocket change for any of the dollars that seemed collectible. Thus I built my assortment of various dates and mint marks—the "O" on the dollar from the New Orleans mint being most likely to catch my eye.

One day Pat mentioned a trip he had recently made on a steamboat from Vicksburg to New Orleans and suggested I try it. This was an exciting prospect to any reader of Mark Twain's *Life on the Mississippi*. Ralph Hilton thought so too, and, after obtaining a dubious approval from our parents (Weren't we too young to venture alone on such a trip? Nobody traveled on steamboats these days, etc.), we made inquiry as to costs and schedules, and at the end of the summer set off.

Buford Yerger drove us to Vicksburg the day before the supposed departure date, since the boat's schedule, it seemed, was somewhat elastic and since the Yerger Ford (in which Buford and I had delivered the Jackson *Daily News*) had seen better days (we did have at least one flat tire on the unpaved Jackson-Vicksburg Road).

We spent the night in a Vicksburg hotel and the next day walking around the town, noting the historic courthouse that had survived the Civil War bombardment, discovering the local library (I remember reading Ben Hecht's *1,001 Afternoons in Chicago*) and periodically checking the river landing for the boat's arrival. By nightfall no boat.

Ralph and I spent several hours sitting on the cobblestones of the sparsely illuminated landing, with our bags, waiting for our dream boat. Finally about midnight it appeared, having had to pick up and deliver more freight on the way than expected. We paid our twenty-five dollars (the total cost for the two- or three-day trip, room and board included) and were shown to our cabin, with its double-decker bunk. Exhausted but still excited with our adventure, we crawled into bed and were soon asleep.

Our craft, as it turned out, was one of the last of the paddle wheelers carrying freight and passengers along the Mississippi. Small in comparison to the pleasure palaces that nowadays transport the well-to-do on vacation jaunts, its name, *Uncle Oliver*, was appropriate to its appearance and amenities.

There were two decks, the lower for the barrels, bales, boxes, and produce taken on and put off at landings along the way, and the upper, given over to a large, central room or salon (if that is not too grand a term) with cabins along the sides. Here meals were taken, and here, at other times, one sat, talked, read or relaxed, listening the while to the throbbing of the engine and the low splat, splat of the paddle wheel. A small pilot house sat atop the upper deck, where a pilot and an assistant alternated in guiding our craft to and from the landings and down the vast, brown river moving slowly to the gulf.

The pilots, one or two crewmen and Ralph and I all ate at one long table, and I seem to remember ham, chicken and eggs at every meal, and sometimes steak. Tomatoes, turnip greens, beans, potatoes, grits, cornbread and biscuits were in ample supply. I also recall favorably the sweet-potato pie. At the front of the upper deck near the railing hung several bunches of bananas in case one needed a snack between meals, and soft drinks (for five cents) were available at any time.

Ralph and I had looked forward to our stop at Natchez-under-the-Hill, our heads filled with romantic tales of outlaws and cutthroats, gamblers and card sharks, maidens in distress or on the prowl—all the characters that the place was famed for. It was after midnight when we arrived, a few lights overhead only faintly illuminating the landing, a few buildings, a warehouse or two. Half a dozen men or more, black and white, stood around, waiting for *Uncle Oliver*. Not a maiden in sight.

A passenger got off, and a bustle began on the landing. Boxes of produce and a crate of chickens were brought aboard, and a large number of bales and barrels were rolled down the landing and across the gangplank. This took some time, and the black workers began a little chant, "Good-bye, old barrel, good-bye-ee," over and over, as they guided the barrels onto the boat and stowed them on the lower deck.

In due time, the pilot sounded a few blasts from the boat's whistle, and *Uncle Oliver* backed out into the dark, mile-wide river and headed for New Orleans. We had seen Natchez-under-the-Hill.

We arrived at New Orleans around dusk and tied up at a wharf some distance above the heart of the city. Ralph and I decided to save a night's hotel bill, spend the night aboard and go into town first thing in the morning. This proved an unwise decision, since we were nearly eaten alive by the mosquitos that swarmed aboard as soon as *Uncle Oliver* docked. We spent a hot and largely sleepless night under our bed covering, trying unsuccessfully to escape these bloodthirsty pests.

After an early breakfast we were happy to pack our bags and flee *Uncle Oliver* and its invading mosquitos, walk some distance across the city's outskirts to Tchoupitoulas Street and take a streetcar into town. We found our way to the hotel my father had directed us to. It was the Lafayette (it faced a square of that name) and was where my father often stayed. In fact, I bore in my suitcase a letter from my father to the manager, whom he knew, commending us to his attention. The result was a fine, large room, and the first thing we did was fall into bed and catch up on sleep.

By afternoon, we were up and headed for the Vieux Carré, the goal of our New Orleans visit. We were not disappointed. The old section of town seemed indeed a foreign city to our eyes; the narrow streets, their names and signs in French, the old low buildings with their wrought-iron balconies, the courtyards glimpsed beyond, all delighted us. The people looked different; their English sounded different. Often the language they spoke was not English at all.

Not so commercialized as today, less crowded, with many of the buildings in a somewhat seedy state of romantic decay, the Vieux Carré was where we spent most of our time for the several days of our visit. That first afternoon we found Jackson Square (where a mounted Old Hickory perpetually doffs his hat to passersby), the triple-spired St. Louis Cathedral, the Spanish-built Cabildo (where an imperialistic President Jefferson, without a congressional by-your-leave, bought half our nation for $15 million) and, at the edge of the Quarter, the vast, old United States Mint, where I knew a large part of my prize silver-dollar collection had originated.

In a small restaurant we had a meal that included our first soft-shell crabs. These so delighted both Ralph and me that we had crabs for lunch and dinner every day, along with a bowl of gumbo, which together cost a little over a dollar. One exception was the day I led Ralph to Kolb's, a fine, old German restaurant, where I had eaten with my father years before, and we had some hearty German food that cost a bit more.

I probably also led Ralph into more churches than he would have sought on his own, not only St. Louis Cathedral, which few visitors fail to enter, but the richly decorated Jesuit Church of Moorish design, just off Canal Street, the Episcopal Cathedral on St. Charles Avenue, the handsome chapel of Loyola University a bit farther out and, even more remote, St. Roch's Chapel and cemetery, where miraculous cures are reported, marriages saved and love affairs given a happy turn by prayers of the faithful.

We seldom passed a bookstore without entering, and when we left New Orleans for home, my bag contained a secondhand copy of George W. Cable's *Old Creole Days*, Sherwood Anderson's *Dark Laughter* and what must have been one of the earliest copies of that author's *Notebook*, with its account of Anderson's New Orleans encounter with a young (though not named) William Faulkner. For my father I brought a menu from Kolb's restaurant, for my mother a postcard picture of the Boston Club and for Miss Flora a tiny image of St. Roch in a little metal container that many New Orleanians carried in their pocket or purse.

I also acquired for twenty-five cents at the Green Shutter Bookshop on Royal Street a copy of Carl Carmer's just-published, little, illustrated book of poems about the Vieux Carré, *French Town*. Years later when Carmer had returned to his native New York, successful author of such best-sellers as *Stars Fell on Alabama* and *Genesee Fever*, and I was working there, I told him I had this early copy of his first book. He said he had no copy himself and suggested I give or sell him my long-treasured copy. Perhaps I should have agreed, but I demurred.

One Christmas, not too long ago, after Eudora had published several New Orleans stories, I sent the book to her. *French Town* has since been reprinted, but the originals that exist now rest in the rare book rooms of the few libraries that have a copy.

I had brought along on the trip Lafcadio Hearn's New Orleans-based *Letters From the Raven*, borrowed from the Yerger family library via Buford and read on the way down. Having previously read Hearn's Louisiana story, *Chita, A Story of Last Island*, I was an admirer of his and became more so in time. His exotic background, strange life experiences and romantic interests perfectly fitted him for the role of New Orleans writer. I wish he had remained longer there and written more about the city. To me he personifies the attraction, atmosphere and quirkiness of New Orleans.

We had maps. We had guidebooks. There were few notable sights or areas we missed. It was still possible to cover the city by streetcar; even in the Vieux Carré the streetcars still ran, including the one named Desire.

With our funds dwindling, we finally realized it was time to return to Jackson, traveling this time by train. When we were checking out of our hotel and asked for our bill, the desk clerk handed us a note from the manager. "It has been a pleasure to have you as our guests," it said. "There is no charge." Had my father sent payment? Was he really such a good friend of the manager? I never knew for sure, though I asked my father about it. My first thought at the time was that we could have afforded more books, more soft-shell crabs. But we sought out the manager, thanked him profusely and set out for the Illinois Central Station and home.

By the time Millsaps opened in September, I had accumulated the $180 necessary to pay the fees and tuition for the year. I continued to work on weekends at Harris Store for Men (I had graduated from high school in a white linen suit, gift of Wiley, a suit that served the same purpose at Sewanee five years later and at the University of Virginia five years after that). On many afternoons I delivered monthly bank statements for the Merchants Bank to major downtown businesses.

These jobs helped to buy books (including textbooks) and supplied a bit of pocket money. I was living at home, where board and lodging were cheerfully supplied by my parents, who were always supportive of my endeavors (however unrealistic some of them were) and ever willing to make sacrifices in my behalf. And belt tightening all around was now the order of the day.

I recall only two of my male friends (but a plethora of female) who entered Millsaps with me, Ralph Hilton and Buford Yerger. George Stephenson, perhaps most brilliant of my high-school classmates, had to postpone his college years and take a job. He replaced me at the Merchants Bank at summer's end. His brother Charles, still at Central High, also went to work after graduation. Marcellus Green was off to the University of Virginia, Bill Wells to Ole Miss.

I entered Millsaps without too much enthusiasm but determined to pursue my interests in reading and writing and see what happened. At Millsaps I found an excellent library, which I made much use of, and four teachers whose personalities I enjoyed and whose classes expanded my horizons.

Latin, the *bête noir* of my high-school years, finally became comprehensible with the skillful and good-natured tactics of Alfred P. Hamilton. Perhaps the considerable amount of late Latin, with its seemingly more simplified structure and occasional Christian elements, made the language more accessible. Hamilton also taught German, and I regret I did not take that subject from him also. (I once asked my friend Frank Lyell, who, as an army officer in World War II, interviewed German civilians and prisoners of war in Europe, if he had learned German in one of those intensive military language courses. "No," he said, "I learned my German in Dr. Hamilton's Millsaps German class.")

A youthful Ross Moore, freshly endowed (or about to be) with a Duke doctorate in history, brought balance and enthusiasm to his classes. He taught us that the little present must not be allowed to elbow the long past out of view, that Tuesday is not better than Monday because it comes later, but also that change is the one constant, and we have to deal with it. Yet history, he assured us, is not about the past but about the present. Or in William Faulkner's oft-quoted phrase, "The past is not dead—it's not even past."

Albert Sanders, from whom I took Spanish (for no particular reason except that Ralph Hilton was taking it, and I had heard that the language was easy to learn), was the most entertaining of my Millsaps teachers. A Rhodes scholar, he had taken on the persona of eccentric professor and enjoyed it. A stocky, somewhat rumpled man, his desk was always piled high with books, papers, publications of all sorts, from behind which, often invisible, he carried on his instruction, chuckling, calling out questions, corrections to our answers and tossing out relevant anecdotes to assure our attention.

He also taught French, and I would probably have been better advised to take that subject as being more useful than Spanish. On visits to the state archives, at that time in the New Capitol, I sometimes encountered Mr. Sanders busily translating the colonial records of Mississippi's Spanish and French periods; eventually published, these were a boon to historians.

I also often saw Mr. Sanders, always prudently accompanied by umbrella and galoshes, at St. Andrew's Church. I don't know if he was an Episcopalian, but he had acquired a liking for Anglican music and liturgy at Oxford. He was a cheerful and cultured man and an adornment of the Jackson scene.

Milton Christian White bore his Harvard English Ph.D. more modestly than some Harvardites I have known. He was a balding, middle-aged man when I encountered him, with a quiet manner and a pleasant but somewhat ironic style. He also taught journalism, looked after the college newspaper and coached the tennis team. He had all the right interests from my point of view.

The course in English literature I took with him was a delight. He made me more appreciative of the authors and writings I already knew and introduced me to many others I have continued to enjoy. Old, neglected authors came to life, and the morning's best-seller received its comeuppance. As for me, I became convinced that when Geoffrey Chaucer, half a millennium ago, wrote of that "clerk of Oxenford," who "hadde but litel gold in cofre" and would "lever have at his beddes heed twenty books clad in black or reed than robes rich," who spent his all "on bokes and lerninge," he had me in mind.

Professor White caused a paper on Sherwood Anderson I wrote for his class to be printed in the Millsaps paper, and, I am sure, was responsible for its receiving the school's annual Clark Essay Prize. I recall he also had kind things to say for an essay I did on Sinclair Lewis but was more restrained in his comments on my paper contrasting the treatment of blacks in Thomas Dixon's *The Clansman* and *The Leopard's Spots* with that in Carl Van Vechten's *Nigger Heaven*, a best-seller at that time. He managed a few smiles, though.

I also had a less memorable English teacher in my first year, who is only mentioned here because of a surprising (to me) event in which she was involved. This lady (on her own or on the administration's behalf) administered to the entire entering class some sort of intelligence or achievement test. The scores were posted on a bulletin board, not with the student's name but with a number, so that each student, who knew his own number, could see how he/she ranked.

I remember consulting this listing with Buford Yerger, and we were both amazed to find the two top scores opposite our numbers. Since neither Buford nor I thought then or ever that we were Millsaps' brightest, this experience convinced us both to cast a skeptical eye henceforth on such testing. Unlike Buford and me, my mother (not surprisingly) thought the test results accurate and obvious.

It was one of the summers about this time that George Stephenson and I decided to visit the Order of the Holy Cross and St. Andrew's School on the Mountain adjoining Sewanee. The Order of the Holy Cross, the largest of the monastic orders of the Episcopal Church (its mother house was located in New York on the Hudson) had conducted St. Andrew's School and St. Michael's monastery for years. Two sons of Bishop William Mercer Green of Mississippi had attended St. Andrew's, and the school, though not as well known as the order's famed Kent School in Connecticut, had a good reputation. This was George's and my first chance to experience the Anglo-Catholic ritual and ceremony that had developed in the Anglican communion generally since the Oxford Movement of John Henry Newman, Edward Bouverie Pusey, John Keble and others had begun in England a century before. It would also be our first opportunity to visit Sewanee.

We were met at the railroad station in the small town of Cowan, nearest stop to Sewanee, by two members of the order, Father Orum (originally from Alabama) and Brother Abishai, and conveyed up the mountain in the monastery Ford to St. Andrew's. This genial pair were our guides and hosts for the several days of our visit.

We enjoyed experiencing life in the atmosphere of an Episcopal monastic community, including the daily round of services in the small monastery chapel, beginning with daily mass and concluding with compline, and often including Benediction of the Blessed Sacrament, a beautiful and solemn ceremony. Meals were taken in the monastery refectory in silence, while a member of the community read aloud from an edifying book appropriate to the day.

We were free to attend or not attend these services and spent some of our time in the monastery library, where an excellent collection of books and periodicals was available. We also spent time on the school tennis courts and hiking to nearby mountain overlooks to enjoy the view across the wooded valley below. Our hosts drove us to Sewanee to inspect the attractive university grounds and buildings, George and I little realizing that we would soon be students there.

Only a year or two before, though we did not know it then, a St. Andrew's student from Knoxville named James Agee had spent four years here. Agee, of course, went on to Exeter and Harvard and to a brilliant writing career that included a highly praised book about the Depression South, *Let Us Now Praise Famous Men*, and the Pulitzer Prize-winning novel *A Death in the Family*.

He also wrote *The Morning Watch* (1951), a lyrical and memorable short novel reflecting his years at St. Andrew's. After leaving the school, he wrote many letters to his St. Andrew's teacher and friend, the Reverend James Harold Flye, letters recording his thoughts and hopes, the achievements and disappointments of his varied career. These letters, edited and published in 1962, after Agee's death, offer, I believe, one of the finest accounts of a writer's life in our time. To all of his writing, whether journalism, movie scripts or fiction, Agee brought a moral earnestness and religious sense of commitment to the truth. These qualities were stimulated and nurtured at that small church school in rural Tennessee and by the wise moral and spiritual guidance of the dedicated Episcopal priest, "my oldest and dearest friend," as Agee calls Father Flye in his letters.

Father Flye was at St. Andrew's during our visit, living with his wife in a small cottage on the school grounds. He was a grave but friendly man, and at a Sunday High Mass in the school's richly ornamented chapel, he delivered one of the most impressive sermons I have ever heard. (I am no admirer of sermons generally, finding them too often more secular than religious and a distraction from the Anglican ritual and liturgy.) Father Flye's subject on that day was the historic authority and continuity of the church from the time of the apostles and of the traditional faith conveyed by their successors, a faith not amenable to the pressures of passing fashion or of divergent times and places. His firm enunciation of this centuries-old ideal was delivered in a restrained but fervent manner that both George and I found most effective. Years later, when George himself was ordained a priest, his mother said to me, "I knew when you two came back from St. Andrew's on that first visit that this was the way it would be."

Sometime in 1927 I became involved with Millsaps friends in a project for a statewide college literary magazine. I don't recall just who first conceived this venture, but among those students taking part at some point were Ralph, Buford, Vernon Wharton (later president of a Texas women's university), and John Maclachlan (eventual faculty member at the University of Florida). Letters were written around to other schools asking for contributions of material, and some were received. Ralph and I visited Jackson College (now Jackson State University) in person, spoke to officials at that then-segregated school and were encouraged by their offer to help. I fired off a letter to Eudora at the University of Wisconsin asking her to draw the cover illustration.

In the fall of the year our magazine appeared. Titled *Hoi-Polloi* (by me) and with my name on the masthead as editor, this venture offered stories, poetry, and humor and existed for one, perhaps two issues. The short life expectancy of such publications was enough to explain *Hoi-Polloi's* early demise. In addition, Ralph, who certainly was a prime instigator of this effort, had left Millsaps and was off at George Washington University.

I myself, after having registered and paid my fees for a third year at Millsaps, decided I had had enough formal education for the moment. The immediate academic outlook was not appealing. I had already taken an afternoon office job with a company in the new Lamar Life building on Capitol Street in order to avoid the Millsaps-required science course that included afternoon lab work. I gave financial need as the reason for postponing this course, and the need was real enough.

I decided that I had been doing too much, going off in too many directions. This, too, was true. I needed a sabbatical, I thought. Again true. A visit to the family doctor confirmed that my pulse was fast, my heart skipping a beat here and there. I needed to slow down, said the good doctor. Digitalis and a few drops of iodine in water were prescribed. Hyperthyroidism was the name of the game. I withdrew from Millsaps, was able to recoup part of the fees paid (not enough, I thought) and entered on my sabbatical. It proved to be one of the most rewarding nine-month periods of my life.

I did not entirely cease college work but took correspondence courses from Southern Methodist University, since it was thought that I might attend that school if the family moved to Texas. One course was in journalism, one in the history of drama. When it came time to take examinations in these, they were administered by my former Spanish teacher, Albert Sanders, and taken at the state archives in the New Capitol, where he was happily engaged in translating the Mississippi colonial records.

I wrote several feature articles for my journalism course based on material in the archives, one on the appointment of Mississippi's L. Q. C. Lamar as Confederate ambassador to Russia (Lamar's commission was on display at the archives at that time). Dunbar Rowland, archives director and an old friend of my family and of my Uncle George, suggested I learn shorthand and do secretarial work for him. I don't recall any women on Dr. Rowland's staff at that time. But the idea of shorthand was not attractive.

Mainly, on my self-proclaimed sabbatical, I relaxed and read. I pored over the pages of the *Saturday Review of Literature* and the original *Vanity Fair* (much different from the revived version), and I remember discovering with pleasure such new writers as John Galsworthy, Lord Dunsany, Hugh Walpole, James Joyce, Joseph Hergesheimer, and Arthur Schnitzler. The latter author's short novels of Viennese life (encountered in *Vanity Fair*) were a particular delight.

I read mostly in the city library, at that time on the corner of Mississippi and Congress Streets, and I purchased some books at Eyrich's but bought more from the catalogs of discount dealers of review copies and overstocks in New York. On the installment plan (perhaps one dollar per month) I purchased through magazine advertisements H. G. Wells's *Outline of History*, Will Durant's *Story of Philosophy*, and a multivolume collection (the title now forgotten) of selections from world literature, a real treasure trove.

There was some tennis playing and some socializing in the neighborhood, mostly with younger friends, since so many my own age were away at school. Saturday evenings at Miss Flora's continued, with new attendees replacing some of the original ones.

George Stephenson and I frequently served as acolytes at the 7:30 A.M. service of Holy Communion at St. Andrew's. On occasion the longtime rector, Dr. Capers, had to reign us in. A wise and kindly man, Dr. Capers was a confirmed low churchman and discouraged any bowings or genuflectings by his servers.

I had been enchanted by the colorful vestments, church furnishings and elaborate ritual observed on my recent visit to St. Andrew's School in Tennessee, and one Sunday morning decided to brighten things up by donning one of the red cassocks only used at St. Andrew's Church at Christmas, somber black cassocks being the norm.

I was out in my bright red cassock lighting the candles before Dr. Capers knew what I was about. Too late to do anything. After the service he cautioned me not to wear the red cassock. "Someone might think this is an Anglo-Catholic parish," he said mildly. I thought it would take more than a red cassock to give that impression. Next Sunday I noticed the red cassocks had disappeared, "packed away," I was told. In any event, our friendship continued.

It may well be that Dr. Capers's advice and encouragement to my parents helped produce the very pleasant surprise that signaled the end of my sabbatical. They told me in the spring that I might go to Sewanee for summer school that year and that perhaps I could stay on and finish my degree there. They would try to manage it.

I expect the managing involved some financial help from my kindly aunts back in Virginia. My father's sisters, Mary and Anna, had never married; they had lived together in Roanoke for years, working for very successful businesses, Mary for a large building-supply firm, and Anna at the headquarters of the Norfolk & Western Railroad (now Norfolk Southern). Through careful management, regular savings and stock purchases in their firms, these two maiden ladies had become well-to-do. They were, I know, frequent benefactors of their brothers, especially in aiding the education of numerous nieces and nephews.

In early summer 1928, then, much refreshed and relaxed from my sabbatical—better educated, too, as a result of my self-directed reading and writing—I set off for Sewanee.

FIVE

"Alma Mater, Sewanee"

Something of Sewanee's history was known to me when I arrived there for summer school in 1928: how on the Fourth of July in 1857 on Chattanooga's Lookout Mountain, bishops and delegates representing Episcopal dioceses in the southern states had resolved to establish a university under church auspices; how other gatherings completed plans for the school, selected a ten-thousand-acre site on the Cumberland Plateau sixty miles from Chattanooga, obtained a charter from the state of Tennessee and raised sufficient funds to begin the project. The name, the University of the South, was suggested by William Mercer Green, bishop of Mississippi.

The founding of denominational colleges was commonplace, North and South, in antebellum days. Most survived briefly, then disappeared. The University of the South was a more ambitious undertaking. It was proposed that a complete university be created, on the model of Oxford and Cambridge, including graduate and professional schools, all on a wilderness mountaintop.

The plan prepared by Leonidas Polk, bishop of Louisiana, furthered especially by Bishop James Hervey Otey of Tennessee and supported by the other southern bishops, called for raising at least a million dollars (a very large sum in those days) before proceeding, half a million to begin operations, half a million for endowment. In the spring of 1859 Bishop

Polk and Bishop Stephen Elliott of Georgia raised half a million dollars in Louisiana and Mississippi alone, and Polk said $3 million could easily be raised in the ten dioceses from the Carolinas to Texas.

Other private colleges—Harvard, Yale, Princeton, Columbia, among them —had grown from small beginnings into major universities. The University of the South was the first to be planned as such from the beginning.

On 10 October 1860, at an impressive ceremony attended by hundreds, a cornerstone was laid. Six months later South Carolina troops fired on Fort Sumter. The ensuing war halted plans for opening the university, wiped out the funds raised and left the school with only its name, its land and its charter.

Among those determined to make the dream of the founders a reality despite the South's wartime ruin was a New York-educated Connecticut Yankee named Charles Todd Quintard, a doctor who had moved to Tennessee in antebellum times, been ordained priest by Bishop Otey, served in the Confederate Army and succeeded Otey as bishop of Tennessee.

At Quintard's right hand was George R. Fairbanks, one of the original founders, a New York lawyer who had moved to Florida before the war and like Quintard had served in the Confederate Army. For half a century he labored tirelessly to guide the development of the ten-thousand-acre domain and the physical aspects of the university to be in harmony with the goals of the founders. His *History of the University of the South* (1905) remains the authoritative, firsthand account of the school's origin and early years.

Finding money scarce in the devastated South, Quintard set off for England, where he preached more than a sermon a day for six months on behalf of the university and received the blessings of the archbishop of Canterbury (and a twenty-five-pound donation), an honorary degree from Cambridge with a scarlet Cambridge gown and ermine hood still worn by the Sewanee vice chancellor on state occasions, one thousand books from the two universities for the Sewanee library and donations of over ten thousand dollars for the University.

With these and other gifts, the school was finally able to open in September 1868 with nine students (one from Mississippi) and four professors. It was well that it did: half of the ten-thousand-acre domain had been given on the condition that the university be in operation within ten years, or the land would revert to the Sewanee Mining Company, which had donated it in September 1858. This long struggle against great odds had always impressed me. Moreover the idea of Sewanee as a southern church university and its link with England, the land of Chaucer and Shakespeare, of Oxford and Cambridge, Canterbury and York, all those kings, queens, saints and martyrs of the storied past—a link demonstrated by Quintard's successful visit—was awesome and appealing to my youthful imagination.

I arrived at Sewanee with great expectations and was not disappointed. I was greeted at the Sewanee station by J. T. Green, a great-grandson of the first Bishop Green and son of the second (my godfather), who escorted me and my baggage to Miller Hall, where I was to stay under the care of its matron, Mrs. Anderson, a Mississippian and relative of Jefferson Davis.

Miller Hall was a frame, two-story residence with room for eight or ten students upstairs and a large dining room and quarters for the matron below. The founders had planned for small, family-sized quarters for the students, with a matron who would maintain the homelike virtues of care and decorum for her charges. Thus the founders countered the fears that in setting the university on a wilderness mountain top, "the manners and dress of professors and their families will become careless, rude, provincial; and those of the students boorish."

The system worked well at Miller Hall. Mrs. Anderson made me feel at home with frequent invitations for refreshments and conversation in her quarters. On that very first day, when I had doffed my coat and was sitting on the front porch enjoying the view, she appeared, and, with the kindliest of smiles, mentioned that at Sewanee one did not appear publicly sans coat.

I received another memorable admonition, never forgotten and scrupulously followed, when I appeared at the registrar's office to sign up for my summer English class. A pleasant young faculty member, whose class it was, asked me why I wanted to take this particular course.

"The reason," I began, "is because—"

"Wait right there," he interrupted. "Never say, 'the reason is because.' 'Reason' means 'because.' No need to say the same thing twice at one time. Tautology, you know." I wasn't sure what tautology was, but his smile relieved my embarrassment. Hundreds of high school students in subsequent years were to hear me urge this bit of grammatical propriety upon them.

The teacher, Abbott Martin, with an M.A. from the University of Mississippi, was as freshly arrived at Sewanee as I. He became a good friend and a Sewanee legend. His often outrageous statements on ideas, activities, personalities, books and authors (past and present) were designed to arouse the listener and evoke response. No one ever went to sleep in his class or was bored in his presence.

I enjoyed and profited from no college course more than from Abbott's Romantic Prose and Poetry that summer of 1928. The words and thoughts of Wordsworth and Coleridge, Hazlitt, Lamb, Byron, Keats, Shelley and all those other worthies, saints and sinners, are forever embedded in my consciousness.

How often in later years have I applauded the wisdom of Lamb's remark that "When a new book comes out, I take down an old one and read it" and Hazlitt's "I am never less alone than when alone" or recalled Byron's cheery couplet when confronting those readers who would understand an author's work while ignoring his life, "Think you if Laura had been Petrarch's wife / He would have written sonnets all his life."

Abbott took a dim view of sociology, economics, progress, Prohibition (then the law of the land), any do-goodism or proposal that ignored the imperfectability of man and man's ever-present need for that forgotten virtue, humility, and at least some infusion of the Grace of God.

It was a small summer school, hardly a hundred students, as I recall. In the winter Sewanee at the time was for males only, but girls were accepted in the summer, and there were also on hand daughters of faculty and of families summering on the Mountain, so there was no lack of social life, such as dancing of an evening in fraternity houses or at nearby Monteagle or drives down to Winchester to see a movie. Abbott, a young and dapper chap, caught the eye of several young ladies in our class, and they laid a wager as to which one could first entice him to a date, a kiss or other amorous advances. I don't recall the winner, but the contest was an example that "sexual harassment," to use the popular cliche, is a two-way street.

Sewanee had long been popular as a summer resort. Originally the regular school year had run through the summer so that students and families could escape the heat and yellow fever of the Deep South, with the long vacation taken in the winter. Among those who came to the Mountain that summer in 1928 were Maj. Frederick Sullens and his wife, who brought along my mother. The Sullenses stayed at the handsome, stone Sewanee Inn and my mother at the large but more modest dwelling of a family recommended by Bishop Green who received lodgers in the summer and students in the winter.

My mother wasted no time in visiting Sewanee's Vice Chancellor Benjamin Finney in his office and pressing my need for a scholarship to attend Sewanee for my two remaining college years. Vice Chancellor Finney, who was facing a continuous struggle in those years to find funds to keep the university solvent and find students solvent enough to populate the halls and dormitories, acceded to my mother's plea. He offered aid from the Lovell Scholarship, founded by a family long prominent in affairs of Sewanee and the diocese of Mississippi. As a result, I was able to attend the University of the South for fifty dollars per month, with tuition, room, board and laundry included. That was cheering news.

At my mealtime table in Miller Hall were Abbott, one or two other students and a guest somewhat older. When I interjected into the conversation the news that some students were in summer school only because they thought the visiting summer economics teacher would be easier than the famed and rigorous Eugene Kayden of the regular term, the older guest amiably responded, "Indeed. I am the visiting teacher."

Despite my early faux pas, ours was a friendly table. The visiting professor was from Clark University in Massachusetts, and he and I shared New England reminiscences. Abbott engaged him in bantering discourse, claiming that economics was no real science or scholarly discipline, just a matter of faith, as variously interpreted as the Nicene Creed and much less comforting. The visitor took this good naturedly, perhaps feeling this was what he might expect to hear on a Tennessee mountaintop.

Among my other table mates was Peter William Lambert, Jr., from Liberty, New York, with whom I was to have a lifelong friendship. Peter, an only child of perhaps overly protective parents, was in summer school seeking to rehabilitate his college career after an unhappy stay at St. Stephen's College on the Hudson. After a year on the Mountain, he was well adjusted and happily playing catch-up.

Red-haired, of medium size, quiet-talking, fast-walking (called "the Dixie Flyer" by fellow students from the name of the express train that streaked through the valley near Sewanee), Peter was from a home where conversation was trilingual: German (the father), French (the mother) and English. Peter managed them all, but his handwriting and his spelling suffered or perhaps were enriched by his creative mixing of the three.

The family base had been Hoboken, New Jersey, then an uncrowded and colorful town across the Hudson from New York, where Germans, French, Italians and other Europeans had created a working demonstration of the American dream, with domestic tranquility, adequate prosperity and as little crime and corruption as human nature can abide. Peter's parents maintained their Hoboken roots after moving to the Catskill resort town of

Liberty, where *der Vater* helped manage a small hotel and *la mère* helped with the local library. Both parents were mainstays of the Episcopal churches in Hoboken and Liberty; Peter was an acolyte and organist. In due time he entered the priesthood. I mention all this because when Peter arrived at Sewanee he was, it seems to me now, not just a New Yorker but a European— perhaps even a nineteenth-century European.

While reveling in English Romantic prose and poetry in and out of class, Peter and I also set about exploring the Sewanee setting: the university, its tiny village and mostly still-forested domain. Not far from Miller Hall was the small, stone building of the university press. Here the director, Albert Chalmers Sneed, and one or two helpers cheerfully labored day after day setting by hand the type for the *Sewanee Review*, other university publications, and an occasional book by a faculty member or anyone with a taste for fine printing. Mr. Sneed also designed widely sought bookplates for libraries and collectors.

He has been called "an artist in type: a fastidious, exacting, patient printer whose handicraft made him known here and abroad." So might William Caxton, England's first printer, I thought, have labored centuries ago over *The Canterbury Tales*, Malory's *Morte d'Arthur* and all those other splendid books from his press. I was delighted with Mr. Sneed and his work and returned time and again during my stay at Sewanee to observe the activity in that small building.

On our first visit Peter and I discovered an offprint of Mississippi poet William Alexander Percy's essay "Sewanee," which I had not previously read. It had appeared in the April 1927 *Sewanee Review* and was to become a chapter in his best-selling autobiographical *Lanterns on the Levee* (1941). I knew that Percy had attended Sewanee around the turn of the century and had returned briefly to teach and edit the *Sewanee Review*. I read his lyrical prose with delight.

"It was a small college," he recalled,

> in wooded mountains, its students drawn from the impoverished Episcopal gentry of the South, its boarding houses and dormitories presided over by widows of bishops and Confederate generals. Great Southern names were thick. . . . The only things it wasn't rich in were worldly goods, sociology, and science. A place to be hopelessly sentimental about and to unfit one for anything except the good life. . . . It's a long way away, even from Chattanooga, in the middle of woods, on top of a bastion of mountains crenelated with blue coves.

A recent Sewanee historian, Arthur Chitty, has called Percy's essay "the best appraisal of the school which has yet been made." Few would question that judgment, though I heard some in my day wish that Percy had not, in his poet's prose, laid quite so bare the romantic aspects of the Sewanee dream at a time when the university was struggling to survive. It was thought a more down-to-earth realism might better appeal to possible benefactors. But no such thought entered my head. I loved the essay and would not change a word.

Peter and I rambled many miles during the summer over the mountains, seeking out those spots especially connected with Sewanee's legendary past, experiencing some small adventures that offered a meaning and attraction of their own. A few clearings here and there were ascribed to Indians who had occupied the Mountain, and sure enough, arrowheads could still be found there. The ubiquitous Daniel Boone may have left his now moss-covered name and the date 1776 on a rocky outcropping beside an old trail. A more plausible tale was that John A. Murrell, infamous outlaw of the Natchez Trace, had committed one of his first murders at Jump-Off Rock.

Civil War skirmishes were known to have occurred, and A. J. Mills of the 42nd Illinois Infantry in July 1863 carved his name in Wet Cave to prove it. Letters of another Yankee invader speak of camping "on the site of the grand Southern University that was to have been . . . a place so delightful and cool that I hoped we might be permitted to spend the whole summer here." Soldier graves (Union or Confederate) were once reported found on the Mountain, but not by the New Yorker or Mississippian seeking them that summer. And Confederate cavalry leader John Morgan's narrow escape from capture is commemorated by Morgan's Steep, a popular overlook.

Will Percy's essay had reported the story of Shake-Rag Hollow, the name given that cove where "a splendid, virile old vixen . . . has always earned a pleasant livelihood, dispensing a beverage called mountain dew." The vixen or customer was supposed to wave a rag (from the cove below or the mountaintop) when "dew" was available or desired. Peter and I had a notable experience involving another variety of liquid refreshment.

On a long tramp out the unused, almost obliterated Brakefield Road that once led from the university across the domain to the valley below, we came to a remote clearing, with a small, ruinous one-room cabin, half vine-covered, its fieldstone chimney collapsed, its one door hanging loose. A few scrawny apple trees bore no fruit. We paused a moment, then entered, walking carefully on the rotting floor boards. An empty room, a closet door ajar.

Half seen on the closet floor was a wooden box, which, pulled to the light, revealed printing on its side: "Booze Whiskey / Philadelphia, Pa." We both laughed, having never heard of Booze Whiskey, named (as I later learned) for its originator, E. G. Booze, a Philadelphia distiller. In the box were several unopened bottles. Without more ado ("finders keepers"), I placed a bottle in the shoulder bag in which I had carried sandwiches and (nonalcoholic) beverages already consumed.

We looked around a little more and started back to the university. As we left the clearing, we encountered a very small black man on a large, brown, rawboned horse emerging from the woods. I don't know whether he or we were more surprised. He greeted us pleasantly and announced, without our asking, that he was on his way to Winchester in the valley below. As we moved on, Peter suggested that the rider might be the owner of the whiskey cache. I stopped to look back. The rider had also stopped and was looking back. Our suspicions somewhat confirmed, we continued on.

When we showed the bottle that evening to my mother and the family with whom she was staying, the latter, longtime Sewanee residents, pointed out that a few local citizens still used the old road to get to and from the valley and that the cabin might well be a drop-off or storage point for the illegal whiskey.

I was also told that the use of the word "booze" to mean whiskey came from Mr. Booze's product. I have since heard this colorful explanation from others, but the dictionaries don't agree, giving a more prosaic Middle English origin for the word and citing examples of its use by major writers since that time. That good Pennsylvania German, E. G. Booze, only did his part to confirm the usage. In any event, innocents as we were, we left our bottle with my mother and her friends.

That summer I also came to know other students: Byrom Dickens, who was to edit the Sewanee yearbook, the *Cap and Gown*, the coming year, go on to teach in an eastern university and himself write for the *Sewanee Review*; Harry Cain, editor of the student paper, the *Sewanee Purple*, and subsequently United States senator from the state of Washington; John Hines, Cain's assistant editor, whose plans to become a doctor were changed at Sewanee and he became bishop of Texas and presiding bishop of the Episcopal Church. I sought out these three students thinking I might be able to write something myself for the student publications. In time I wrote for all three and became editor of one.

Byrom Dickens was also preparing for the installation at Sewanee of a chapter of the Pi Kappa Phi fraternity, to consist of a group he had assembled the year before. Before summer was over it was agreed that I would join this Pi Kappa Phi group. The student body was small and fraternities numerous; almost everyone, it seemed, was a fraternity member. The fraternity houses offered no living quarters, only meeting places for talk, games and recreation, most of it harmless.

I found pleasure in my Pi Kappa Phi membership and wore my diamond-shaped pin faithfully for years, until it was stolen while I was teaching at St. Christopher's School in Virginia. When Thomas Wolfe, a Pi Kappa Phi member from the University of North Carolina, became famous as the author of that American classic, *Look Homeward, Angel*, I felt somehow elevated, though my own writing improved not a whit.

With me installed on the Mountain for the coming two years, my parents decided to rent our Boyd Street home in Jackson (or sell it if a likely offer turned up) and move to Texas—something Mississippians had been doing for a century. Houston was the town selected, as my father's best business was in that area and up the Rio Grande Valley.

He worked hard, seldom taking time off, returning on his infrequent visits home as brown as a berry from the valley sun, and slowly emerged from his indebtedness. He often regretted that he lacked the funds to participate in the Texas oil boom that was making overnight millionaires of hardscrabble cotton farmers precariously surviving on a dozen red-clay acres, as well as cattle ranchers already doing well on a thousand. He had many a tale of opportunities missed but told them with a wry smile, without self-pity.

I took no more courses from Abbott Martin but continued to be educated by him. He accompanied Peter and me on our extensive explorations and encouraged me to take French, which he knew well from having served in France during World War I and in French-speaking Beirut for the State Department. He and Peter often spoke French when we were together, which increased my own interest and skill. I was well aware of the American writers who were flocking to France, and that also whetted my interest.

Abbott had already begun to write for the *Sewanee Review* while he was still at Ole Miss. Other essays ("Patriotism and Fried Chicken," "On Marrying a Southern Lady" to name two) followed, all amusing, thoughtful and provocative, projecting their author's devotion to traditional values and culture. The southern way of life was defended but not uncritically.

For some years he wrote a column, "Abbo's Notebook," for the school newspaper with maxims, aphorisms and commentary that were a delight (the "Abbo" derived from the French pronunciation of his name). Today a landscaped, beflowered pathway just off the campus, begun and maintained by Abbott and his friends (during World War II assisted by volunteers from a nearby German POW camp) is a university showplace, marked with the sign, "Abbo's Alley." He became a legend.

I took a course that first year from William S. Knickerbocker, English department head and editor of the *Sewanee Review*. Dr. Knickerbocker was a bustling New Yorker with a Columbia doctorate and a somewhat scornful air. He enlivened the *Sewanee Review*, was an early promoter of the Fugitives and Agrarians and, in my day, was a stimulating presence on the Mountain. He achieved, but survived, a certain notoriety by not permitting one of his children to participate in a community parade (Memorial Day, Lee's or Jefferson Davis's birthday or some such) because a Confederate flag was to appear, was even to be carried by his child, I believe.

Mrs. Knickerbocker, too, I remember. She was a frequent and dependable critic for the *Sewanee Review*. Her review of Helen Waddell's *Wandering Scholars,* in the fall of 1928, introduced me to one of my all-time favorite books. I borrowed Mrs. Knickerbocker's review copy and was enchanted, as she had been, by Waddell's account of those little-known twelfth-century poets, monks and scholars who produced a considerable body of verse, serious and satirical, in and out of the universities of Germany, France and England. I soon bought a copy for myself and have reread Waddell's sophisticated translations and poetic, witty descriptions many times.

A more reclusive but excellent teacher, with a wry but friendly manner, was Tudor Seymour Long (what a name!), from whose course in literary criticism I received great benefit. In his class we worked through one book of critical essays after another, and often he would have a student conduct the class and lead the discussion, while he participated as a student with an occasional comment or question. One of the books we worked through was Joshua Reynolds's *Discourses on Art.* Reynolds, of course, was talking about painting, but his comments on style, form, point of view and talent were equally appropriate to literature.

Mr. Long was a great hiker and often accompanied Abbott, Peter and me on our excursions. His summers were sometimes spent hiking in Germany's Black Forest. It was his idiosyncrasy that, despite (or because of) his great love for England—its culture, history, literature and traditions—he would never visit that country. He did not want his image of that land, derived from his reading, to be affected by twentieth-century reality.

In due time I took Eugene Kayden's feared economics class and found it as rigorous as reputed, but also rewarding—and found Mr. Kayden himself to be a remarkable man. He was short and bald, with a large head and a Harvard M.A. His analysis of the American economy and its probable course in coming months was amazingly accurate. He predicted the stock-market crash of November 1929, the resulting Great Depression and the inauguration of federal social programs and expansion of federal bureaucracy that we know as the New Deal.

But I also discovered Eugene Kayden to be a friendly and kindly man, a great lover of books and literature. His frequent reviews in the *Sewanee Review* were of great variety and wisdom. Of a Jewish background, he found Sewanee's expression of Christianity congenial; he was baptized and confirmed and became an active Episcopalian. His memorable short poem "Betrayal in Lent," published in the *Sewanee Review*, artfully encapsulates the real meaning of that penitential season and would have found favor with that seventeenth-century Anglican clergyman-poet Robert Herrick, one of whose most famous poems has the same theme.

Years later I became accustomed to seeing Mr. Kayden's name as translator on the title page of books by Boris Pasternak and other Russian authors coming to the *New York Times Book Review*. Not your everyday economist. I still have his copy of Legouis and Cazamian's fine history of English literature. He sold me the book for five dollars—an economist after all.

One of the most entertaining Sewanee teachers was historian Sedley Lynch Ware, holder of degrees from Oxford and Johns Hopkins. A tall, slender man with white hair and beard, he demanded full attention at his lectures, calling out sharply when a student's attention wandered, hurling chalk or even an eraser at the culprit, not angrily but determined that education should prevail.

He had Mississippi connections and was a relative of Susan Dabney Smedes, author of that southern classic *Memorials of a Southern Planter*, which recounts her father's removal in antebellum times from Virginia, with his family, slaves and possessions, to a Mississippi plantation and tells of their experiences through good times and bad (including the Civil War), presenting a microcosm of the nineteenth-century agrarian South. The book was admired by England's Prime Minister Gladstone, whose praise did much to enhance its popularity. Mrs. Smedes spent her last days at Sewanee and is buried in the university cemetery.

In the course of time, I happily wrote for all three student publications at Sewanee: the student newspaper, the yearbook, and the humorous magazine, *The Mountain Goat*. In my first year, I found myself managing editor of *The Mountain Goat* and in my senior year, editor-in-chief.

I am not sure how as a new student I became managing editor. I had early submitted material to the editor, Hurlbut ("Tony") Griswold, a Connecticut Yankee, mover and shaker on campus, active in every possible organization, a "theolog" (student in the School of Theology) even a college instructor in Bible. Tony read my *Mountain Goat* submissions, liked them, and without more ado told me I was managing editor. I don't recall whether I was more pleased than surprised.

It is possible that my friends Abbott and Byrom Dickens, the latter being yearbook editor and consummate campus politician, had put a bug in Tony's ear. Anyway, I spent many hours in that first year sitting in Tony's quarters in St. Luke's Hall at his typewriter, editing, writing and typing *The Mountain Goat*. Tony was into so many activities that he had little time for this one and largely left me to my own devices.

I learned more than a little about deadlines, errant staff members, make-up and other matters that served me well in later years. *The Mountain Goat* was not all humor, at least during my regime; an occasional article, poem or book review was included. When Stark Young's novel *River House* appeared, I wrote a review praising the book and informing our readers that Sewanee was mentioned in the narrative and that Stark Young had once taught on our Mountain.

St. Luke's Hall, where Tony, Abbott, and Peter lived, was the most comfortable and attractive student quarter at Sewanee in my day. The four-story, stone structure housed the library, classrooms and common room of the School of Theology on the first floor; on the upper floors were roomy student suites, each with two bedrooms and a large living room with fireplace. To my romantic eye, St. Luke's, with its dormered, slate roof and touches in its facade of Victoria's gothic and France's moyen-âge was most appealing.

In Peter's top-floor rooms a coterie of like-minded, book-reading, literarily inclined students and an occasional faculty member were wont to gather on many an afternoon and evening to talk of writers and poets, living and dead, of ideas and philosophies, also living and dead, and much else besides.

These gatherings went on for hours, and I expect I learned as much there as in my classes.

Our world views were mixed and contradictory, ranging from the Anglo-Catholic rearguard of Oxford to the avant-garde modernism of Greenwich Village and the Paris Latin Quarter. I bought paint and created swirling comets, spinning planets and meaningless batches of color on the walls. Very modern, very futuristic, I thought. But I was no modernist, no futurist. My artistry caused comment, caught attention, so I was satisfied. It should have brought a bill from the university for the expense of repainting.

It was also in St. Luke's that I was initiated into Sopherim, mother chapter of the literary fraternity Sigma Upsilon. Though founded years before at Sewanee and with many chapters nationwide, Sigma Upsilon's officials, headquarters and bank account were now elsewhere, and neither the fraternity ritual, if any, or the significance of the name Sigma Upsilon was known to us at Sewanee at that time. An improvised ritual of initiation designed to instill humility in fledgling writers was in use, and meetings were lively and vociferous.

Members read their own stories, poems or nonfiction, which were then subject to criticism, serious, bantering, laudatory or belittling—good experience for all concerned. A Sopherim faculty member usually turned up, or a nonmember might be invited. Ironically, Abbott Martin, the new, young English instructor, was an early member, but department chairman W. S. Knickerbocker was not.

In any event, at one meeting I read a story presenting a highly romanticized version of my visit to Natchez-under-the-Hill, by which Dr. Knickerbocker, an invited guest, claimed to be impressed. He declared he might like to print it in the *Sewanee Review*. I was dubious about the merit of the story, which had been hastily put together, and since Dr. Knickerbocker never said anything more about this, neither did I.

By coincidence, years later a very fine story with the same title turned up in Eudora Welty's volume *The Wide Net*, though she, of course, off in Wisconsin at the time, had never heard of my youthful tale. The title was "At the Landing." That Welty story, in my judgment one of her very best, mingling as it does so many of the elements at which she is a master, has never received the critical praise it deserves.

My "At the Landing" never saw print, but Peter and I and others did publish a parody of the trendy extremes in literary fashion. Our spoof appeared in a 1932 issue of the *Sewanee Review* as "L'Exil, A Tertiary Review," described on SR's cover as "A Satire on Current Literary Freaks," its author one "Pierre Lambert." "L'Exil" consisted of several pages of experimental prose and poetry by some very weird contributors. Staff members named were Ignaion Neerg, Dimitri Nottap and Hashi Regrub (real live participants, their surnames spelled backwards). I was identified thusly: "Hashi Regrub was born on board ship in the Aegean. After studying at the University of Themopolis he was instrumental in promoting home industry among rug weavers in Arabia and Afghanistan. He is temporarily engaged in teaching Aramaic at the University in Porto Gulfo on the Gulf of Mexico." When "L'Exil" appeared, I was indeed teaching on the Mississippi Gulf Coast.

We had fun with "L'Exil," which proved, at least once, that even the *Sewanee Review* is not entirely without humor. Regrub has several other times appeared in print, usually as Hsan Regrub, for example, in the "Queries and Answers" column of the *New York Times Book Review*, the letters column of the New Orleans *Times-Picayune* and the Spruce Pine (N.C.) *Tri-County News*. I would not be surprised to come across his name again.

On Sunday mornings at Sewanee most students slept late, read the Chattanooga *Times* or the Nashville *Tennessean* and emerged in time for midday Sunday dinner. Some attended the midmorning services in the university chapel, with a few even rousing themselves for the earlier Holy Communion services. A handful of the more ritualistic-minded (I among them) were apt to be found at Father Adkins's early service at the university hospital chapel. Here also Wilson Bevan, a teacher in the theological school with a doctorate from the University of Munich, would on occasion indulge us with a mass in French, German, or Latin.

Dr. Bevan's services not only helped develop our language skills (and was my first acquaintance with German, its gutterals, umlauts and amazing compound words) but created a feeling of unity with the wider church, both in time and space. In affirming our belief in English in the Apostles' Creed's "Holy Catholic Church," in French "la Sainte Eglise Catholique," in German "die heilige katholische Kirche" and in Latin "sanctam, catholicam Ecclesiam," we felt that though the language differed, the church was not divided, but was indeed one.

Sometime in my senior year Peter and I decided that we would go to France after my graduation and take a bicycle trip through that country. I counted on the anticipated small profit from my *Mountain Goat* editorship (an entirely student-operated activity) to pay at least for my steamship ticket ($198 round trip, as I recall).

At graduation time my parents came to the Mountain to witness the great event, my father combining his visit with a trip to his employer's headquarters in Chattanooga. Peter and I set off for *la belle France*. My mother accompanied us as far as New York on her way to a summer with her sister Mae and family in Massachusetts. My father returned to the cities and small towns of a hot Texas summer, hoping to convince store owners that even in the Great Depression, now getting underway, Miller-Smith's socks and stockings were essential to survival.

Sewanee, like most schools, has a revered school song in not-too-perfect iambics, always to be heard at commencement and other momentous occasions, its opening words, "Alma Mater, Sewanee. . . ." When I sang it for the last time as a student that commencement day in 1930, I knew Sewanee had indeed been to me a nurturing mother.

SIX

Aller-Retour: U.S.A.-France

When the *Ile de France*, pride of the French Line (La Compagnie Générale Transatlantique), delivered us to Le Havre at the mouth of the Seine, most passengers disembarked to take the train to Paris. Peter and I, innocents abroad, found our way to an inexpensive hotel in the port area to prepare ourselves for our trip—the first and most important thing being to buy bicycles. After some inquiries and shopping around, Peter doing the talking while I listened (beginning my summer objective of learning French), we purchased two similar bicycles. Each cost, as I recall, about thirteen dollars.

Trying them out in a quiet, nearby street, we encountered one difficulty: Peter could not really ride a bicycle. He had never owned one and had only seen others riding them. It looked simple enough. He thought you just got on and rode. So for two or three days, I supported him while he pedaled and tried to keep his balance. He had several falls despite my help but made good progress. Soon we decided it was safe to set out.

Meanwhile we had learned more about Le Havre, France's second largest port, than we had planned. For one thing, the steward who had tended to our tourist-class needs in our cabin deep inside the *Ile de France*, and who had been a friendly sort, was a native of Le Havre. His family owned the small Restaurant du Port near the docks, and he had urged us to visit him and the restaurant. This we did, not once but several times.

They served us what I considered fine food, excellent *potage*, much *fruits de mer*, including mussels (my first) and cider and calvados (the Coca-Cola of Normandy). On our first and last visit they declined payment, and at other times I felt the prices were tempered to our obviously modest means. I knew that the French fleet that had come to the aid of the American colonies in the Revolution had sailed from Le Havre, and I thanked them for that, and they laughed and thanked Peter and me for the American aid in the 1914–1918 war (not yet called World War I).

We followed the Seine through Normandy and the Ile de France (the province surrounding Paris) to the French capital, some two hundred miles by the winding river. One of our first stops was at Villequier, where I knew Victor Hugo had spent some time and where his daughter and son-in-law had drowned in the Seine. There we visited the Victor Hugo Museum. Before our trip was over, Peter and I decided that Hugo must be the most popular French writer of all time, as every town has a Rue Victor Hugo.

I was surprised by how much open country there was along the river, how many fields and forests, farms and villages, and picturesque castle and monastic ruins atop the steep chalk hills, as well as some not in ruins. We explored the abbey ruins at St. Wandrille and Jumièges, halfway to Rouen, and visited the fine abbey church of St. Ouen in Rouen itself, as well as Rouen's great Cathedral of Notre Dame, longer and taller than Notre Dame in Paris.

All of these buildings and sites were centers of art and learning in the Middle Ages, and as we visited them I was thinking of Helen Waddell's wandering scholars, knowing that many of the poets, chroniclers and others of whom she wrote had enjoyed these marvelous buildings when they were new. Rouen itself had known many writers in more recent times, and the novelist Gustave Flaubert was born here. To commemorate the fact, I bought a copy of *Madame Bovary* in a Rouen bookstore, and it became one of the volumes I read on our trip. Maupassant also lived and wrote in Rouen. We discovered that both of these authors have streets named for them, and that Flaubert has a museum. It's different at home we thought, not many streets there named for writers.

My most vivid memory of the Normandy countryside and the Seine is of an early morning as we paused for a breath, a forest at our back, and across the sparkling river the view of a small village: a few low, red-tiled or thatched-roof houses, stone, half-timbered, a row of trees, a bit of mist still on the river. It was a postcard view, or better, a painting from a medieval *Book of Hours*. And the name of the village, Pressagny-l'Orgueilleux (Pressagny-the-Proud), if nothing else, would have made the scene memorable. Why Pressagny was proud I was never able to learn. The village is not even on most maps.

Not far away on the top of a white chalk cliff were the ruins of a castle with another of these splendid French names, the Château Gaillard (Jolly Castle or Saucy Castle) built by Richard Coeur de Lion in the twelfth century to protect his Norman realm from the French. A few miles farther on Peter and I crossed the Rive Epte where it enters the Seine, leaving Normandy and entering the Ile de France.

We decided not to attempt cycling through the Paris suburbs and struggling with the traffic of the Paris streets, but to take a train when we were closer to the city and then seek out the hotel recommended by theological school professor Wilson Bevan before we left Sewanee. A misadventure occurred just before we were to take the train. Riding through a small village, Peter, not yet the world's most skillful cyclist, lost his balance and ran off the road and into the fence of an adjoining yard, miraculously doing no damage to himself or his vehicle, but knocking some of the fence askew.

An excited citizen ran out in high dudgeon, pointing to the *dommage* and demanding reparations. His dudgeon did not diminish (perhaps the reverse) when he learned we were crazy Americans, twentieth-century wandering scholars, ill-prepared to pay for fence repairs. Not wishing to face the local *gendarmerie* or do further damage to Franco-American relations, Peter handed over a portion of the unreasonable sum demanded, and we departed.

We arrived without further mishap at Paris's Gare St. Lazare and made our way to the Hotel d'Athéné on Rue Gay Lussac, hard by the Jardin du Luxembourg, where we were warmly received by *la patronne* as friends of the esteemed *professeur Américain* Bevan. American students, writers, and artists had been finding their ways to Paris since colonial times, but there had never been anything like the number flooding the French capital during the score of years between World Wars I and II.

Paris was the literary capital of America. Ezra Pound and T. S. Eliot, Gertrude Stein and Ernest Hemingway, William Faulkner, Sherwood Anderson, Sinclair Lewis, James Farrell—it would be hard to name an American writer of fame or talent who did not take at least a brief part in that migration. And there were even more hopeful wannabees (including now two from Sewanee) haunting the intersections of the boulevards Raspail,

St. Michel, and Montparnasse and the area around the Café du Dome, Select and Rotonde, hoping to catch a glimpse and breathe the same air as those great ones.

Whether Peter and I ever even saw any of these literary personages, I cannot say, but we thought we saw them, and at least we were there. In Paris. And that was enough. What we certainly did see were the milling crowds and festivities of Le Quatorze Juillet, France's equivalent of the Fourth of July, that took place a few days after our arrival. High point to us, and a wonder to many Parisians, no doubt, was the sextet of black musicians we encountered on a Latin Quarter street giving forth enthusiastically with such Dixieland classics as "Tiger Rag," "Milenburg Joys," and "High Society."

Our plan from the first was to see Paris, as much of France as we conveniently could, and then find an out-of-the-way village in an inexpensive area, read, relax, and (in my case) learn French. By the time we left Paris, our route was roughly in place. We would go first to Chartres to see the famed cathedral, south to Orléans on the Loire for a trip through the châteaux country, then farther south to Bordeaux on the Atlantic coast and follow the coast on down to the Spanish border (if we and our bicycles held out).

We hoped to find in that far, southwest corner of France some attractive coastal village on the Gulf of Gascony (the Côte d'Argent, as it was called in the tourist brochures) that would be far enough away from Biarritz, then at the height of its fashionable fame, to be affordable. There we would settle in the country of the Basques, those restive, mysterious people with language like no other in Europe and a history as mysterious as their language.

Before leaving Paris, Peter and I made one diversionary excursion. We met a mutual friend from Sewanee, John Hickman Whaley, Jr., of Nashville, now a student at Dijon, in the picturesque medieval city of Troyes. The center of the old city was a maze of narrow streets and timber-framed houses, the upper stories protruding, even touching, overhead, and at the end of every street it seemed, was a fine, old Gothic church, the finest of all being the thirteenth-century St. Urbain's, named for the pope born in Troyes, a soaring creation of pinnacles and flying buttresses supporting enormous stained-glass windows, magnificently colored.

We returned to Paris and departed that city as we had entered it, by train, going first to Chartres. Dating from the twelfth century, the magnificent cathedral on its hill above the Eure River occupies a site that has been used for religious worship since Druid times. A Druid well in the cathedral crypt can still be seen.

As Peter and I were admiring the cathedral's interior, we encountered a group of chattering schoolgirls being shown around by a guide. I heard American English with a definite southern accent; looking closer, I discerned the blonde and ebullient Winifred Green, from Jackson, sister of my good friend Marcellus. There was some excitement at our encounter, but Winifred's guide was not to be deterred. He continued his progress and his remarks; the young ladies regrouped and followed. Winifred has later said that her interest in gourmet cooking (evidenced in her recipes in *Southern Living* and in her acclaimed cookbooks) stemmed in part from her gustatory experiences in this summer of 1930.

The fine weather that had accompanied us from Le Havre to Paris and Chartres now took a turn for the worse. Setting out for Châteaudun on our way to the Loire, we encountered a day of heavy rain in open country with no shelter in sight. We had only lightweight, inadequate ponchos, and we pedaled along for some time, cold, wet and dripping.

Finally we came to a farmhouse where we thought we might find protection under the eaves or inside an adjacent barn. However, a cheerful wife not only invited us inside but took us into her kitchen. We gratefully accepted splendid soup from a pot bubbling on her stove and warm bread from her oven. She seemed happy to have guests from America, indeed had a sister, married and living in Detroit. Did we know her? With the weather clearing and after many *merci's* to our benefactor, we went on our way.

Reaching Châteaudun at near dark and exhausted from our long, wet day, we chose a somewhat better hotel than usual, where we could be assured of plenty of hot water, good food, and a chance to recuperate. At Châteaudun also, we caught up with our bags, which had been sent there from Paris. Our custom was to send the bags to a town two or three days ahead and live out of a shoulder bag in the intervening days. Thus we could attend to laundry, the stowing of small purchases of books or knickknacks and other logistical arrangements. This plan only failed once—here at Châteaudun, when a teen-age youth languidly pedaling a three-wheel baggage carrier did not arrive until after our train had come and gone.

We had not planned to visit Châteaudun's fortress-like castle that gave the town its name, but our missed train left us with several hours on our hands. Indeed, we had planned to visit fewer historic sites than we did along the Seine. They were time consuming, required payment from our small funds, increased our expenses generally and slowed our progress. But we made an exception for Châteaudun.

A guide showed us around, and we found the château's interior courtyard and chapel more attractive than the austere exterior. On a large mural of the Last Judgment on the chapel's interior wall, our guide was careful to point out, a bishop or pope or two (mitres on their heads but otherwise unclothed) were being cast to the lower regions by a judgmental God. This touch of anticlericalism we found not uncommon in France, even among practicing Catholics. Their faith might be strong but did not extend to all its emissaries. A touch of Gallic realism.

On our way again, we cycled through the Loire Valley: Orléans, Blois, Amboise, and Tours, noting the handsome châteaux, the extensive vineyards as neat and well arranged as the châteaux gardens, vineyards that made the gardens and châteaux possible. Only at Blois did we relent from our austerity and enjoy a tour of the castle, admiring the thirteenth-century hall and towers and the great interior rooms and eye-catching, open spiral exterior staircase (duplicated in George Vanderbilt's handsome Biltmore mansion in Asheville, North Carolina).

I believe it was at Tours that after a stop for lunch we were given a lesson in proper tipping by our waiter and shown the French concern for every centime. Peter, who handled our financial matters, left what he considered an adequate *pour-boire*, and we departed for a stroll before resuming our travels. Half a block away, our waiter caught up with us, out of breath, his face red with exertion. He thrust his hand at Peter, showing the coins. "The church begs for money!" he exclaimed. Peter looked at the waiter, then at the coins, and (he wasn't red-headed for nothing), annoyed by the waiter's comment, said, "*Merci bien, mon vieux*," took the coins, put them in his pocket and turned away. We continued our walk, followed by further commentary from the garçon.

Farther south, we only braved the urban sprawl of Bordeaux, the large port and a center of the French wine trade, because Peter's father had an old friend there and we had been urged to pay him a visit. This gentleman was a wine merchant with offices and a large adjoining warehouse of several floors, some underground, in the wine district; the building and cellars were crowded with rows and rows of wine barrels filled mostly with the white wine for which the city and region are famous. We were received cordially, taken to lunch in a very grand nearby restaurant, then given a tour and a tasting of some choice vintages in our host's cellars. We nodded sagely at the explications offered in excellent English and made occasional polite responses, but the most pleasure was in the wines themselves. It was a wonder that we made our way safely through the Bordeaux streets after so many fine vintages, but we did.

A day or two south of Bordeaux we entered the ancient province of Gascony. We rode for miles and miles through pine forests, planted long ago to halt invasion of sand dunes from the gulf, the largest dunes in Europe. The road was relatively level; the pines offered protection from the summer sun, and this portion of our trip was the most pleasant of all for cycling.

Despite the careful husbanding of our resources, it became apparent that our funds were not going to last the summer. We took lodgings at Bayonne, an attractive port, and cabled to Liberty for help (my own parents being less accessible, and I to repay my share later). The transactions took several days, during which we explored Bayonne and environs. Gateway to the Basque country, Bayonne (which gave its name to the bayonet, invented here by an enterprising Basque), with a thirteenth-century cathedral, two castles, a seventeenth-century citadel and many attractive houses and buildings, was a refreshing rest stop.

Happily infused with funds, we resumed our trip and found, farther south along the coast beyond Biarritz, what we had been looking for. The Basque village of Bidart was situated on a low, rocky bluff above the sea and was built around a pleasant, tree-shaded plaza consisting of church, village hall, a small shop or two and the attractive, well-maintained, little Bidartenia Hotel. We settled in and remained there until time to return to Paris and home.

At the Bidartenia, operated by an efficient Basque couple (with a six- or eight-year-old son whose off-color vocabulary was incomprehensible to me but, in its French elements, was astounding to Peter), Peter and I were befriended by an Irishman, Mr. Thomas, a teacher, and his daughters, Rose and Fiona. We often went to the beach with the three, scrambling down the path from the bluff to a small sheltered beach. Occasionally on a Saturday evening we watched an ancient American western movie projected on an outdoor screen erected on the village square.

One Sunday we attended mass together (the Thomases were members of the Anglican Church of Ireland), but, having taken our place in the nave, Mr. Thomas, Peter and I were politely escorted by an official to a seat in the balcony with other males, while the daughters remained below with the women—apparently an old Basque custom.

On another Sunday, at Mr. Thomas's suggestion, we all took the little coastal train to Biarritz to attend Anglican services and to lunch at an expensive outdoor restaurant, with Mr. Thomas paying the bill. We found Rose and Fiona shy but attractive, their lilting Irish accents charming. *Malheureusement*, we never managed to see the daughters apart from their father.

We did not ride our bicycles much at Bidart. We were in the foothills of the Pyrenees, and the terrain was quite hilly. We walked a great deal along the bluff, which was often very high with spectacular views. Small farms with low, stone-walled farm houses topped with red tiles ran inland up and down the hillsides. Orchards and vineyards, pastures with many sheep and some cattle were green and lush. Atop the bluff at the edge of the village was a small stone chapel with room for about a dozen people, dedicated to some obscure Basque saint or to some legendary, pre-Christian miracle worker transformed into a Basque saint.

Once we took the little streetcar-train even farther south, to St. Jean-de-Luz, to see the town and seek out the grave of English novelist George Gissing, who had died nearby and whose *Private Papers of Henry Ryecroft* I had read at Sewanee. Gissing's long struggle to overcome misfortune and to succeed as a writer I found as moving as any of his books. The owner of a small bookstore directed us to the cemetery, and we found Gissing's grave, overlooking the sea and with a view of the Pyrenees above the town.

Each day I recorded events in French in the pocket notebook I carried, and we spoke French entirely insofar as my abilities permitted. On the beach or elsewhere I improved my skills by reading what newspapers and magazines were available along with my *Madame Bovary* and a copy of André Maurois's *Ariel ou la Vie de Shelley*, picked up in Paris. Meanwhile Peter studied his Basque textbook and claimed to be making progress.

Finally came September and time to end our pleasant stay in Bidart. The owner of a local bicycle shop gave us, to our surprise, about ten dollars in francs for each of our bicycles (about as much as we had paid for them). From the nearby town of Dax, we took an all-night train, third class (comfortable enough but fleas galore) to Paris.

We settled at a small inexpensive hotel near the train station and for several days resumed our walking exploration of the city. We crisscrossed Paris, walking miles each day, finding the usual must-see places: the Louvre, Notre-Dame, the Champs-Elysées, Arc de Triomphe, the basilica of Sacre-Coeur atop Montmartre with its fine view over the city. We ventured into the Folies-Bergère and were not impressed.

We were more intrigued by the Cimetière du Père-Lachaise, that city of the dead, where many of the inhabitants rest in handsome, small stone maisons, temples and chapels, as well as in elaborate tombs and more modest graves. A mixed company indeed, on those steep slopes and cobbled avenues: Molière, Balzac, Oscar Wilde, Proust, Héloïse and Abelard (together at last).

On the Seine's Ile Saint-Louis we saw the seventeenth-century Hotel Lambert (no hotel, of course, but a residence), built, Peter claimed, for a distant relative, a building connected as well with both Rousseau and Voltaire. We browsed in the book stalls along the Seine, where I found a bargain in a leather-bound copy of the *Maxims de La Rochefoucauld* and a popular account of François Villon, that poet, scamp and romantic figure from Paris's medieval past.

We also made our way to Sylvia Beach's Shakespeare & Co. bookshop on the Rue de l'Odeon to purchase a copy of Joyce's *Ulysses*, still under censor's ban in the United States. Fred Whittlesey, a Sewanee friend, had given us the money for this purchase before we left the Mountain.

At some point the idea occurred to me that I might return from Le Havre to my native land at New Orleans rather than New York. I exchanged my ticket and even received some money back. I accompanied Peter to Le Havre, saw him board the *Ile de France* for his six-day trip to New York and passed several pleasant days in Le Havre (during which I observed my twenty-second birthday) waiting for my three-week voyage to New Orleans to begin. Joyce's *Ulysses* accompanied Peter, its cover concealed by the jacket from a more innocuous volume, lest the book be seized by a zealous customs inspector.

When my ship *Niagara* came in and began to load and unload, the officials good-naturedly let me go aboard a day before departure (thereby saving me a night's hotel bill). The *Niagara* was an ancient vessel, half the size of the *Ile de France*, if that, and seemed to have a permanent list to starboard, but it was clean and neat, and the food was good. There were perhaps no more than a score of passengers, and only half a dozen, all males, with me in tourist class.

I came to know several memorable individuals who can only be described as extremely colorful and who ranged from attractive to disquieting. At my mealtime table was an aged retired priest, Father Huber, a native of one of those originally German villages on the Mississippi River above New Orleans that dated back to the days of John Law and the French and English kings, an area called *Côte d'Allemand* on colonial maps and still called the German Coast today.

As a boy in parochial school Father Huber had been fascinated with the study of language (he heard enough different ones around him every day, he said), and he had devoted his life to the subject, especially the changes within languages, the drift of words from one tongue to another, changes in pronunciation. He had emerged with degrees from the Sorbonne and the German University of Göttingen and still spent his summers in Europe; he was returning now from three months in Göttingen.

My other tablemates were an erect, overbearing Swiss hôtelier of some sort who claimed to be on his way to a job in Houston; a mild-mannered, darkly handsome Iraqi graduate of the American University in Beirut on his way to further study at Texas A&M; a high school teacher from Memphis whose hobby was the prehistoric caves of western Europe; and a merchant from Mexico, who had been on a buying trip.

Our mealtimes were pleasant enough except that the Swiss had a fondness for critical and confrontational remarks and for the narrating of anecdotes I thought inappropriate in the presence of Father Huber. Father Huber thought so too and said as much on one occasion. The Swiss (I never knew his name) seemed especially to feel the need to comment on the table manners and spoken English of the Iraqi, who often appeared to be unaware of what the Swiss was talking about.

Sometimes at the table Father Huber and the Swiss spoke German, and once, after the others had gone, the priest said to me, "You know, that Swiss is no Swiss." "No Swiss?" I asked incredulously. "No Swiss," he replied firmly. "Swiss German," he continued, "sounds a bit different from other German, but no Swiss speaks German like our contentious friend. Our Swiss, despite his fluent and knowledgeable German, is a Slav, perhaps a Russian—but that doesn't justify his bad manners." Well, well, I thought, what's going on.

"Can you tell my nationality by my accent?" I asked.

Father Huber, who knew I was a Mississippian, replied, "I can tell you are no imposter but an American from somewhere well south of the Mason-Dixon line." We both laughed at that.

We had passed through the English Channel, around the great western bulge of Africa and into the smoother, warmer regions of the Atlantic by the time we reached Teneriffe in the Canary Islands. Out from shore came a number of small boats with islanders holding aloft items for sale: yellow canary birds in wicker cages; small, fluffy white canary dogs; various local handicrafts. We were all surprised that our sardonic Swiss was one who purchased a canary. He held it up for us to see, wiggled his finger through the cage at his little pet and even seemed to smile.

Life was more than canary birds on the *Niagara*, however. On the first Saturday of our trip, as I was walking around the deck, I heard a piano being played in the ship's modest salon, a Strauss waltz, a favorite of my unsophisticated, untrained ear. I took a seat outside the open window and enjoyed the view of a tranquil ocean, the gentle motion of our ship and the tuneful melodies that continued to be heard. Very nice, I thought.

I saw at the piano an attractive girl. She played on awhile and then departed from the other side of the room. I know it was Saturday, because the next morning I was up early, about 7 A.M. for a mass Father Huber was having at a portable altar on the foredeck. It was a bright morning, with the sun reflecting on an ocean calm as a millpond and a slight breeze. The congregation consisted (besides myself) of a teen-age youth I hadn't seen before, a woman everyone called *la Baronne*, because no one knew her name and she was said to be a baronness—and my concert pianist of the day before, looking better than ever. In a blue-and-white dress, with a little blue beret on ash-blonde hair and with eyes on her missal, she seemed in this world, but not of it. Abelard's Hélöise? Faust's Gretchen? Obviously I wasn't paying full attention to Father Huber's mass.

Lara, a Newcomb College music student from New Orleans, had made a *tour de France* (and Germany) with a college friend, very similar to the look around just completed by Peter and me. When Richard Wagner's widow, Cosima, died in April of that year, Lara, a worshiper of the great German poet and composer of operas, decided she must go to Europe, visit Bayreuth, and see the *Festspiel Haus* and other sites connected with the Wagners. By the time we reached New Orleans, my mind was a pleasant jumble of Wagnerian information imparted by Lara, including the (was it three?) illegitimate children of Wagner and Cosima (daughter of Franz Liszt) given ex post facto legitimacy by a delayed marriage.

By coincidence, Lara, like Peter, had some knowledge of both French and German, as her mother was a New Orleans native in a French-speaking household and her father German-born. Under the tutelage of Lara and Father Huber, my French made great progress. And I acquired another teacher, *la Baronne*. She frequently appeared, took a nearby seat on the foredeck where we gathered and engaged me rather sternly in French conversation, not permitting any indolent relapse into English. "*Parlez Française*," she demanded when I took the easy way out. I wondered at her zeal.

When she learned that I also knew some Spanish (four years of college Spanish, after all) and had no job but was planning to teach, she began suggesting that I continue to Mexico, her destination. I assured her I had no interest in going to Mexico, no funds, and no Mexican contacts. "Doesn't matter," she said. "I will take care of it. I have many friends there, in the schools, in the colleges. You can repay me later if you want. It will be very fine for you."

I mentioned all this to Father Huber. "She has the funds and may have the influence," he said, "but she is no *Baronne* and is probably not even French." And he began to talk again of accents, vowels, Grimm's Law, dialects, and the rest. "Perhaps a *Baronin* or a *Gräfin*," he concluded with a chuckle. I knew both those words were German. Was she German? I asked. He shrugged, his little blue eyes twinkling.

I was flabbergasted. Here was another of our companions identified by Father Huber on the basis of language alone as being other than pretended. Were his revelations entirely language-based or were they derived from other sources? And why the deceptions?

There was another thing that puzzled me about *la Baronne*. She never spoke to the Swiss. If he was present with our group on the deck when she walked up, she kept going. If he appeared when she was talking to us, she moved away. Yet once, I came upon them in a corridor talking animatedly, even angrily, in no language that I recognized. They glanced at me, ceased to talk and walked separately away.

Day after day, the sun shone, no rain, scarcely a cloud in the sky. Nights were bright with a million stars and constellations I identified from my Boy Scout days. The *Niagara* moved slowly southwestward. Then one day the ship ceased to move. In the middle of the Atlantic, a thousand or so miles from land, it came to rest. No explanation. Officers, crewmen, shrugged their shoulders. A strange interlude in an increasingly strange voyage.

We passengers ventured hypotheses: a storm ahead of the aged *Niagara*; the vessel's machinery had broken down; some act of espionage or international hugger-mugger was afoot or had been detected. Lara was certain she had heard some banging or clashing against the side of the vessel in the night. In a day or two, *Niagara* began to move again. Still no explanation. A week later we pulled into Havana and docked.

While most of the passengers were ashore to shop or sightsee (my funds were low), I witnessed a small adventure the others missed. In the middle of the warm afternoon as I was lounging at the rear of the ship, observing activity in the harbor and ashore, two young men I had never seen before emerged onto the deck, clambered over the rail and dropped into the water. A strange time and place for a swim, I thought. A short time later I saw the Swiss walk down the gangway to shore, a bag over his shoulder. Normal enough—except that he never returned. Most of his few possessions remained in his cabin, his wicker canary cage hanging by the open porthole, the door also open.

There was much excitement aboard ship that evening, the crew seeking the Swiss from stem to stern. It was known he had gone ashore, and it was thought he might have returned unobserved. But he had not. I mentioned the two young men I had seen drop in the bay. More excitement. I was quizzed endlessly. Why had I not reported this earlier? Reported what? I asked. To whom? I was given dark looks. The *Niagara* pulled out and headed for New Orleans. On the night before reaching port, Lara and I stayed up, discussing our future and the future of the world and the universe. At dawn we watched the ship's slow progress up the Mississippi, a morass of marshes and mile-wide meanderings of slow-moving water.

Lara and I were met by her mother and a male friend of Lara's with a car. A photographer from a New Orleans paper appeared and took several pictures. (Lara appeared on page one the next day.) I was introduced and invited to come along. As we all piled into the car, I waved to Father Huber, who, seemingly in no hurry to disembark, was standing on the ship's upper deck. He smiled and waved.

I was transported by Lara's friend (with no enthusiasm) to the Pi Kappa Phi house at Tulane where I found hospitality and (as arranged) a letter and check from my mother. I knew enough to keep out of the way for the time being and took the train for Jackson the next day.

Three weeks on the *Niagara* had been a relaxing and pleasant ending to a strenuous summer of bicycling and land-based activity, and no less rewarding. The disparate characters and mystifying events of those shipboard days would make an entertaining tale, I thought. Katherine Anne Porter thought so too. In 1962 she published her novel *Ship of Fools*, which was the same story with different characters and different incidents; her ship was a German one crossing the Gulf and Atlantic from west to east. The novel was set at a time one year later than my voyage on the *Niagara*. Once again, life had gotten the jump on art.

SEVEN

Wandering Scholar Meets the Great Depression

My mother and father were in Jackson when I arrived there from New Orleans after my *tour de France*. They were taking room and board on President Street, in a house just behind Davis School, and I joined them— but not for long. I had determined to return to New Orleans and find a job, any job, and in that city's French atmosphere pursue my study of French culture and language.

I gathered up some letters of introduction, packed my bag and set off. I knew that La Louisiane, one of the French Quarter restaurants, rented a few rooms on the second floor of its historic building, and I established myself there, in a large, bright, high-ceilinged room overlooking a patio with a banana tree or two and attractive shrubbery. It seems incredible now, but the cost was only a dollar or two a day and included a breakfast of croissants and coffee.

I wasted no time in setting out job hunting, visiting banks, bookstores and men's clothing stores (in which enterprises I had some experience), plus French restaurants (where I touted my knowledge of the language) and movie theaters (ushering was not beneath me). I also visited the Soule Business College (the Soules were relatives of my Jackson friend Flora Walthall) and Tulane University (where former Sewanee teacher and *Sewanee Review* editor John McBryde was on the faculty).

Everywhere, I met Deep South courtesy, often with a special Gallic flair, but the same response: the Depression was indeed a reality; no one was hiring but, rather, letting people go, trying to survive.

To keep up my spirits I lunched once or twice at a Royal Street bookshop-restaurant with a young lady I had known at Sewanee summer school (whose family owned the bookshop and much else in New Orleans) and resumed of an evening my dialogue with Lara. My friend from the *Niagara* and her mother knew of my meager funding and often fed me as well. Some mornings I early rode the St. Charles Avenue streetcar out to Lara's house and walked her to Newcomb College before resuming my job hunt.

Yet I could not expect my parents to support me in New Orleans for the weeks or months it might take to find any sort of employment, so I reluctantly gave up my quarters at La Louisiane, bade farewell to the Vieux Carré and Lara and joined my family in Dallas, where they were now settled. Though my first Depression venture was unsuccessful, I was not downcast. It had been a learning experience, a fitting introduction to the real world of the thirties. Over sixty years later I still drink my morning coffee from a cup marked with a distinguishing monogram and the words "*La Restaurant de la Louisiane.*"

In Dallas my parents were living on Gaston Avenue, at that time a wide, tree-lined street of large family homes, some of whose owners were now forced to offer food and lodging to survive. I resumed my rounds of stores, banks and businesses, looking for a job. I read the want ads and was out every day looking, talking, applying. In my remaining time, I wrote letters to colleges and universities from Harvard to Tulane, inquiring about graduate scholarships. I did not think I wanted to stay permanently west of the Mississippi.

The Episcopal cathedral was nearby, located at that time in the chapel of a dormant girl's school while the diocese sought to raise funds for a large, new cathedral. In his quarters adjoining the cathedral, the dean had an excellent library which he welcomed me to use.

There I found much fine reading. I made acquaintance with the novels and religious writings of Dorothy Sayers, of Sheila Kaye-Smith and her priest husband T. Penrose Fry and others. A little volume by Ralph Adams Cram, *The Catholic Church and Art*, in a series edited by Hilaire Belloc, so impressed me that I sought out and bought a copy, which I still have. Cram, best known as the architect of the final plans for New York's great Cathedral of St. John the Divine, examines the basis and stimulus of all art (including literature)—"the expression of emotions and aspirations so high in character that they admit of no other voicing." Simply written, yet knowledgeable and wide-ranging, his book remains a tract for the times.

My job search was finally successful, as so often happens, not on the basis of what I knew but whom I knew. I had early on left a job application at the Adolphus Hotel, one of Dallas's finest. Nothing happened, but weeks later a priest I knew at the cathedral mentioned my name to a friend with some hiring authority at the Adolphus. In no time at all I was a key clerk at the hotel, placing guests' mail and keys in the proper pigeonholes and disbursing them on demand.

The pay was sixty dollars a month, the same I had received as a high-school student at Jackson's Merchant's Bank, but the Merchant's Bank itself was now bankrupt (or about to be) along with many others, and I was glad to take any job. I saved every penny I could, looking forward to graduate study, my parents taking care of my room and board. As usual, they supported me in what I wanted to do.

Among the letters I sent here and there seeking a teaching job or graduate scholarship was one to the Mississippi Education Association, which periodically sent out a list of prospective teachers, with brief biographical data, to state principals, in case a teacher was needed. Here again it was whom I knew. The principal of the school at Ocean Springs, on the Mississippi Gulf Coast, happened to be a friend of one of my Sewanee classmates from New Orleans. She had a high opinion of him and from him, of Sewanee.

She wired me, someone with no teaching experience whom she had never seen, an offer to teach at Ocean Springs, starting in the fall, at a salary of one hundred dollars per month. Elated, I accepted by wire the same day. My application to attend summer school at the University of Virginia went off almost as swiftly. I knew an M.A. degree could be taken at Virginia in three summers (it took me four, with one summer off to write a thesis).

No problem in getting into the esteemed University of Virginia (or any other school) in the depressed thirties if you turned up with the money and proper credits. After about six months at the Adolphus Hotel, with a hundred dollars borrowed on a small insurance policy, I caught a ride with my Dallas dentist, who was driving to Washington.

The university gave the appearance of a country club in those days, especially in the summer. The handsome, Jefferson-designed, red-brick and white-columned Lawn, with its facing rows of one-story student rooms and two-story pavilions (some faculty residences, some offices and classrooms) was framed at one end by the Rotunda, famed centerpiece of Jefferson's plan, and at the other by Cabell Hall, a non-Jeffersonian but handsome addition. A row of similar buildings, East and West Range, parallel to those on the Lawn, completed the original plan. Most of the present university buildings had not yet been erected.

Neatly trimmed green lawns (unmarked by student footpaths), lush gardens scattered among the buildings and curving, one-brick thick walls (a Jefferson innovation) added to the attractiveness of the Lawn and grounds. As at Sewanee, coats and ties for men were de rigueur. Women students in hats and gloves were not unknown. Cars were few. Students walked, rode bicycles or took the five-cent streetcar.

My budget for the three months was three hundred dollars, including books, tuition, a second-floor room in an East Range pavilion (larger and cooler than the regular student rooms), and inexpensive and excellent meals at a restaurant (later cafeteria) across from the university or in the University Commons. The library at that time was in the Rotunda, and I early learned that first summer to head for the Rotunda as soon as I knew what textbooks I would need so that I could put a copy of each text on reserve, thus seldom having to buy a book.

There were many women at the university in the summer (though the regular term was still all male), most of them public-school teachers, some working, as I was, on a master's degree. However, most of the students in my graduate English classes were men, and all the teachers were.

That first summer my old Sewanee teacher Abbott Martin turned up (he had done some work at William and Mary at one time and was a great admirer of Virginia and its university). We shared a course in Chaucer, taught by a noted Anglo-Saxon and Middle English scholar with a Harvard doctorate, by whom we were not enchanted. Too much dissection of Chaucer's language, too little discussion of Chaucer's content for our taste. I later read how this dichotomy divided Oxford scholars J. R. R. Tolkien and C. S. Lewis, and I was certainly on Lewis's side.

There was a custom at the university in those days that if a student or even a professor was talking too randomly or too outrageously, the class or the disaffected portion thereof would shuffle their feet vigorously on the floor to create a diversion and register disapproval. Abbott, a great talker and not infrequently the expounder of startling opinions, was the recipient of this shuffling on one occasion. I don't know if the students were annoyed at having their brain cells disturbed so early in the day or were just being boorish, but Abbott continued his remarks unfazed.

Joe Scott, a fellow Sewanee student, also attended the university that first summer to take a master's degree, guided there, as I had been, by Abbott— though my father's Virginia birth and my numerous relatives still in the state were also factors. Our favorite teacher, from whom, first to last, we took the most courses, was Armistead Gordon (Elizabethan drama, Restoration drama, modern English drama).

A native Virginian, Gordon was acting dean of the graduate school in those summers, a fine and personable scholar, with a constant and intelligent interest in his students' progress. He approved Joe's thesis subject, the Oxford Movement (observing its centennial), and steered me from my first choice of the Edmund Spenser-Sir Walter Raleigh relationship to Mississippi's Sherwood Bonner.

From eminent James Southall Wilson (for whom a large university building has since been named) I took a memorable Shakespeare course and with Abbott paid a call on Mr. Wilson at his home on the Lawn. (All teachers were "Mr." at Virginia, not "Dr." or "Prof.," since "Mr." was good enough for founder Thomas Jefferson, who is always "Mr. Jefferson.")

Joe Scott spent a summer or two and a full academic year at Virginia, perhaps thinking of a doctorate, but Armistead Gordon called it "wool-gathering." Joe's wool-gathering (he could afford it) took him to Sewanee for some teaching after his M.A., to the London School of Economics, to naval intelligence in World War II, and thereafter to the State Department and posts in several countries. We corresponded for years (using as noms de plume Shakespeare's Dogberry and Verges) and met occasionally right on to postwar years in New York. Always with a car in our Virginia summers and an unflagging interest in discovering and entertaining attractive young women of the town and university, Joe added much to my enjoyment by often inviting me along on an evening drive through the hills of Albemarle. I have heard him, after a mint julep or two, lecture his companion on aspects of Shakespeare's *Othello*, though some of these I am sure had never read the play. He was obsessed by *Othello* and expected everyone else to be.

It was Joe who discovered at my first summer's end a young woman teacher with a car who was driving home to Mississippi and would take me along with Joe. As Joe and I were sitting on the Rotunda steps a few days before our departure, enjoying the view of the long, green Lawn, with handsome Cabell Hall at one end and the statue of Homer and his little lad just before it, a woman's voice behind us was heard to say, "And this year I'm going to teach at Ocean Springs." Since this was where I was also going to teach and Ocean Springs was a tiny town, a thousand miles away, this seemed more than a coincidence. Perhaps it was, but I didn't turn around.

My ride to Mississippi with Joe's teacher friend worked out well. My mother was in residence at our Boyd Street home in Jackson, for my parents had found that renting the house in those Depression years was difficult and collecting the rent even more so. With me now teaching in Mississippi, it had been decided to return family headquarters to Jackson and see what developed.

Ocean Springs was an attractive town with a few thousand inhabitants, the original site of Biloxi, founded in 1699 and the oldest settlement in Mississippi. Spreading live oaks lined the quiet streets, some paved, some surfaced with crushed oyster shells. The inhabitants were a mix of often long-settled French, Spanish, Anglo-Saxon and black families, tradesmen, fishermen, a few merchants and professionals, plus a handful of retirees from the North and Midwest.

On the north edge of town, Gulf Hills (there really were a few low hills at Ocean Springs, a rarity on the coast), a development of homes and small estates, had been begun, where sailing and golf were available and a few families had moved in. On the east, the talented Walter Anderson family from New Orleans had for some years been conducting their Shearwater Pottery and were well on the way to gaining the national fame they enjoy today.

The Ocean Springs School, grades one through twelve, was new and well-maintained. The principal had decided that a second male presence in the junior-high school grades was desirable, hence my appearance. I taught English, history and a course in agriculture (about which I knew little, though I considered myself an Agrarian of the *I'll Take My Stand* persuasion; I had a textbook and managed to keep ahead of my students).

I had been out of public school for half a dozen years and couldn't remember what was supposed to happen on that first day of class, how you got started. Inquiry of other teachers evoked some amusement and elicited the suggestion that I write my name on the blackboard, identify the course subject, take the roll and proceed from there. This seemed to work fine, and I was soon teaching.

I naturally enjoyed the literature the most, and, as a result, the students did too (Stevenson's fine story "The Sire de Maletroit's Door," Galsworthy's "Quality," bits and pieces of Masefield, Noyes, Twain, Sidney Lanier, and so on). In this class we also wrote poems and prose of our own, using, as I emphasized, local and familiar material. I still recall one eighth-grader's contribution:

The Crab

The crab is a lucky fellow.
He lives on the beach all day;
He swims and eats when he pleases,
And he loafs his life away.
When he sees you coming, his eyes
Pop out, and that's not easy to do.
Some crabs are unlucky:
Some are made into stew.

In my agriculture class a student's diversionary question about the Gothic lettering that appears on the masthead of some newspapers and elsewhere led me willingly from talk of crop rotation and insect control into the teaching of the alphabet known to Chaucer and Wycliffe. I had the blackboard strewn with such letters, which the students seemed to enjoy learning, when a mother came to visit the class. If she wondered at the Gothic script in an agriculture class, she did not say so.

I lived in the French Hotel, operated by Mrs. Edwards, a German woman married to a Scot, the latter a ship's officer usually at sea. The hotel was a comfortable, two-story, beach-side, frame building, operated with German efficiency. The meals were good and everything well in hand. Guests were scarce. I lived on the second floor with three young women teachers and was not bored.

One of my neighbors was the teacher I had overheard at the University of Virginia saying she was to teach at Ocean Springs. She was the only one of us who had a car (convenient on rainy days, the school being some distance away), and I am afraid I monopolized her and the car for trips to Biloxi and for exploring the countryside. And she was the generous and welcome source of more than one trip to and from summer school in Charlottesville.

We would drive regularly to Biloxi on a Tuesday night for a copy of the just-arrived Sunday *New York Times*, so that I could read the *Book Review*, and on other nights for a movie or a look around. On weekends we might take a sail in the Gulf Hills sailboat with the pleasant young manager, who seemed to have little to do, play a few holes on the unpopulated golf course and sample the various alcoholic beverages he seemed always to have on hand. Whether these Prohibition-era products were produced in the backcountry above Ocean Springs or imported from New Orleans or Chicago, I never knew.

There was a little group of ladies who met monthly of an evening at the Walter Anderson Shearwater Pottery home for talk, refreshments and the reading of members' poems and stories. Mrs. Edwards, our hotel hostess, was a member, and I was invited to attend. The senior Mrs. Walter Anderson had a talent for writing, as did her attractive daughter-in-law, wife of Walter Anderson, Jr. None of the Anderson men attended, although Walter, Jr., wrote and illustrated one of the finest of all children's stories, *Robinson: The Pleasant History of an Unusual Cat.* I enjoyed the meetings of this lively group and contributed a few poems and a forgettable story, "Brother Junipero's Miracle," clearly influenced by Willa Cather's *Death Comes for the Archbishop*, which I had just read.

At Christmas time, my mother and father came to the coast for the holidays. Peter Lambert came down from Sewanee, and a merry time was had by all. We spent most of our time in Biloxi in the handsome beachfront home of the Garner Greens, that Jackson family having offered the use of the home for the occasion. Peter and I were back and forth to Ocean Springs, visiting several of the teachers remaining there over Christmas.

There were parties, the practicing of carols at St. John's Episcopal Church and carol singing on the streets of the town. Abbott turned up with a Virginia friend, both on the way to a Kappa Alpha convention in New Orleans. They spent the night with us, then took Peter and me with them to New Orleans. There was a chance for Peter to meet Lara; French, German and English were spoken cheerfully and inaccurately. A quick look at New Orleans followed—the churches, streets and sights of the Vieux Carré. There were trains in those days, and one took us back to Biloxi.

I enjoyed my first year of teaching, which turned out to be not quite a year, for the Depression-era town ran out of funds and the school closed. I returned to Jackson with the eighth-month pay not yet received, though it arrived shortly.

What I remember of the year with most pleasure, perhaps, is sitting on the porch of the French Hotel, the sunlit waters of the gulf only a few yards away, on a Sunday morning after returning from the early mass at St. John's Church, having enjoyed a good hotel breakfast, listening to the syncopations of the New Orleans radio and reading John McClure's literary page about books and authors in the *Times-Picayune*. McClure knew all the

New Orleans writers, living and dead, and wrote about them (and others of the time) with charm and intelligence. Some day I hoped to know such writers, too, and to write about them and their books.

I arrived at Jackson in the late spring of 1932, without a job and with only a portion of the funding for my second graduate summer at Virginia. I heard of an opening for an English teacher at Central High School, where I had graduated seven years earlier, and immediately applied. Many other teachers, I knew, most with more experience than I had, were also applying.

I visited a longtime friend of my father (also a traveling salesman), D. C. Hester, and asked him to lend me two hundred dollars to help pay for summer school, repayment to begin when I got a job. No questions asked, nothing to sign, he wrote me a check. (My parents had obligations of their own, and I did not want to add to them.) I left my godmother Gladys Eyrich and my father, both good friends of school superintendent Edward L. Bailey, to nourish my application at Central High, and took off for Charlottesville and the same room at the university in East Range that I had had the summer before.

Joe Scott was again on hand, and we again took courses together, including two from the Middle English specialist whose Chaucer class had annoyed us the previous year. That worthy seemed to have moderated somewhat, and we agreed on a policy of peaceful coexistences—besides, we loved the material ("Troylus and Cryseyde" and medieval prose and poetry). Armistead Gordon was a delight as usual (we read so many plays with him that even today I would rather read a play than see it performed—the reading giving more time for appreciation).

Most summers I managed to tuck in a course in education along with my graduate English, since a license to teach in the public schools required such courses. I was educated but had no Education. I took a course in Health (all about measles, mumps and tooth brushing), which taught what I had learned in grammar school. And I took a worthwhile course in teaching English from a sensible, young Virginia graduate, Horace Alvey, who went on to become president of Mary Washington College.

The legendary Emma Ody Pohl, from Mississippi State College for Women, accompanied by several lissome young lady assistants, appeared each summer to teach various sports education courses. I took a course in tennis and received education credits for playing tennis each afternoon.

Sometimes on weekends I would catch a ride or hitchhike to visit my aunts Mary and Anna in Roanoke, always carrying a textbook along (a lot of concentrated reading in those summers). Those good ladies would often arrange to have a pretty, distant cousin on hand (of whom I had never previously heard) for me to meet. Invariably when I returned to Charlottesville, I found an encouraging note, accompanied by some United States currency, tucked in my textbook. Splendid aunts!

Before the end of that second summer, Jackson School Superintendent Bailey offered me the job I had applied for. I was lucky again. Often in those Depression years I felt like Harriet Beecher Stowe's Eliza crossing the Ohio by leaping from ice floe to ice floe, often in peril, but never drowning. But there was always the possibility.

I found Central High very much as I had left it. The teachers were still mostly women, efficient, dedicated, middle-aged, unmarried. One or two were widows. There were several young, unmarried women teachers, fresh out of college, who would soon either marry and depart or not marry but stay and replenish the ranks of the veterans. There were now two or three men teachers. Principal John Luther Roberts remained at the helm, maintaining the traditional order and decorum and the educational standards I remembered. In front-corner offices of the building, Superintendent Bailey, more ancient in appearance than ever but still spry, presided over all the city schools, keeping the mayor, taxpayers, principals, teachers, parents and students in a reasonably harmonious relationship.

I soon became one of four congenial Central High teachers, all Central graduates, who were much together, sharing similar tastes in ideology (Confederate), reading (*I'll Take My Stand*, *The Forsyte Saga*, *Anthony Adverse*), recreation (travel, exploration, talk, mint juleps) and other matters. History teacher William Baskerville Hamilton, Spanish teacher John Knox Bettersworth (who later moved to history), mathematics teacher Robert James Landis and I found much to enjoy in those low-salary Depression years.

Among our reading was *Time* magazine. When we discovered errors therein, we boldly suggested corrections. A letter Bill and I fired off to the movie review editor was published:

> We wish to protest most vigorously against the sentence in your Feb. 19 review of the cinema *Carolina*, wherein you say: " . . . Lionel Barrymore plays a sniveling old Confederate veteran."
>
> For your information, sir, we would have you know that there were no "sniveling" Confederate veterans. With more perspicacity you might have said, "The sniveling Lionel Barrymore played a Confederate veteran."

We, of course, signed our full names, followed by "Jackson, Miss., C.S.A."

Our chief pleasure, however, was traveling together over the state, seeking out forgotten or little-known historic sites and overlooked spots of scenic and recreational interest. Vicksburg, the Natchez district, the Gulf Coast, and New Orleans were our most frequent destinations.

Once, early in my first months at Central, there came a tapping at my Boyd Street door, and I responded to find Eudora Welty, of whom I had seen little since we graduated from high school. We both had been in and out of town in different colleges and, in my case, jobs. We had a visit and brought each other up to date on our plans and hopes, our reading and writing. Later I had a meal or two at the Weltys' Pinehurst Street home and soon was joining others of Eudora's friends there for evening gatherings of fun and games and literary talk.

The group I encountered largely consisted of Frank Lyell, Hubert Creekmore, Lehman Engel, and Baron Ricketts, though seldom all at the same time. Bill Hamilton was frequently on hand, as was Ralph Hilton, when he was in town. With Eudora, Hubert and Margaret Harmon (a Welty neighbor), I made outings to such spots as Natchez, Port Gibson and the Mississippi Delta, some details of which I have detected in later Welty fiction. It was a shifting and eclectic group from among the many friends who were welcomed at the hospitable Welty home.

More frequent were my explorations with Bill, R. J. and John. On a trip to the extreme southwest corner of Mississippi, the sparsely populated area of Fort Adams and Pinckneyville, south of Natchez, we encountered an old, black man puttering around on the site of Fort Adams. Over the years he had come across an old brass bullet mold, a powder flask, arrowheads, and a few military buttons. These he was more than willing to turn over to us for a dollar or two. We thought we would donate them to Dunbar Rowland, director of the Department of Archives and History at the New Capitol, for the State Historical Museum.

I had known Dr. Rowland since the days when, as a small boy, I had wandered through the museum located on the capitol's first floor (and about to overwhelm it). It contained documents and artifacts (an Egyptian mummy, Confederate flags, Indian pottery, old swords and uniforms) displayed in glass cases in the rooms and corridors, and on the walls were large paintings of historic events by my friend from days at the Crafts', the Paris-trained, local artist Nesbit Benson (an illustrator for national magazines, as well).

A native of north Mississippi and originally a lawyer, Dr. Rowland was a friend of my lawyer uncle, George Leftwich, and always had time for a smile and small talk when I encountered him in the capitol. Dr. Rowland was also a friend of George W. Christian, a school principal in Grenada County, which adjoined Dr. Rowland's native county. This latter friendship with a man I never met was to have more effect on my life than the friendship with my Uncle George. It came about this way.

On a Saturday morning soon after our trip to Fort Adams, I arrived at Dr. Rowland's office to deliver the items we had obtained there. As I walked in, there, to my surprise, talking to the esteemed state archivist, was my Central High student, Marjorie Williams. She was about to leave, holding a fat volume in her hand. The book turned out to be the second volume of Mrs. Rowland's *Varina Howell: Wife of Jefferson Davis*, which had recently appeared.

Marjorie had read and returned the first volume and was now borrowing the second. The occasion was the writing of a term paper on the comely Varina for my English class. After some smiles and explanations all around, the young lady departed. It turned out that Marjorie had known Dr. Rowland about as long as I had, having met him as a little girl on visits to the Rowlands' with her grandfather, the above-mentioned George W. Christian.

At the time, Marjorie and her family were living on President Street across from the Rowland home facing the capitol at the corner of President and Mississippi. She was later to recall other visits to the Rowlands', including one in which she was waltzed about the living room by the tall, slender, gray-haired historian to the sound of music from the large, hand-wound Victrola.

My unexpected meeting with Marjorie Williams in the capitol that Saturday morning somehow lingered in my mind. That she was attractive and intelligent I had been aware, but that was in class, not the real world.

Yet now extracurricular meetings with Marjorie seemed to occur. She had been friends in her President Street days with a housebound neighbor, Mrs. O. J. Waite, wife of the president of Jackson's First National Bank. Mrs. Waite had somewhere known Mississippi writer Sherwood Bonner, and nothing would please Mrs. Waite more (according to Marjorie) than to see the painting of that writer hanging on the living-room wall of my friend Mrs. Ruth Stephenson, Sherwood Bonner's niece. The picture came down, and Marjorie, Mrs. Stephenson, Sherwood Bonner and I paid a visit to Mrs. Waite.

Marjorie, standing in the rain of a West Street corner, could not be left to drown but must be picked up and taken home. There were evening encounters at the Jackson Public Library, where the no-nonsense librarian, Mrs. Annie Parker, more than once had to shush our conversation. Somehow we ended up sitting together at a Saturday morning screening for French students at the Century Theater of Sous les Toits de Paris. Reared a Methodist, Marjorie expressed a desire to join the Episcopal Church and was confirmed at St. Andrew's. Our meetings grew more frequent. She breezed through Central High in three years instead of four, winning a scholarship to Belhaven College, and our social life became easier and less haphazard.

In some juggling act involving college credits, Marjorie returned to Central High for a summer math course under the formidable Miss Annie Lester. One weekend I took Marjorie on an extensive bicycle trip in the hot Mississippi sun. She returned to class on Monday red and blistered. Miss Lester expressed concern and when told the cause, responded, "Well, I knew Nash didn't have any sense, but I thought you did." I was never one to question Miss Lester's judgment. With summer schools and correspondence courses from the University of Alabama, Marjorie finished college in three years, as she had high school. And her grades were always better than any I ever made.

Meanwhile I was busily engaged in teaching the pleasures and benefits of literature and the proper usage of the English language to some 150 teenagers five days a week for about $100 per month (raised to $120 when I was made English department head), and teaching a class in journalism when it was decided to introduce that subject to the curriculum (this included producing a page of student-written school news for the Sunday editions of Jackson's two daily newspapers). On my own initiative I started a student magazine, Pegasus, which published prose and poetry by Jackson's junior-high and senior-high school students, with student-produced linoleum-block illustrations.

The literature classes influenced the writing produced for Pegasus, and the writing increased the interest for the literature. Sometimes the writings of adult authors were too influential on our teenagers and were followed too closely in the zeal to achieve a place in Pegasus. Eudora, who several years helped judge the entries, lamented one year, "Why didn't you ever tell me I awarded the prize to a big hunk of plagiarism? Max Schulman seems to have written the piece I thought was the best high-school writing in the stack." Evidently neither Eudora nor I recognized Max Schulman when we saw him.

Yet there were certainly pleasures and benefits for students and teacher alike. *Pegasus* produced a number of journalists, editors, and writers of one sort or another. At least one well-known poet, Turner Cassity, is a *Pegasus* alumnus.

Once, suggesting possible subjects for a *Pegasus* piece, I mentioned Earl Van Dorn, the dashing Mississippi Confederate cavalryman. Van Dorn did not survive the war, dying, as I supposed, in defense of southern independence. A hand went up in class. "I'll write about him," the hand's owner said. "My grandfather killed him." And so he had. It was not a skulking Yankee who had laid Van Dorn low but a jealous southern husband.

Out of class I wrote a story of my own now and then and read books, old and new, that caught my fancy or filled gaps in my summer graduate study at the University of Virginia. I read the *New York Times Book Review* and the *Saturday Review of Literature* and other periodicals faithfully. Current books were discussed and sometimes bought from Mrs. Curtis Herbert, the pleasant lady who ran the book department at what had been Eyrich's, but which by now had had a series of owners and names.

Mrs. Herbert and I shared our pleasure with DuBose Heyward's *Porgy* and *Peter Ashley* and with Joseph Hergesheimer's *Quiet Cities* and *Swords and Roses*, disagreed somewhat over Lillian Smith's *Strange Fruit*, puzzled over T. S. Eliot's praise of Djuna Barnes's *Nightwood*, and rejoiced at the success of *So Red the Rose*. We enjoyed and took in stride such best-sellers as Caldwell's *God's Little Acre* and the well-made historicals of Mississippi's James Street. Sinclair Lewis, John Steinbeck, and Ernest Hemingway were not neglected.

One year a group of my students were inspired (with some nudging from their teacher) to prepare a series of thirty-minute radio playlets, each based on an episode from English literature or an author's life, the series emphasizing both the continuity and the variety of this literature. The plays ran from *Beowulf* to John Galsworthy and were produced on Sunday afternoons over the local station WJDX. This early version of "Masterpiece Theater" went over very well.

The director of WJDX, none other than my old friend Wiley Harris, now ascended from his first-floor Harris Store for Men to a studio office in the same Lamar Life Insurance Building, was so impressed with our little dramas that he summoned Bill Hamilton and me to his office and suggested that we do a similar series on the history of Mississippi, Bill being a historian. He even proposed to pay us fifty dollars each for our trouble (not for each episode but the entire series). We were flattered, but Bill thought there would be too much labor involved, and my enthusiasm for radio drama had by now been sated. We thanked him but declined, shook hands and departed.

I believe Bill at that time was already contemplating a move from Central High to Duke University, where he was to spend the rest of his days. Jackson's durable superintendent, Edward L. Bailey, had finally retired, his place taken by a superintendent intent on introducing into the Jackson system the latest theories of John Dewey, Columbia University's Teachers College and Nashville's George Peabody College for Teachers.

Method and technique (though constantly shifting) were the things for teachers to master; content was on the back burner. Two or three non-teaching administrators were installed to see that the new insights were implemented. A Peabody professor with a doctorate in education came down once a month to conduct a night class for Central High teachers to tell them how to teach.

All teachers, veterans and neophytes, after a long day of work, were expected to turn out for meetings to learn how to teach. Basically, it seemed that the teacher was to conform to the perceived desires of the student rather than seek to impose traditional standards of order, discipline and the three R's. Students were to be kept happy, their self-esteem nurtured. The dumbing down of American education had begun. I remember Mary Lee Boyd, longtime Central history teacher, shaking her head. "It's all wrong," she said. "We'll see the results in the years to come."

Bill Hamilton was, indeed, soon off to Duke. John Bettersworth followed, en route to a long and brilliant career as author, teacher and administrator at Mississippi State. Meanwhile I slugged away in the classroom, continuing to enjoy some of it but aware that a new day had dawned. On one occasion our new superintendent, a portly gentleman and product of Peabody College, I believe, wandered into my classroom and took a seat to observe proceedings.

We were studying the writing of business letters, the punctuation thereof, the importance of correct grammar, spelling, and sentence structure. The students had written on the blackboard letters of application for a supposed job. We discussed the merits and demerits of these letters. The bell rang; the students departed. The superintendent made no comment but just sat there.

I asked him what he thought. "That's all right for those who are going to college," he replied morosely. Taken aback, I suggested that everyone has to write letters from time to time, college or not, and it's better to write them correctly and in the King's English. Didn't he think so? He only mumbled something, rose from his seat and ambled away.

In my summers at the University of Virginia I had early decided that I would write my master's thesis on Mississippi's Sherwood Bonner, and I worked on this from time to time while teaching. Bonner was the nineteenth-century author of two volumes of short stories, *Suwanee River Tales* and *Dialect Tales*, a novel of Reconstruction times, *Like Unto Like*, and many uncollected stories and articles in magazines. She spent much time in the publishing centers of New York and Boston, charming more than one editor and author (including the aging Henry W. Longfellow, to the alarm of his family), and traveled widely in Europe, sending back travel articles to supplement her income. She was a pioneer in the writing of Negro dialect stories and local-color narrative, introducing more realism than was customary at the time and that sometimes scandalized her readers. She died in Holly Springs at the age of thirty-four.

Mrs. Ruth Stephenson, Bonner's niece and mother of my good friends George and Charles Stephenson, had a diary the youthful author had kept, as well as numerous letters, reviews of her books, articles and so on. I copied or made notes from these, pored over Bonner's several books and ran down other of her stories and articles in bound volumes of nineteenth-century periodicals at Millsaps College. Bill, who had taught at Holly Springs, Bonner's home, and had written his M.A. thesis on that town, took me on a visit there and introduced me to several people with material and recollections of the Bonners.

In the summer of 1934 I spent some time in New Orleans libraries, where even more periodicals were available, reading and making notes on other stories. Ralph Hilton, who was with the Associated Press bureau there, was living in a French Quarter apartment. Hospitable as ever, he urged me to stay with him, and I did so for several days; it had been almost ten years since he and I had first visited New Orleans together. However, his work day ran from afternoon to midnight, after which there was much traffic through the apartment and other nocturnal activity. It was fun, but I wasn't getting any sleep, so I moved to the least expensive hotel I could find and continued my researches. By summer's end I had Sherwood Bonner pretty much in hand.

Years later at a gathering in New York's Cathedral of St. John the Divine, I met Sherwood Bonner's only living descendant, her granddaughter Martha Hammond, who had become Sister Frideswide of the Episcopal Church's

Community of St. Mary, with schools at Peekskill, New York, and Sewanee, Tennessee.

There was irony in Martha's becoming a nun, since Sherwood Bonner had said when her daughter Lillian McDowell was born that she didn't know whether she would have Lillian baptized. At that time, Bonner (perhaps as a result of too-long exposure to New England Unitarianism) considered baptism a somewhat outworn custom. Lillian, however, was baptized as was Lillian's daughter Martha. Sister Frideswide eventually became, as the Reverend Mother Frideswide, head of the Episcopal order. Man proposes, God disposes.

I took a final course or two at the University of Virginia in the summer of 1935, survived an oral exam by Armistead Gordon and other professors, demonstrated my ability to read a foreign language (French) and was pronounced worthy. Mr. Gordon, indeed, declared I had performed well, "but had some of the strangest pronunciations of proper names" he had ever heard. I didn't explain that many of the names I tossed about had only been encountered in books, that I had never heard them spoken. Years later when I put him to work reviewing for the *New York Times Book Review*, I reminded him of his remark. "Did I really say anything so brutal?" he asked. He remains high on my list of excellent teachers.

There was an end-of-summer commencement one hot August evening in Cabell Hall; my mother and Aunt Anna came up from Roanoke for the occasion, and the next day I departed Mr. Jefferson's university as Magister in Artibus. It was the first such degree in my direct family line since the Reverend William Eddy, vicar of St. Dunstan's Church, Cranbrook, Kent, was so endowed by Trinity College, Cambridge, in 1586.

Clara Isabel Eddy Burger and Nash Kerr Burger, Sr., parents of NKB, about the time of their marriage, Boston, 1902.

NKB in wagon in yard at 511 Amite Street, Jackson, being pulled by a little boy brought to the house by Eddy Harper, my nurse, who is stand-ing on the porch. This was about the time (c. 1912) a teen-age William Faulkner also pulled me in the same wagon on a visit to Jackson (as my mother told me). Credit: Mississippi Department of Archives and History

Right: NKB, c. 1915. This picture was printed in the Jackson *Daily News* as part of a Sunday feature, "Future Belles and Beaux of Jackson."
Credit: Mississippi Department of Archives and History

Below: Senior pictures from Jackson Central High School annual *Quadruplane,* 1925.
Credit: Louis Lyell

NASH K. BURGER—
"I am not only witty in myself,
But the cause that wit is in other men."

RALPH HILTON—
"His words, like so many nimble, airy
servitors, trip about him at command."

GEORGE ROYSTER STEPHENSON—
"He adorned whatever subject he wrote
or spoke upon
By the most splendid eloquence."

WILLIAM CALVIN WELLS—
"Whose words all ears took captive."

EUDORA ALICE WELTY—
"Of talents and good things she owns
such a store,
You'd think where they come from
there'd never be more."

BUFORD YERGER—
"He was a scholar, and a ripe and good
one;
Exceeding wise, fair spoken and per-
suading."

Left: NKB as Mad Poet taken by Eudora Welty, Jackson, c. 1935; *above:* NKB on terrace of Rotunda, University of Virginia, Charlottesville, c. 1934.

Hubert Creekmore (front), Eudora Welty, Margaret Harmon, and NKB, at Brown's Wells, c. 1930s. Taken with Eudora's camera on automatic.

River

a magazine in the deep south

Volume I, Number 1   *March, 1937*

25c a copy   *$2.00 a year (12 issues)*

River, a magazine in the deep south, Box 111, Oxford, Mississippi. Published monthly and copyrighted by Dale Mullen. Manuscripts should be accompanied by an addressed envelope for their return. Although every care will be taken of them, no responsibility can be assumed for the return of unsolicited manuscripts. River does not pay for contributions.

Cover of the first issue of *River* with stories by Peter Taylor, NKB, Eudora Welty, and Hubert Creekmore, March 1937.

Credit: Mississippi Department of Archives and History

Left: NKB and Marjorie Williams Burger on their wedding day with Rev. George Stephenson, rector of St. Stephen's Church, Indianola, Mississippi, 26 December 1938, St. Stephen's Day; *right:* NKB teaching at St. Christopher's School, Richmond, Virginia, 1938.

NKB with the *Ingalls News,* at the Ingalls Shipbuilding Company, Pascagoula, Mississippi, 1943.

Credit: Mississippi Department of Archives and History

Above: NKB with sons Nash Kerr Burger III (left) and Peter Eddy Burger, Cathedral Choir School of St. John the Divine, New York, 1950.

Right: Peter Lambert, son Stephen Burger, NKB atop Mount Mitchell, North Carolina, about 1957.

Hubert Creekmore, Eudora Welty, Lehman Engel, March 1954. Credit: Louis Lyell

NKB and Eudora Welty at the Southern Literary Festival, 1963. Welty gave an early version of "Words into Fiction" and read "Powerhouse." NKB gave a talk entitled "Southern Writers and New York Publishers," and Shelby Foote spoke on "Faulkner and the Craft of the Novel."
Credit: Millsaps College Archives

Book Review staff meeting, c. 1970. From upper center moving right around the table: editor Francis Brown, Ray Walters, NKB, Nona Balakian, Roger Jellinek (back to camera), Charles Simmons, Walter Clemons, John Leonard, William DuBois. Credit: Maggie Berkvist/NYT Pictures and Mississippi Department of Archives and History

Right: NKB at the *Book Review,*
c. 1970. Credit: Maggie Berkvist

Below: New York Times building
at 229 West 43rd Street.
Credit: Lorna L. Stark

EIGHT

Wandering Scholar
Meets World War II

I believe it was in the fall of 1934, with the Great Depression still burdening the nation, that my father gave up his long effort to retain the property at North State and Boyd Streets, where we had been living for some fifteen years. Both the Boyd Street house and the large adjoining North State lot had always carried a mortgage, had to be maintained, interest and taxes paid. He had planned to build a small apartment house on the lot for income in his retirement (a popular ploy in those days), but there was to be no retirement for my father.

We moved to a one-story duplex on High Street, across from the home of Mrs. Annie Parker, city librarian, and her two middle-aged daughters. The Parkers were good friends and neighbors, and we never lacked for news and gossip, much of it true. Some of my father's financial troubles were eased, but debts remained. More worrisome was his health.

Years of overwork in a depressed economy had taken their toll. He did not complain or moderate his work schedule, but he was not able to perform as he once had. I gave what financial help I could, which was little enough. After a few weeks in Jackson for the Christmas holiday of 1935, he returned to Texas. I took him to the bus station for the trip to Dallas (buses cost less than trains) and was worried by his appearance. He smiled at me through the window and waved.

Dallas had remained his Texas base, and it was from Dallas that business friends wired us in March that he had collapsed from a heart attack and was in the hospital. He had urged his friends not to inform us of his condition, preferring to die (as he expected to do) with the least possible expense and distress to his family. A characteristic gesture. My frail, ninety-five-pound mother, not too well herself, took the next bus to Dallas and wrote me a letter:

Dear Nash–

When I came into your daddy's room he seemed to be sleeping but a very disturbed sort of sleep, so I did not wake him right away but the nurse said he was going to have his breakfast so I waked him. He looked at me in a dazed sort of way, but smiled a little, and then paid no attention to me. After a while he woke again and said he had a terrible night, no sleep and that they wouldn't give him anything. He seemed to be in pain with his heart and he groans with every breath. He looks *terrible*. But I just talked with the doctor and he says he has improved a lot but I could see he thought he was not doing quite so well to-day. He said last Tuesday he had a terrible sinking spell and they thought he would die, but the next day he had improved rapidly. I let him understand I thought he should have let me know but he says your daddy would not give them my address or let them send me any word.

This is a Catholic hospital and the sisters are very sweet and restful. It is very quiet here, unlike Jackson hospitals. I remember we passed it in walking several times, down toward town on a back street. They are going to put a cot in his room and let me sleep here, but guess I won't sleep much if he continues to groan all the time. He says his heart hurts him all the time is the reason he groans.

The trip over was terrible, especially from Shreveport on, as the second bus was a cramped up little thing with hardly room to stretch in, and the road was terribly rough. I never slept a wink, and at 3:30 got a bowl of delicious crab & gumbo soup, but almost choked on it as I had to hurry. We got into a terrible rain storm out from Tallulah and to-day it is awfully cold. My eyes are so full of sticks I can hardly see, so please send this letter on to the girls [my father's sisters, Mary and Anna, in Roanoke] as I cannot write any more until I have had some rest.

Take care of yourself and don't get lonesome. I will try to write you a note every day.

Lots of love–
Mother

Soon my mother was able to bring my father home, by train. I met them at the station. He was carried from the train on a stretcher, with an ambulance taking him, my mother and me to our High Street home. He was able to smile and say, "I knew someone would be here to meet me." My Aunt Anna soon arrived and stayed until my father died weeks later.

He knew he was dying, spoke calmly of it and mentioned a number of practical matters for my attention. Though never given to emotional display, he reminded me several times of my obligation to care for my mother. His last words to me were, "Be good to mama." He died on the morning of Sunday 14 June 1936. After the Reverend Walter B. Capers read the Prayer Book's "Order for the Burial of the Dead," at St. Andrew's Church, he was buried in the family plot at Cedarlawn beside his and my mother's firstborn child.

He was a most remarkable and devoted father. He would speak firmly to me on important matters, but I never knew him to lose his temper or display anger. No arguments took place between us. He expressed his opinion and his reason for it, and left it at that. No vulgar or profane word ever crossed his lips in my presence. He never punished me, that I recall. He expected me to do what was right, and I sought, not always successfully, to do it. Courteous and helpful to others, no one, it seemed to me, had more friends. One of these friends, redoubtable Jackson *Daily News* editor Fred Sullens, wrote a tribute to my father a few days later:

> The passing of genial and lovable Nash Burger, Sr., removes from the scene of earthly action one of the veteran traveling men who was a star shoe salesman in the olden days when knights of the grip toured the state with huge sample trunks and on returning to Jackson for the weekend were hailed with glad acclaim by hosts of friends. In common with his contemporaries Nash Burger was a hail fellow well met, beloved by everybody. Most of them have passed into the Great Beyond . . . [Their] names are now only precious memories mingled with dear dead days gone beyond recall. They played well their parts in human affairs.

It is a coincidence that Eudora's story "Death of a Traveling Salesman" was being completed, submitted for publication and accepted during the early 1936 months of my father's illness and death. That now-famous story (her best, Reynolds Price has said) begins, "R. J. Bowman, who for fourteen years had traveled for a shoe company through Mississippi . . ."—as my father had done for nearly a quarter of a century.

In no sense is R. J. Bowman a portrait of my father, yet the coincidences are striking and obvious to me at least. It has been argued that the making of pure fiction is impossible, that all "fictional" characters and events partake of their author's experience. It is what the author does with this material that matters, that distinguishes the classic writer from the lesser. Eudora, as "Death of a Traveling Salesman" shows, has been from the first among the classic writers. Many years later her most autobiographical and fictional work, *The Optimist's Daughter*, with its moving account of another father's death, was to receive a Pulitzer Prize.

In *One Writer's Beginnings* she has told us, "The characters who go to make up my stories and novels are not portraits. . . . I don't write by invasion into the life of a real person," though she agrees with Elizabeth Bowen that " 'Physical detail cannot be invented.' It can only be chosen." And of the "passionate and strange" music teacher of her story "June Recital," she writes, "I realized that Miss Eckhart came from me. There wasn't any resemblance in her outward identity. . . . What counts is only what lies at the solitary core. . . . What I have put into her is my passion for my own life work, my own art." Beyond that, she adds, "Any writer is in part all of his characters."

During the months after my father's death I coped with the added responsibility of a widowed mother. In an effort to minimize expenses, we moved to somewhat smaller quarters, a second-floor, two-room apartment in a large frame house on President Street. Here we had a wide front porch overlooking the New Capitol grounds across the street and conveniently close to the public library and Central High School. My mother told me that our new home reminded her of the North Street house where I was born.

I had never taught in summer school but realized summer teaching with its extra income was now in order. Principal Roberts obliged and put me to work. That helped, but not enough. My good aunts in Virginia were generous as usual, and that helped, too.

During my summers at the University of Virginia my regular Sunday morning attendance at St. Paul's church had produced a good friend in Robert S. Bosher, rector of the church in nearby Stanardsville, who often visited Charlottesville. He was much more attuned to my own high-church, ritualistic and Catholic sympathies than most Virginia clergymen, and he was determined that my desire to teach in a church school be fulfilled.

Bob set to work on Churchill Gibson Chamberlayne, founder of St. Christopher's school in Richmond, which he had attended. In the summer of 1937, Dr. Chamberlayne offered me a job teaching English and French; it paid more than I was making at Central High and included room and board. We moved to Richmond, a city where my father and grandfather had also lived for a time. My mother for the next several years divided her time between Richmond, Roanoke and Jackson, passed around, as she noted uncomplainingly, from relative to relative, town to town, as she had been as a little girl in Massachusetts and New Hampshire.

I left my friends and familiar scenes in Jackson with some reluctance. On the night before setting off, Marjorie, about to become a Belhaven senior, consoled me, and I, her. Early the next day, in a car packed with belongings, my mother and I departed Jackson. But not before a final drive by the Williams home. Marjorie, looking none too cheerful, stood leaning against a porch column. She managed a smile. We waved. "I know just how she feels," my mother said—she had seen my father off on so many long trips.

Like many a distinguished American private school, St. Christopher's was the lengthened shadow of a remarkable man. After the University of Virginia and the University of Halle-Wittenberg in Germany, where he earned both M.A. and Ph.D. degrees, Dr. Chamberlayne returned to Virginia, married a descendant of Pocohontas (a respected custom in old Virginia families) and founded Chamberlayne School (later renamed St. Christopher's) in 1911.

When I arrived at St. Chrisopher's, I found Dr. Chamberlayne to be a pleasant, courteous, slightly built, somewhat intense man in his sixties. His wife, a substantial lady, was, I gathered, the power behind the throne, protecting her spouse from the rigors of the everyday world, keeping a watchful eye on the maintenance of the school's plant, the operation of residences, dining hall and classroom buildings. She was vigilant in thwarting the depredations of errant students and the foibles of a faculty for which, she early made clear to me, she had no high regard. I hoped to escape such judgment and did manage to maintain good relations in that quarter.

Oddly, though a church school, St. Christopher's had no chapel. I suggested to Dr. Chamberlayne that a chapel fund might be started to dramatize the need. He acquiesced. Pence cans were prepared (the labels printed by a student with a printing press in his parents' basement) and distributed, and the project was advertised in the local press.

A reporter called with questions about the fund—how it was going, how much had been raised, and so on. He droned on and on, far more than was needed, I thought. Finally I detected something familiar in the voice. And it dawned on me. This was my old Jackson friend, Ralph Hilton, now in Richmond with the Associated Press. Neither of us had known that the other was in Richmond, but he had seen my name in the chapel publicity and had decided to play a little prank. Henceforth, I saw much of Ralph, his pretty New Orleans wife, Mary, and their infant daughter.

There was a further, and, to me, very pleasant result of our chapel project. It involved the renowned American architect Ralph Adams Cram, especially known for his splendid designs in Gothic style at Boston University, New York's Episcopal Cathedral, Rice University and elsewhere. Cram, son of a Unitarian minister, was a convert to the Episcopal Church under the influence of the Oxford Movement. He wrote many articles and over a score of books in support not only of the Gothic revival in architecture but of the religious spirit and convictions it expressed.

A few weeks after our project began, I was amazed to be invited to a dinner with Bob Bosher's parents, Dr. Chamberlayne and the famous Ralph Adams Cram himself to discuss plans for the chapel. Cram agreed to do some preliminary sketches for a possible chapel and talked in a fascinating way of the development of church architecture over the centuries and of Gothic as an expression of Christian doctrine involving all the arts—not just architecture but painting, sculpture, stained glass, and metal working. High mass in a medieval Gothic cathedral, he thought, brought together these material arts with man's finest developments in drama, poetry, music, and spirituality. It was a virtuoso performance by a very great man that ran some time into evening and left us all impressed, though Dr. Chamberlayne told me the next day that at his age he couldn't survive many such late-night Anglo-Catholic seminars.

In such spare time as I had at St. Christopher's, I made the acquaintance of the very fine Virginia State Library and its extensive collection not only of books but of documentary records dating from colonial times. I became aware of the drama to be found in such seemingly prosaic documents as wills, land deeds, and court records, where high crimes and misdemeanors were laid bare—and dealt with in much less lenient form than today. I encountered many a tale that called out for elaboration and retelling. Even in the old church records, many of which were preserved in the library, tales of human passion, weakness and conflict were to be found. Dr. Chamberlayne encouraged me in my visits to the library and my desire to find out more about my own and related families' history. "Get on with it," he said. "It takes a lot of time and eyestrain, but it is worthwhile."

Meanwhile Marjorie and I were making full use of the postal service. During the spring holidays of 1938 I made a quick dash to Mississippi to see her, and we made plans for the summer. Peter Lambert, now chaplain and head of the Appalachian School in the mountains of North Carolina, agreed that Marjorie and I would help with the school's summer camp.

This worked out fine. The mountains were spectacular, much more so than the more modest Virginia Blue Ridge. The area was still remote and uncluttered. Adjoining the school was the Penland School of Handicrafts, where weaving, pottery making and other crafts were taught and a few permanent residents and summer artists of one sort or another lent a modest cultural note. There were thirty or forty boy and girl subteen campers. There was much hiking, swimming in the clear, cold waters of the Toe River, outings to such nearby peaks as Grandfather Mountain, Mount Mitchell and towering Roan Mountain on the North Carolina-Tennessee border. There was a bit of Anglican liturgy in the school chapel and inculcation of Anglican doctrine (at which I assisted).

Marjorie and I had a splendid summer, and I hope the campers were not neglected, for our major interest was obviously elsewhere. Peter was benign and supportive. But the summer sped by and the thought of separation for another year was not to be borne. Plans were made.

Back in Richmond, I rented from a retired doctor the third floor of a nineteenth-century, brick townhouse on tree-lined West Franklin Street. At the Christmas holidays I drove down to Mississippi. Marjorie and I were married by George Stephenson in Indianola on St. Stephen's Day (December 26) in St. Stephen's Church where George was rector. Marjorie had been born in the tiny nearby town of Sunflower; her father had been mayor, her mother postmaster. Friends and relatives were on hand, and George's mother supplied a marvelous feast in the rectory. A first marriage makes an impression. If it's your only marriage, it makes more.

West Franklin Street was only a streetcar or short automobile ride from St. Christopher's, and I was now able to escape the chores that came with living at the school with students overhead. Marjorie did some tutoring and helped out in the library. It was a state of affairs that we enjoyed and seemed only likely to improve. There would be time for writing and traveling in the summers at least, perhaps more schooling.

Then in the spring Dr. Chamberlayne, after only a short illness, died. He was a fine headmaster and a fine scholar. The assistant headmaster, a faculty member, took over as acting head, and we completed the school year, but it was clear to me that St. Christopher's would not be the same.

Marjorie and I had already decided we would spend the summer in Jackson. Her parents were building a home there and, anxious to see their only child again and become better acquainted with her sometime English teacher, urged us to stay with them. Ralph and Mary Hilton also went down from Richmond to summer in Jackson. Bill Hamilton appeared from Duke, Frank Lyell from North Carolina State. Hubert Creekmore and Eudora had been working with the Federal Writers' Project. It was Old Home Week for the summer.

It was about this time that Maj. Frederick Sullens (he was proud of his full name and military title from World War I), editor of the Jackson *Daily News*, was in full flower. A native of Missouri, a sturdy, handsome man in his prime, a lover of ladies, old bourbon and the Presbyterian Church, Sullens was a fiery, hard-hitting journalist of the old school. He had married into a well-to-do Jackson family, allied himself with the more prosperous elements of city and state and waged unremitting warfare against such populist leaders as James K. Vardaman, Theodore G. Bilbo and Gov. Paul B. Johnson.

Not only politics but literature and the arts fell within purview of editor Sullens: William Faulkner he cast into "the Garbage Can School of Literature" (he may have read or heard of *Sanctuary*), and Eudora believes she may have shared a similar fate. This seems unlikely unless it was part of Sullens's quixotic campaign against WJDX, her father's Lamar Life radio station, for which Eudora wrote the program notes. Sullens even refused for a while to carry the station's radio schedule in the *Daily News*, lest it steal away some of the paper's advertising.

Be that as it may, by the spring of 1940 Governor Johnson had had enough of Sullens's editorial slings and arrows, and there occurred the famous encounter in Jackson's Walthall Hotel between the editor and the governor. I say famous because in faraway New York on 3 May the bemused *New York Times* gave the following report on page one:

> Governor Paul B. Johnson and Major Frederick Sullens, editor of the Jackson *News*, bitter personal and political enemies for more than twenty years, fought tonight in a crowded hotel lobby.
>
> The Governor's face was bruised severely. Major Sullens suffered a head injury.
>
> Witnesses said that Governor Johnson attacked Major Sullens without warning, and struck the editor on the back of the head with a walking stick.
>
> Despite the force of the blow, which caused him to bleed profusely, Major Sullens whirled and shoved the Governor and jumped on him after he fell over a chair in the lobby of the Walthall Hotel.
>
> The editor pounded the Governor's face with his fists until bystanders separated them.

It was too much for the *Times*. Two days later they returned to the story:

Jackson recalled that there had been bad blood between the two for years. Strong words—"polecat," "hyena," "buzzard,"—have passed between them. Once the Governor sued the editor for libel, obtaining an apology. After last week's battle Editor Sullens thought he was due an apology. Sullens's reporters next day covered the capitol attired in football helmets and shin guards.

Not to be outdone, the Jackson *Daily News* reported that the chair over which the editor tossed the governor suffered eight dollars worth of damage, which the editor paid.

As it happened, while these historical events were taking place in the Walthall Hotel, across Capitol Street at Primos' restaurant, Eudora and Hubert, Seta Alexander (not yet married to New Orleans novelist Thomas Sancton) and James Wooldridge (state archives staffer) were having a snack. Sensing a commotion, they investigated and became early near-witnesses of the event. And chroniclers of it, as I was later to learn.

In 1972, while I was laboring at the *New York Times Book Review*, a note from Eudora included this paragraph: "Found what looks like the original copy of a local ballad composed by 4 anonymous merrymakers in Jackson, Miss., circa 1938 (?), celebrating an event that supposedly took place in 'the old Walthall,' a mythological meeting place, between two celebrated antagonists who may or may not have been human." Just a bit of it here:

> It was on May the second in the Old Walthall
> When these two men fought a fight in the hall,
> They met by a pillar, they met by a post
> It was hard to tell who was whacked the most.
>
> Old Fred Sullens he was 63
> Short & stocky and a sight to see
> Came in the lobby as the clock struck 6
> Where Old Man Johnson was hiding with a stick.
>
> Little recked he of the fate in store
> Once he took & opened that Walthall door,
> Little recked he that words unkind
> Would bring to him a blow from behind.
>
> 13 days behind a post
> Johnson had waited for Sullens's ghost,
> 12 days behind the desk,
> Johnson had waited without any rest.

There was much meeting together, partying, swimming, talk. There was writing, of a "serious" nature. Hubert was producing stories and poetry. Eudora was writing stories and taking photographs. We never managed to repeat Hubert's 1934 *Southern Review* "success" nor were we ever again published together as in the previous spring issue of *River*, a little magazine under the charge of Dale Mullen in Oxford. His first number, in March 1937, included "Prosefiction" by Peter Taylor (then a student at Vanderbilt, this his first published story), Hubert, Eudora, and myself (my only story to see print).

Mindful of my recently augmented interest in history and the admonition of Dr. Chamberlayne that I continue it (to which Bill Hamilton added his bit), I set to work reacquainting myself with the resources of the Mississippi Department of Archives and History and the considerable library and documents in the possession of the Episcopal Diocese of Mississippi.

Little had ever been done with the fascinating material in the diocesan archives on the destructive effects of the Civil War on the state's religious and secular life, and I made use of this in an article, "The Diocese of Mississippi and the Confederacy," for the *Historical Magazine of the Episcopal Church* (March 1940), my first venture in historiography. There were to be many others for this quarterly and *The Journal of Mississippi History* in the years to come.

What with one thing and another (the death of Dr. Chamberlayne and the expected arrival in late September of an addition to our family), Marjorie and I gave thought to remaining in Jackson. A job with the Historical Records Survey, one of the innumerable New Deal agencies set up to do good works and aid the economy, turned up.

The HRS located and described records of historical value in governmental and private institutions and issued the results in mimeographed or printed volumes. State headquarters in Jackson received material from over the state, which was then edited, written up and published. When I arrived, the HRS was working chiefly on county records, and several volumes had appeared.

Church records were also in our purview, and for a year and a half I did little else than run down and identify records and evidences of Anglican and Episcopal Church life in Mississippi from 1763 (when much of what is now Mississippi became part of British West Florida) to 1940. My work saw light in the HRS volume *Inventory of Church Archives of Mississippi, Protestant Episcopal Church, Diocese of Mississippi*.

The book was more history than inventory, since that was what appealed to me, and was well received. With its historical narrative and notes, it was in effect a history of the Episcopal Church in Mississippi. Bishop William Mercer Green, my godfather, pleased with the results (for which he had written an introduction), proceeded to set up the office of Historiographer of the Diocese with me as first incumbent, a post I held until 1959. I was now a historian. From somewhere in the empyrean, perhaps Dr. Chamberlayne was nodding approvingly.

Meanwhile, Nash Kerr Burger III arrived on schedule in September 1939, and Marjorie's parents cheerfully gave us shelter until we were able to buy a home of our own the following year. (How does anyone ever raise a child without grandparents?)

Our little Fondren Place house was on a hilltop at the then-northern edge of Jackson. I remember being taken there several times by my father when I was small. The site was at the end of Jackson's now-extinct streetcar line and was only open country overlooking a valley, Millsaps College and the straggling town. I think my father liked to go there because it was the nearest thing around to a mountain, and the view vaguely reminded him of his boyhood home in the Virginia Blue Ridge.

The 1941 Japanese attack on Pearl Harbor presaged the end of such New Deal programs as the Historical Records Survey. The government had other uses for our tax dollars. Two other important events marked the year: the birth of our second son, Peter Eddy Burger, and the delivery to me by Frank Lyell, at Eudora's request, of the manuscript of *The Robber Bridegroom* to see what I thought. I thought then, as I do now, that it is a masterpiece.

I said as much in a review for the *Journal of Mississippi History* when it became her second book and my favorite. I recall still our enthusiastic gatherings under Bill Hamilton's tutelage, reading, laughing, discussing, walking Mississippi's past with excursions to Natchez, Rodney, Grand Gulf, and through reading Robert Coates's *The Outlaw Years*. Eudora was, in fact, as I sometimes was, engaged in occasional Duke-financed research of the Natchez area for Bill. Eudora's 1975 report, in a talk to the Mississippi Historical Society, of her writing of this remarkable story, what she set out to do and how she did it, offers a revealing glimpse of the creative process.

Meanwhile it was necessary to shift gears again. With a growing family to support, the Historical Records Survey itself about to become history and the nation at war, I took a defense job with the Ingalls Shipbuilding Company at Pascagoula, a sleepy little Depression-ridden town at the mouth of the Pascagoula River, where ships had been built since French colonial times. But Pascagoula was sleepy no more. Ten thousand shipyard workers from far and near jammed the town, bringing high wages and new ways. Aircraft carriers, troop and cargo ships and other vessels were being built not only for our own country but for France and England.

I soon found myself editing the weekly *Ingalls News*, house organ of the shipbuilding company, our aim being to keep the workers informed of the course of the war, the importance of what we were doing in helping to win it and such shipyard happenings as seemed newsworthy. Government information agencies in Washington kept us supplied with relevant pictures and features, and our small staff scouted for town and shipyard news. An official shipyard photographer took pictures, and our staff took others.

Yard-based military censors were a problem. Every picture had to be cleared by an intelligence officer, lest some wartime secret be revealed. These officers tended to be young, freshly minted and zealous. Once we printed a picture that showed the small flagstaff at the bow of a ship under construction. An officer hot-footed it over with a rebuke; the flagstaff indicated that this was an aircraft carrier, information that would give aid and comfort to the enemy.

Even our prose caused problems. An article I wrote told of an eccentric veteran of World War I with a silver plate from a war wound in his head living on a little yacht on a Pascagoula bayou. My friendly intelligence officer called again. I was quizzed: How did I know his story was true, had I checked it out, etc.? Perhaps naval intelligence had its eye on this self-proclaimed veteran of an earlier war and wanted to know if I knew more than they did. But they didn't say.

My only other problem was finding Coca-Cola in the town or shipyard. All the military offices had Cokes galore; ordinary folk drank Nu-Grape or Orange Crush. I solved this emergency by striking up a friendship under the guise of news gathering with a navy petty officer who had the usual Coke machine in his shipyard office. Henceforth I fared better.

I found time to read and write on the side. I reviewed Eudora's third book, *The Wide Net*, for the *Journal of Mississippi History*. It was a watershed book, I thought, that linked the earlier stories of *A Curtain of Green* with the longer, more complex stories that showed increasing maturity, as well as the influence of her brilliant and understanding agent, Diarmuid Russell and her friend Mary Lou Aswell of *Harper's Bazaar*. I noted in the review (as I have continued to notice) Eudora's fondness for the word "little." (It appears on almost every page.) Along with this writer's great talent, intelligence and sophistication, I always sense the unsullied freshness and innocence of a child, for whom "little" is the essential and revealing word.

At Pascagoula I managed to assemble and publish the second of my reprints of the early journals of the conventions of the diocese of Mississippi. These little booklets, only ten or fifteen pages in length, included added biographical and historical material I hoped gave life and interest to the record. Easton King, editor of the Pascagoula *Chronicle-Star*, on whose presses the *Ingalls News* was printed, aided in this second publication. Easton set the type for the 1827 reprint himself and published it free of charge. Three others (1826, 1828, 1829) eventually appeared. I have found examples of this small project in the New York Public Library and in the libraries at Columbia, Princeton, the University of Virginia and other places my travels have taken me.

The Ingalls ships were among the nation's first to be welded, not riveted, and were stronger and faster as a result (or so we claimed). At the *Ingalls News* we created a cartoon character, Winnie the Welder, to compete with the better-known Rosie the Riveter of those wartime years. We eventually published a collection of these Winnie cartoons for shipyard distribution. Even so, the thousands of welders needed were hard to find.

A welding school was set up in the shipyard and would-be welders, men and women, were put on the payroll while learning the skill. Newspaper ads in nearby towns and cities brought in trainees of all shapes, sizes and backgrounds. Among the trainees I talked with while gathering news and human interest stories were several sturdy young ladies whose previous employment had been in the *maisons de plaisir* of the New Orleans French Quarter.

Making no secret of what had been the only work they had previously been able to find, they were now happy with their good welding wages (plus ample overtime), were saving their money and looking forward to better days. At least one soon married, settled down in nearby Lucedale and began raising a family, events reported in the *Ingalls News* (the settling down part, at least).

But sometimes things worked the other way. One of our trainees, chosen (so I was told) as the prettiest girl in her senior class at the crossroads high school in a nearby county, one day failed to appear at work. Nor did she appear on subsequent days, or ever again. "Gone to New York with a British officer," her roommate confided. Several years later, now in New York myself, I was surprised to see her name in Walter Winchell's nationally syndicated gossip column, an aspiring actress, linked with well-known males. One day, looking little changed but much more prosperous, she walked unannounced into the *New York Times Book Review* offices to see me. She had seen *my* name, in the *Times*. After some chitchat, she left her card with an East Side address and telephone number. "Call me some time," she said. "I'd love to see you."

During my year or two at Ingalls my family remained in Jackson two hundred miles away, and we got together as often as gas rationing and other hindrances permitted. Marjorie had charmed her way into the State Tax Commission at the New Capitol as an auditor (a lifetime of economic austerity similar to my own had well prepared her for this job), but came down to Pascagoula several times with the children, and I managed frequent trips to Jackson on weekends and on Ingalls business.

Having dependents and a defense job, there was no chance of my being drafted; but most of my friends were being shot at, and I applied to the navy. They said stay in the shipyard, and Dallas Smith, my eager-beaver boss at Ingalls, spoke of the importance of my work, its future potentials in war and peace, of salary increases, pie in the sky, and so on.

I stayed a while longer until the fall of 1943, then returned to Jackson, my family and Central High. The school needed teachers as much as the shipyard needed an editor—especially since as a result of my efforts we seemed to be winning the war. "How long will you stay this time?" asked Kirby Walker, school superintendent, pleasantly. We both knew we were embarking on a marriage of convenience, while the war wound down.

I was given some English to teach, as well as something called Consumer Education and Radio Code (wartime innovation, the Morse code via records). None of these were very challenging to students or teacher. I stirred up interest by introducing some Shakespeare, buying enough paperbacks with my own funds to go around: *Twelfth Night*, *Hamlet*, *The Merchant of Venice*, as I recall.

I *was* simply waiting for the war to end, thinking that if it didn't end soon, I would be in uniform myself. Hubert was back from the navy and the South Pacific about this time, but Frank was in the army, Lehman in the navy and others of our Jackson group were also scattered. Eudora would be off to New York in 1944 to work with Robert van Gelder at the *New York Times Book Review*, where he was editor.

In the early summer Eudora had van Gelder send me books to review for the *Times*. This was exciting and remunerative: reading books and writing about them—and being paid for it! Heavenly! I was startled at being invited to come to New York to do this full time.

I had always planned to teach as a way of earning a living and to write on the side until the writing could replace teaching. I had visited New York and didn't know if I would like living there, and the logistics of moving were awesome. I wrote van Gelder, "Thank you, but I believe not." Marjorie, visiting relatives in Arkansas, on returning to Jackson and hearing of the offer, said, "No way! Of course we'll go."

I wrote to van Gelder and asked if the offer was still good. Some time elapsed. I thought the deal might be off, and I had decided I really wanted the job. I conferred with Mrs. Welty, asking her to check with Eudora on the prospects in their frequent telephone talks. Eudora busied herself. A deal was struck.

It was agreed that I could finish out the 1944–45 school year at Central, then come to New York. I continued to review some books. Meanwhile, All Saints College and Episcopal School offered me a job. Too late now. I was never to be a college teacher, although later, when they were in positions to do so, both John Bettersworth at Mississippi State and Bill Hamilton at Duke gave me the opportunity.

Many years later when I was at the *Book Review*, Mrs. Welty came with Eudora to see me and the place where I was working. I reminded her of her part in the process of getting me to New York and thanked her again. She smiled. It was the last time I saw her. She died in 1966, a wise, courageous, and gracious lady.

NINE

To West 43rd Street

One of Eudora's assignments when she went to the *New York Times Book Review* had been to seek out "new, young, bright reviewers," and she has said I was first on her list. I remember I was more than willing to cooperate. I was certainly new, at thirty-five not yet old and, I hoped, bright enough to pass muster. Soon *The History of Rome Hanks and Kindred Matters*, a first novel by Joseph Stanley Pennell, arrived in my Jackson mailbox for review. I gave it my best shot. My comments appeared on page one of the *Book Review* and *Rome Hanks* became a best seller.

I had left Sewanee in 1930 convinced more than ever that I wanted to write. I was innocent, but I had sense enough to know that making a living by writing was a chancy thing. I decided that teaching would offer more time for writing than almost any other work. Even high school teaching, public or private, might fit the bill. Had not Thornton Wilder taught at prep school and had a successful writing career? So I reasoned.

It did not work out as it had for Thornton Wilder—or for Eudora. Yet from 1930 and into the years of World War II, Eudora and I both had spent most of our time in Jackson, working at writing of one sort or another. We both came to know Mississippi better than ever through jobs that took us to every crossroad, she for the Federal Writers' Project as a publicity agent (well illustrated now in her photographs), I for the WPA's Historical

Records Survey. She wrote for WJDX and society notes for the Memphis *Commercial-Appeal* ("Mr. Nash Burger has been in Charlottesville attending the University of Virginia. He's back now—once more Mr. Burger to the English students at Jackson High School"), and, of course, she published her first story, "Death of a Traveling Salesman." I wrote articles for such as *The Journal of Mississippi History* and the *Historical Magazine of the Episcopal Church*, a story for *River*, an article on Sherwood Bonner in Hubert's *Southern Review*. Curiously, both literary reviews died after my appearance in them; my success with publishing fiction ceased also, but not my desire to write and to be read.

My first book review, in the Jackson *Daily News*, of Stark Young's *So Red the Rose*, a book I had not yet read, appeared in these trying-out years. I knew enough about antebellum Mississippi and the Civil War to write a paean of praise for the Old South, and that was the review. Nobody asked me to write it, but I did, and editor Fred Sullens, fire-eating editor of the *News*, an old friend of my father's, published it, as he did other unsolicited contributions over the years, including an editorial in praise of another publisher of mine, a piece that began firmly, "No boon-doggling project is WPA's Historical Records Survey. . . ."

The *News* didn't ordinarily run book reviews, but Bill Hamilton and I decided the Jackson population should be alerted to *So Red the Rose*. I wrote the piece and gave it to Sullens. I knew a little about Young and told about the setting and the timing of the book. I don't recall if I had ever even seen the actual book. "Oh fine, thank you," Sullens said and put the piece in his desk drawer. About a month later, I saw him in the drugstore across from the Old Capitol and I asked him about it. "Oh yes, it's in my desk drawer." A day or two later, it appeared under the boxed heading: "So Red the Rose by Nash K. Burger." He hadn't read the review then either.

Now, ten years later, and after other forays into reviewing, here was *Rome Hanks*, another book about the Civil War, to review for a far more eminent newspaper. This time I read the book first. Then I carefully read a page-one piece in the *Book Review* that had appeared a little while before and analyzed it. (Moreover, I'd been reading the *Book Review* all my life, it seemed.) And then I sat down and wrote a review of *Rome Hanks* based on my analysis. The review I had modeled mine on was written by the *Book Review*'s immediate past editor, J. Donald Adams, who I thought was a fine writer.

Nonetheless, I had a telegram from Eudora commending my effort but conveying the wish of van Gelder that I do thus and so to the review, send other material by wire, which I did, and she tucked the thing together. So you might say the review was a collaborative effort.

Perhaps my pleasure in reading *Rome Hanks* was in part due to its finely drawn first narrator, Rev. Thomas Wagnal, a retired Episcopal clergyman and sometime surgeon to the 117th Iowa Regiment in Grant's Army of the Tennessee, or to the fact that the modern man searching for answers through his ancestral stories is named Robert Lee Harrington, Lee for short. The book became a classic of its kind because, as I noted then, "Shiloh becomes once again reality, one with Tarawa, Salerno, and Normandy," evoking universal shades of Chaucer, Joyce and Proust.

Eudora had said it was a page-one book, perhaps on van Gelder's instructions, so I wasn't surprised when the review showed up there. It gained a bit of office notoriety when a story circulated that the editor, Lester Markel, called upstairs to find out the identity of the Nash K. Burger on the front page of his Sunday *Book Review*. Eudora says van Gelder responded by saying simply that Nash K. Burger was the writer of the review he was running on page one. I believe *Rome Hanks* is the best Civil War fiction I had ever read up till that time.

Later, at the *Book Review*, I reviewed Ben Ames Williams's Civil War best-seller, *House Divided*, a more impressive book in a way, and long, long, long. Bill DuBois of the *Book Review* staff wrote a piece for the "In and Out of Books" page titled "Outsize Dept." calling Williams's book "monumental . . . super-jumbo." Without naming me, DuBois wrote that "our stalwart reviewer, who has been working overtime since late June and is now on Page 902, with a mere 612 to go, lifted his eyes and offered us a plucky smile."

It didn't seem excessively long to me because I thought it a very good book. I did comment, however, that *House Divided* "could swallow up *So Red the Rose*, *Rome Hanks*, *Bugles Blow No More*, and still have room for a book club dual selection and a couple of volumes of fugitive verse." Mr. Williams, a Mississippi native and relative of General Longstreet, was sympathetic toward the South, but I thought he concentrated too heavily on the Confederacy's faults. I quoted Stark Young's lines: "Out of any epoch in civilization there may arise things worth while, that are the flowers of it. To abandon these, when another epoch arrives, is only stupid."

Eudora and van Gelder continued to send me books to review that first summer, so that I was reading and reviewing about two books each month on average. In late August, two of my reviews appeared the same Sunday. It was *Times* policy to discourage staffers filling up the *Book Review* with their bylines, so one of my reviews appeared under the pseudonym of Michael Ravenna, a name invented by Eudora for one of her reviews. After I had gone to work at the *Book Review*, I asked Bill DuBois why they had cut so heavily one of those pieces, a negative review of Gilbert Gabriel's novel *I Got A Country*. His response was sensible: "If it was so bad, why write so much about it?" Over the years I used other bylines, including Peter Eddy, my second son's names. That review, of a book by New York's Cardinal Spellman, earned Peter Eddy an invitation to apear on a USIA radio program, but Peter, about six at the time, was obviously unable to accept.

Marjorie and our two sons had stayed in Jackson while I spent the summer of 1945 getting oriented to New York and the *Book Review*, living in easeful comfort at the General Theological Seminary, the church's oldest, a stone, gothic establishment built around a quadrangle (reminiscent of Sewanee, in fact). Clement Clarke Moore had written "The Night Before Christmas" while teaching there. Hubert Creekmore was in New York and visited me at the seminary and at the *Book Review*. Eudora was back in Jackson.

Two remarks made to me that summer comforted and amused me. Van Gelder told me, early on, "The *Times* never fires anybody." That was comforting. Ellen Lewis Buell, who had been J. Donald Adams's secretary and was now handling children's book reviews, told me that I was the first person ever invited twice to join the *Times*. That was amusing.

Ellen and her husband Hal Cash became our good friends. They were the first persons to take me out to dinner in New York, and Marjorie was to review many children's books for Ellen including the Walter Farley *Black Stallion* stories, Danny Dunn titles, and *Blue Cat of Castle Town*, her favorite. Harold Cash was a Paris-trained sculptor, member of a well-to-do, land-owning family in Georgia, just south of Chattanooga. Hal commuted between their Georgia place and his New York studio. They were friends of Allen Tate (Hal had done a bronze head of Tate in a Confederate cap that I would love to have had), Caroline Gordon and other literary figures, including the Sherwood Andersons.

When I first arrived, I thought, "Here's the *New York Times*. A huge paper, world famous. Since it is ten times the size of the Jackson *Daily News*, the people must be ten times the size." But they weren't. They were the same size. Or smaller. I soon relaxed and rejoiced that I was paid what seemed to me a nice salary to read and write about books or read articles about books (our reviews) and put in an occasional comma, eliminate four-letter words and otherwise make the reviews fit to print. Moreover there was a certain prestige to this. Once you are at the *Times*, you and your byline known, you become an oracle. Your views are published in advertisements across the land. You and the *Times* both profit. An aura builds up.

The *Book Review* is the very eye of the publishing hurricane (at that time twenty thousand or more reviewable books were published each year, half of these, at least, coming across our desks). I became all too conscious of the varieties, even contradictions, of truth held by authors, editors, and publishers. And since I also observed the Best-Seller List each week and read the reviews, I marveled no less at the versions of truth firmly established in the minds of readers and reviewers.

The *Times*, like most large organizations, had its rivalries, both between departments and between individuals within departments. At the time of my arrival, Lester Markel, the dynamic Sunday department editor, was busily creating his own empire, expanding the various departments (travel, Review of the Week, art, the Sunday *Magazine*, gardening, you name it) and making the *Book Review* more popular by replacing the literary-type editor J. Donald Adams. That explains Robert van Gelder, who came from the daily *Times* to replace Adams. It must be said that Markel was successful, making the *Book Review* and the *Magazine* dominant in New York and in the nation.

In 1945 the *Book Review* was located in a small space on the tenth floor of the *Times* building at 229 West 43rd Street. The space adjoined the offices of the editorial board of the *Times*, each editor having a spacious office and secretary, where he had his thoughts and wrote editorials, assembling with the others once a day to plan the next day's paper. The *Book Review* space was not much larger than that, van Gelder having about an editor's space and the rest of the staff of five or six people in some adjoining space.

Some years before, I was told, the *Book Review* was run by one editor and a secretary. When the editor asked for an assistant, the reply came back, "What does the *Book Review* need two people for?" By the time of my arrival, the *Book Review* had grown to half a dozen people. Lester Markel and his Sunday department had three times that many on the eighth floor, and he wanted more influence over the *Book Review*. After all, it was the Sunday *Book Review*, wasn't it?

The managing editor of the *Times* on the third floor had an even larger staff of skilled editors and reporters, some of them qualified to do anything as well as or better than any of those assembled at the Sunday department. So there was tension over control of the *Book Review*. There were confrontations. Memos flew back and forth.

When Eudora was hired by van Gelder, she had to submit to an interview with Markel. When I innocently arrived from Mississippi, this did not happen. I do not recall anyone arriving at the *Book Review* after that who escaped this intimidating interview, and the *Book Review* soon moved to the eighth floor, adjoining the other Sunday departments where Markel could keep a closer eye on us. When Meyer Berger, Pulitzer Prize-winning reporter from the third floor, was commissioned to write a centennial history of the *Times*, a fat volume, it was said that the section dealing with Markel and his Sunday department had to be extensively revised at Markel's demand.

Despite Markel's reputation, I got along with him well enough, perhaps because we had little contact. Soon after I came to the *Times*, I was sent to some major bookstores to inquire what they thought of the Best-Seller List (one of Markel's innovations of which he was proud). I reported back to him that they didn't like it, saying it helped a few books and hurt many. He and I kicked the idea around harmoniously. On several occasions he had kind words for one of my reviews, perhaps because my pieces tended to help sales rather than hurt them (sales meant ads for the *Book Review*). Once he had another editor try to get me to moderate a review I had done (I gathered the book was by a friend of his), but I declined, without ill effects.

Once, years later, I deliberately needled Markel and the Sunday *Magazine*. I wrote a "Topics of the Times" on oysters and began by saying that a sentence in the *Magazine* had recently puzzled me, "as sentences in the *Magazine* frequently do." I thought that would please Charles Merz, who handled the editorial page. He published it, and Markel fired a memo to him, asking what was the big idea. Merz told him to ask the author, Nash Burger, in his *Book Review*. Markel fired a memo at me. I replied soothingly and all was well.

On a Monday morning around nine o'clock in early summer 1945, I arrived at the *Book Review* to begin work. I found no one on hand except Carolyn Wood, van Gelder's secretary, a pleasant young woman from, I believe, Maine. She sat me down to wait, and soon van Gelder came in, shook my hand, and took me to meet the other staffers.

John K. Hutchens, who seemed a sort of assistant editor to van Gelder, wrote a weekly page for the *Book Review* on books and authors. He also had a hand in making review assignments, wrote an interview now and then, and helped out with copy reading, makeup, and odds and ends as everyone else did, I was to find out. He came to the *Book Review* from the third floor where he had reported on radio and other cultural matters, and had come to the *Times* from the highly esteemed (until it folded) Boston *Transcript*. He was a native of Montana, pleasant, restrained and intelligent.

William DuBois handled most of the makeup and putting together of the *Book Review*, much of the copy reading and some review assignments. He was a born newspaperman, tough, intelligent, energetic. He could do more in less time than anyone I ever knew. He did any *Book Review* assignment willingly and quickly—and still had time to write novels and plays of his own as well as to write or rewrite novels by other people, including those of Frank Slaughter, many of which became best-sellers. All this in the office. He was a believer in "creative copy reading," as he called it, making extensive changes, even "running a review through the typewriter," as he put it, whence it emerged greatly changed and much more readable. This habit did not always sit well with the reviewer or the *Book Review* editor.

Bill was a Columbia graduate, born in Florida, and came to the *Book Review* from the morgue on the third floor. His typewriter was never silent. This meant that he was the only member of the staff who passed up one of the fringe benefits: invitations by publishers and authors to go out with them for lunch, very high-powered lunches, too, at New York's top eateries. (I learned quickly that such affairs lasted too long and made me too sleepy for productive afternoons.) Bill was a real character, and very kind to me when I turned up at the *Book Review*, fresh from Mississippi, helping me adjust to *Times* style, *Times* customs, and New York City.

Tom Lask, born in London, a graduate of City College, had been an office boy for the editorialists adjoining the *Book Review* before the war. Now returned from the navy, he was given the opportunity to try his hand in the *Book Review*. He wrote and edited, and he also became poetry editor for the *Times*, choosing each day a short poem for the editorial page of the daily *Times*, and eventually editing a *New York Times Book of Verse*. He stayed for some years and eventually moved down to the third floor where he dealt with news and cultural matters.

Nona Balakian, a native New Yorker, had been hired two years before I had; fresh out of the Columbia School of Journalism, she had been recommended to van Gelder by her teacher John Chamberlain, who had also been a daily reviewer with the *Times*. She once described van Gelder as a "maverick with ideas of his own." These ideas often differed from those of Markel and made his tenure as *Book Review* editor a rocky and abbreviated one. Nona had introduced Eudora to the *Times* style and customs during her months at the *Book Review* and kept in touch with her throughout the years.

Nona worked diligently, writing and editing, and eventually published a collection of her reviews and articles.

In the *Book Review,* but not of it, in a sense, since she operated at her own speed and by her own rules, was a dignified maiden lady of some years, Hazel Felleman, a relation of Adolph Ochs; she was sole proprietor of a page at the back of the *Book Review* called "Queries and Answers." Each week, readers wrote in with questions about poems and authors of poems; other readers wrote in to answer them. She had a glass-walled office in a corner of the *Book Review* lined with cabinets of drawers filled with three-by-five inch cards, thousands of poems, and the queries and answers, with dates, pertaining thereto.

Mr. Ochs, creator of the modern *Times*, had suggested this feature, and it was quite popular with *Times* readers. Miss Felleman compiled a selection of these poems into a volume called *Best Loved Poems of the American People* that sold thousands of copies and was once to be seen on the shelves of most public libraries—perhaps still is. The Q&A page continued long after Miss Felleman's marriage and her later retirement.

Miss Felleman and I became friends. She had some southern connections down Chattanooga way, where Mr. Ochs had made the Chattanooga *Times* flourish, and she insisted that only I should handle her page while she was away or on vacation. (There was no competition for this job.) Eventually I had to tell her I just did not have the time for the task, and she was forced to permit others to handle it in her absence.

Another staffer from an earlier day who was also somewhat "out of the loop," was an aged, gray-haired, quiet gentleman by the name of Isaac Anderson. He sat by a window, day after day, tranquilly reading mystery stories and four or five times a week turning to his typewriter and writing a short review. His reviews were always clear, written with a restrained humor, and exactly the same length. Bill DuBois, who handled the layout, as I have said, knew in advance just how much space to allow for Mr. Anderson's contribution, since he knew how many words each short review would contain.

Nobody needed to edit Mr. Anderson, and he never edited himself. At the end of the day, he rose from his desk, said, "Good night," put on his hat and walked out. If spoken to, he was always polite in reply, but he was not one to initiate conversation or to engage in small talk. He was a delightful character, an ancient gentleman of the type they used to have at the *Times*. He would have made a marvelous character himself in someone's mystery.

During my first year at the *Times* I wrote forty-three reviews and read countless books for assignment and hundreds of pieces for editing. Most of the time, we all did a little of everything. In the 1940s, under van Gelder, things were quite informal with no staff meetings. Galleys and review copies poured in each day and were shelved in van Gelder's office. The major books had already been anticipated, with reviewers even signed up in many cases, and the galleys or books went right on out to the reviewer. Staff members were free to suggest reviewers to van Gelder, especially on the many books of secondary importance, or he might consult a staffer. He would read or look over reviews when they came in, and perhaps pencil a suggestion to the copy editor. (We all functioned in this capacity.)

Copy for editing was parceled out more or less in terms of staffer interest or specialty. A staffer might query a reviewer by phone or letter, but usually not. Usually a reviewer knew nothing about the fate of his review until he saw it in the *Book Review*. No review galleys were sent to the reviewer, not even a copy of the *Book Review* containing the review. Later, under Francis Brown as editor, review assignment, copy editing and proofreading were much more systematic.

The *Times* was a "closed shop," its workers required under its contracts with various unions to be union members. In our case this was the Newspaper Guild, C.I.O. Union dues were withheld from paychecks and paid to the Guild. Each type of work was defined in the Guild-*Times* contract and placed with others of comparable skill and difficulty in a numbered and graduated pay scale. The top, grade 10, included copy editor, my job. The base pay when I began was a weekly seventy-five dollars with annual specified increases. (Executives and supervisors, such as van Gelder, were excluded from Guild membership and accompanying pay scales.) A worker, of course, was free to ask for a raise and might sometimes receive one without asking. Overtime above the contractual thirty-five-hour week was paid at time and a half. At the *Book Review*, we were paid extra for reviews (thirty-five to fifty dollars in 1945), theoretically done on our own time (and I did read many a book on the subway).

I was happy with the pay, which was more than I had ever made before (and it hardly seemed like work, reading). Prices were low. The *Times* itself cost five cents, bus and subway the same. New York apartments (scarce as hens' teeth because of the war) were rent-controlled; before my family came up in the fall I had found a five-room apartment near Columbia University for sixty-two dollars a month.

No one at the *Book Review* before I arrived was classified as copy editor;

in fact, everyone seemed involved, and problems with this system were evident. Van Gelder said I was to have a breaking-in period, learn the specific *Times* requirements and shibboleths and eventually give some uniformity and order to the proceedings.

Only one snafu: I had not been told when or how I would be paid and had not asked (southern politeness?). I worked for a week, two weeks, no word or sign of pay. I had been used to a monthly pay schedule so did not think much about it—though my funds were slim, and dwindling. Finally, after about a month, I made inquiry. General amusement on the tenth floor. We were paid weekly, by check picked up on Monday on the second floor. I went down and picked up four weekly checks and about as much in payment for several book reviews. I was rich.

By this time another Mississippian, Turner Catledge, had risen from his small-town origins to become the paper's assistant managing editor. A graduate of Mississippi State, he had been a reporter for the *Neshoba County Democrat* and other Mississippi weeklies, correspondent and reporter for the Memphis *Commercial Appeal,* where he had impressed then-Secretary of Commerce Herbert Hoover on the latter's visit to assess damage from the great Mississippi River flood of 1927. Hoover praised Catledge to Adolph Ochs, and the Mississippian was invited to join the *Times* staff.

All of this was known to me, it having been well reported in the Jackson *Daily News* over the years (local boy makes good) and told to me by others. As soon as I learned my way around the *Times*, I descended one day from the tenth-floor *Book Review* to the third-floor newsroom to introduce myself to Catledge, where he sat at his desk near gruff, no-nonsense managing editor Edwin L. (Jimmy) James. I took along several copies of the Jackson *Daily News* (to which I continued to subscribe for some years), thinking that Catledge would like to be brought up to date on local affairs in his home state and sample some of Fred Sullens's colorful prose.

Catledge must already have heard of me from van Gelder and had no doubt been consulted on my hiring. (I have often wondered whether van Gelder's insertion of a Mississippian into the increasingly Markel-dominated *Book Review* was a small part of a larger plan. There were certainly talented members of Markel's Sunday staff who would have relished a move to the *Book Review*.) In any event Catledge and James had seen my reviews and byline and knew that I existed. It was nearly two in the afternoon when I introduced myself to my fellow Mississippian, and the vast city room was not as noisy and busy as it would soon be. Catledge received me and the copies of the *Daily News* cordially and had me tell him something about myself. We made a few comments about New York, Mississippi and mutual acquaintances, including Fred Sullens and my old Jackson friend Ralph Hilton, whom Catledge had known in Washington and elsewhere.

As we talked and I observed him, I felt that there was something familiar about his appearance and manner, though I knew I had never seen him before. It was sometime after I left that it dawned on me: Catledge was very like Ralph Hilton. Both were stocky and a bit below average height, with the same hair and eyes, but more than anything else was the similarity in manner: an amiable and relaxed way of giving you the feeling that knowing you, speaking with you was a pleasure.

It was a southern manner, and one that did much to explain the success of both men in their different (but really similar) fields: editor, on the one hand, State Department official on the other (though Ralph, too, began and ended a journalist). Both were, in the best sense, to put it bluntly and meaning nothing derogatory, politicians. Not calculatingly, perhaps, but out of a natural instinct of good will and the ability to get along. Either could have done well in elective office or have switched roles with the other. Curiously, this is the same way that Lewis Nichols of the *Book Review* would characterize me nearly thirty years later, upon my retirement. After suitable quips about my Episcopalianism in the "age when God is dead," Nichols suggested that "if at any time" I "had played the office politician," I "was so good at it that no one ever noticed." Perhaps such is a distinguishing mark of a Mississippian gone north.

There were other characteristics Catledge and Ralph shared: beneath their pleasantness and a certain aplomb were an intelligence and toughness to be revealed as needed. Cross them, deceive them, and they knew how to respond. Growing up in the spare economic world of red-clay Mississippi, they knew what it took to survive.

Among the acclaimed writers Catledge added to the *Times* staff was the stylish and cherub-faced Craig Claiborne, food news and restaurant critic. Craig reviewed cookbooks regularly for the *Book Review* and became wealthy and internationally famous from the writing of his own books in the field. He wrote with humor and panache but was not amused when I told him that his recipe in the *Times* for bourbon pie produced for Marjorie and the Burger table not one but two of the lucious desserts. (We had no complaints.)

Catledge seemingly had not known before he interviewed Craig for the job that his new hire was another Mississippian and had attended Mississippi

State as Catledge himself had. Nor did Marjorie and I realize for some time that she and Craig (incredibly) had been born in the same tiny Delta town of Sunflower, and that as a child she had played in the Claiborne home with Craig's older sister while an infant Craig kicked and cooed in his cradle, watched over by his faithful black nurse, Aunt Catherine.

When the Claibornes moved to nearby Indianola, Aunt Catherine, on occasion, cared for Marjorie, and later, when Marjorie's parents moved to Jackson, Aunt Catherine's daughter came along as cook, and, in time, as nurse for our sons. Craig has recalled this remarkable coincidence in his best-selling 1982 memoir, *A Feast Made for Laughter*, and when Marjorie wrote him a letter adding a few details to his account, he reported himself "utterly fascinated, entertained and made sentimental."

Over the years at the *Times*, I seldom had contact with Catledge as he rose ever higher both in the *Times* hierarchy, to the post of executive editor, and in the esteem of the publisher, Arthur Hays Sulzberger, son-in-law of Adolph Ochs and head of the prospering newspaper. Sulzberger had been chosen by Ochs's daughter Iphigene (and Arthur's wife) over a favorite Ochs nephew, Julius Ochs Adler. Between Catledge and me, a few words passed in the elevator, a phoned request now and then for a book (I or the publisher glad to supply).

After I reviewed Burke Davis's life of Lee, *Gray Fox*, in the daily *Times* (May 5, 1956), he asked for a copy. He did the same for my and John Bettersworth's *South of Appomattox* (1959), which he then praised highly to *Book Review* editor Francis Brown (which did me no harm). I have a feeling Turner Catledge was never fully reconstructed.

Around 1970, when Catledge was about to retire, he called me in for a talk, spoke of his retirement and asked that I mention this to Bettersworth, then a dean and vice president at Mississippi State University. Catledge thought he might do some teaching and lecturing and was wondering about the disposal of his papers. I did as he suggested, and there was, I believe, some lecturing, and his papers are now at his alma mater. When Catledge and his wife retired to the handsome home they had built in New Orleans, he continued as a director of The New York Times Company until his death in 1983.

Another southerner who helped ease my way was Henry Irving Brock ("Captain Brock," from World War I), the preceding Sunday editor. Brock was an ancient character with long Virginia roots. Once he knew of my southern roots, particularly as relating to the Hessians in Virginia, he sought me out, and we became friends. More than once he made favorable points for me with Markel. I once heard the volatile Markel speak of "Captain Brock's gentle southern manners"—manners that became increasingly rare in the power struggles at the *Times*. Markel, although brutal with his staff, was otherwise pleasant enough. My tranquil association with him may have been fostered by kind remarks from both Brock and Catledge.

People tended to come to the *Times* and stay in those days. It was a benevolent institution, highly esteemed in the city and by the people who worked there. They had a great loyalty to it. People came as office boys, as Tom Lask had, and stayed until they retired, moving up step by step. When someone retired, they'd hire another office boy at the bottom and the previous office boy went up one step. If you stayed thirty or forty years, and many did, you might do very well.

Because of World War II the *Times* staff had grown smaller, and now after the war the paper was hiring a great many people at various levels. Some of the newcomers didn't have the old-time loyalty; they busied themselves furthering their careers (they hoped), competing against each other. Turnover, once a rarity, was common, as disgruntled newcomers moved on.

One who came, stayed and made a name and fortune for himself (and a reputation for uncivil behavior even exceeding that of Markel) was A. H. ("Abe") Rosenthal. He arrived at the *Times*, just out of City College, a few months before I did. He was managing editor by the age of forty-seven and eventually became executive editor, finally taking the less hectic job of *Times* columnist in 1986. He is often credited (or discredited) with creating what has been called "the new *New York Times*," a paper with more features, simpler writing and an expanded reader base.

I had only one slight encounter with Rosenthal (and that via interoffice mail). Soon after our mutual arrival at the *Times*, I reviewed favorably for the daily paper a volume by the English historian Arnold J. Toynbee. The next day I received a memo from the third-floor newsroom signed "A. H. Rosenthal," of whom I had never heard, asking "Have you read the review of *Civilization on Trial* in the [London] *Times Literary Supplement*?" I took this to be a pert question, implying that I hadn't known what I was talking about in my review of that book the day before and also that I was probably unfamiliar with the august London paper.

I contemplated a pert answer, saying that, yes, I had read the unfavorable review in the *TLS*, and also the favorable review in the English *Church Times* and *Daily Telegraph*. But I thought, what the heck, and made no reply at all—rebuke enough, I felt.

Before going to New York, I used to scramble at the Jackson newsstand each week for a copy of the Sunday *Times* to see if my review had appeared in the *Book Review*. I, like other reviewers, used to wonder why one review appeared promptly, another weeks later, why one appeared as written, another drastically changed. After I was on staff, reviewers used to ask me about this, fearful they had done something wrong and had endangered their reviewing future with the *Book Review*, their reputation and income. There was no one answer. It was in the laps of the gods—which only added to the piquancy and suspense.

I remember my astonishment down in Mississippi at the size of my first check: forty dollars! Forty dollars for reading a fine book and writing about it! Awesome. Later, four hundred dollars was not uncommon for such a review, which did not decrease the pleasure. Now, at West 43rd Street, I read and wrote with some leisure, much enjoyment, and fine profit.

At the *Book Review* one not only read good books (and bad) and was paid for it, read and edited reviews and literary essays by masters of the art, but often saw and talked with authors as they appeared at the *Book Review* for one reason or another. Somerset Maugham's cigar remains were preserved for days by an admiring secretary until the odor brought complaints. Poet Robert Frost, impressed by the seeming industry of the *Book Review* staff, paused to inquire what exactly was going on and departed with words of praise for the product. Anaïs Nin, girlfriend (one among many) of Henry Miller and high priestess of the erotic, appeared on her visit to the *Book Review* to be as demure as a vestal virgin.

Ben Ames Williams, born in Macon, Mississippi, but long a resident of New England and grown wealthy from a score of best-sellers and movie sales, dropped in when his jumbo Civil War novel *House Divided* was about to appear. I had been a Williams admirer since the days of his early *Saturday Evening Post* short stories and first novel, *All the Brothers Were Valiant* (which I had read as a teen-ager). I introduced myself, showed him the copy of *House Divided* I was reading for review and talked to him for some time about the business of writing. Our talk continued later at his hotel over some "bourbon and branch." I recall his advice that an aspiring writer should stay out of New York (the same advice that Stark Young gave Allen Tate). I also recall his statement on another occasion that "I believe in the potency of place and the impotency of man." Williams's credo, to me, contains more truth and meaning than the frequently noted words of another Mississippian, William Faulkner, in his Nobel speech that "I believe man will not merely endure;

he will prevail." But then, I've never been able to figure out exactly what Faulkner had in mind.

On another day a tallish, slender figure in blue jeans, T-shirt and old-fashioned, low-quarter tennis shoes hurried past my desk on the way to deliver an overdue review or article. I recognized W. H. Auden. I had in my desk drawer a postcard received only a few days earlier from Frank Lyell, still in the army in Germany. Among other things, it said, "Wystan is here." I had not known that the English Auden had held a commission in the United States Army and served in the same intelligence unit as Frank. Wystan Hugh Auden had evidently made a swift return from overseas.

I showed the card to Auden as he came back by. He chortled, seeming pleased, and we had a few words. (You can see a picture of Auden in American uniform at the wheel of a jeep in the ruins of Nuremberg taken by Frank in Stephen Spender's book *W. H. Auden: A Tribute*.) Later, when Frank himself was out of the army, we visited Auden at his New York lodgings in St. Mark's Place, and I enjoyed hearing the two reminisce about their army experiences. Each of the two was among the most entertaining talkers I have ever heard. Taken together they were matchless.

Among their wartime duties was interrogating German civilians and POW's on "how they liked being bombed," as Auden expressed it. They didn't like it, since, as I learned, the entire hearts of major German cities had been blown to bits, more civilians (thirty-five thousand) being killed in the British-American carpet bombing of Dresden alone than in all the more widely publicized Luftwaffe blitz on England. Auden, who had lived in Germany before the war and knew and liked the people, was especially sympathetic to their plight.

Auden, who had by this time returned to the high Anglicanism of his youth and was a regular worshipper at nearby St. Mark's Church (where Peter Stuyvesant, last Dutch governor of New Amsterdam, with his peg leg, was interred) and Frank, grandson of a rector of St. Andrew's Church in Jackson and faithful Episcopalian, were equally dismayed at the increasing "goofiness" (Auden's word) and secularism of the church both in England and America. This was, of course, well before the Episcopal Church's general convention had invented women priests and replaced its traditional Prayer Book with a trendy modern version.

I saw and heard Auden once again when he spoke at the Anglo-Catholic St. Ignatius Episcopal Church on New York's Upper West Side. His talk was an account of his own spiritual odyssey, a mixture of history, theology and Audenesque humor, a telling indictment of current Anglican tinkering with ancient and established doctrine, tinkering that only revived old heresies under newfangled names. His oft-quoted opinion that "the Episcopal Church in America has gone stark, raving mad" was yet to come—but was clearly on the way.

When crime, drug traffic and other neighborhood changes, including those at St. Mark's Church, forced Auden to leave St. Mark's Place, he returned to England and the Oxford he loved. His last piece for an American periodical appeared in the October 1973 issue of *Vogue* magazine. It began: "I have a ferocious bee in my bonnet that is enraged by the contemporary liturgical reforms and new translations of the Bible." It was the old Auden, witty, scholarly, devout. His poems, accessible and admired by the common reader, were no less esteemed by critics and scholars. But for the American citizenship he had taken on, he might well, and justly, have become England's poet laureate.

Auden continued to write for the *Book Review* off and on, and at his death in Vienna in September 1973, he left uncompleted the review he was doing for our Christmas Book Issue of a book of folk tales by the German Brothers Grimm. He was buried in the village of Kirchstetten, where he had a home, at a service conducted by both Anglican and Roman Catholic priests. An *Audenstrasse* commemorates his residence in the village.

In that first summer at the *Book Review*, when I was living at the General Seminary, I had ample time on weekends to explore New York. This remained over the years my chief recreation in the city—not the theater, the concerts, the museums (though we experienced those things), but the ever-changing spectacle of city life and the people themselves. Of course, not every weekend was work free. On more than one occasion van Gelder handed me a book on Friday with a request for a review by Monday. Such was the case with the memoir of a famed Harvard physiologist Walter B. Cannon, *The Way of an Investigator*, a man of whom I had never heard.

Van Gelder wanted twelve hundred words for an upfront review. I did my usual research in the *Times* morgue, read every word (thinking more than once of the British critic who had said he never read a book before reviewing it, "it prejudices the mind to do so"), wrote my piece and handed it in. Van Gelder was pleased with the result, but my good friend Peter Lambert wrote from the Appalachian School in Penland, North Carolina (he was probably the only person in Mitchell County who subscribed to the Sunday *Times*) that my review was overwritten. Oh, well, I thought, you can't please 'em all.

Charles Poore, *Times* daily book critic and assistant *Book Review* editor, always claimed that New York City, with its five sprawling boroughs, especially the island of Manhattan at its heart, wasn't a city at all but a congeries of towns and neighborhoods. On the other hand, the view often expressed by my fellow southerner, Captain Brock, who was in and out of the *Book Review* several times a day, was that New York was "no longer a place fit to live in." (I noticed though that Captain Brock, who could have retired at any time and returned to his native Virginia, never did.)

I ventured into Brooklyn, Queens, the Bronx, and Staten Island, and I explored Manhattan relentlessly. Mostly I walked. The streets of New York were safe in those days. Especially did I seek out those spots where important events had taken place, where authors and publishers had plied their trade. I found out-of-the-way foreign restaurants with exotic foods and low prices. In small book and coin shops, often tucked away on side streets, I found bargains for my collections. The dislocations of war had produced an increase in the number of rarities available.

Sometimes my discoveries led to an article for the *Book Review*, daily *Times* or Sunday *Magazine*. In other cases my wanderings provided a thought or detail useful in composing or buttressing a review. In a Brooklyn shipyard after much subway, bus and foot travel, I found the remains of the French Line vessel, *Normandie*, its superstructure burned away, giving the ship the look, at a distance, of an aircraft carrier. I wrote an article for the Sunday *Magazine* on the inglorious end of this luxury liner. I discovered a rare Jefferson five-cent piece in a small Greenwich village coin shop and, an anniversary of this coin being at hand, I told the *Times* readers all about it.

In the case of both the ship and the coin, my encounter with the *Magazine* subeditor assigned to steer my article through the Sunday department maze was memorable. On the *Normandie* piece, one of Markel's zealous young men bedeviled me for days with questions and demands for changing this and that. "It's the little Markels that are the problem," Charles Poore always said. "They are so afraid of letting something get by that will arouse his ire that they become paranoid." I made some cosmetic changes, and the piece survived. (Poore was offered the job of *Book Review* editor before the arrival of Francis Brown but had the good sense to decline.)

On the Jefferson nickel piece (Monticello on the obverse), my editor was P. W. Wilson, an aging, white-haired English gentleman with a bit of a walrus moustache, a former member of Parliament and author of several novels in his younger days. He wanted especially to be sure all facts were correct, examined my documentation and departed amiably. He was a member of the Plymouth Brethren, a small English religious sect, and for some years prepared a column of brief comments on religious books once a month for the Saturday *Times*. These comments eventually became so incomprehensible that they were discontinued. How he happened to have found residence in Markel's Sunday department was a mystery, but such picturesque staffers were not unusual at the *Times* in those days.

One Saturday after a lunch at a Chinese restaurant on Broadway just beyond Columbia University (a restaurant I had sought out because I had learned it was long favored by novelist Thomas Wolfe), I walked on to 125th Street and east for some blocks to a coin shop nestled almost under the elevated railroad tracks. I had made one or two purchases there, and the owner had told me that if I came by this particular afternoon, a friend of his would show me some interesting coins.

The friend was there. The coins, he said, were in his car parked in a garage just beyond the tracks. This seemed odd, but I accompanied him to the garage and up the ramp to his car. He raised the lid of the trunk, exposing a wooden chest about two feet long, perhaps a foot high and about as wide. He took a key from his pocket, unlocked the chest and lifted the lid. I was staring at a chest full of gold coins, hundreds of them, many thousands of dollars worth.

Amazed, I said, "Those look like gold coins." "They are," he said. I became aware that the garage was very quiet. No one else was in sight. My companion stood watching me, saying nothing. I began to feel nervous. Were these stolen coins, coins pilfered from wartime Europe perhaps? Was I being set up for a robbery, a scam, a "sting" of some sort? Perhaps a scoop for the *New York Times* was being offered by someone seeking notoriety. I decided I was in the wrong place.

"Oh," I said as calmly as possible. "I only collect silver coins. I couldn't afford any of these." He smiled. My alarm increasing, I turned and walked, not too briskly, I hoped, down the ramp and into the safety of the Harlem streets. I heard the trunk door slam down. I did not look back. Or visit that particular shop again.

At the end of my first New York summer Marjorie and sons Nash and Peter rode "the rattler" (as we Jacksonians called the Southern Railroad's New Orleans-New York express) to join me. We spent our first weekend in the famed old Chelsea Hotel on West 23rd Street, a writer's haven, where

Mark Twain, Tennessee Williams, Jack Kerouac, and a host of others had preceded us and where Dylan Thomas would follow. The Chelsea, with its nineteenth-century facade and grillwork balconies, had a New Orleans look that pleased us.

We dined well at the esteemed Cavanagh's, a block away, went to church on Sunday at the Little Church Around the Corner on East 29th Street (where longtime rector Father Ray, from Canton, Mississippi, greeted us warmly and displayed his Mississippi fig bushes in the churchyard). We saw Central Park, the Battery at Manhattan's southern tip, and the Cloisters overlooking the Hudson at the borough's northern end. We walked and rode bus, subway and elevated until we could do no more.

On Monday we moved into our apartment at 417 W. 120th Street, with Columbia University across the way. We were New Yorkers now—and like most New Yorkers had come from somewhere else.

TEN

New York Times Book Review

My first year at the *Book Review* went smoothly, but there were always rumblings from the eighth floor. Lester Markel and his minions in the Sunday department were never satisfied. When I began, the staff was so small and the books so numerous that we all did a lot of reviewing. I was writing so many (thirty-three in the first year) that van Gelder said he had to make the decision to pay for only the more important reviews. I'm sure this was initiated by Markel, but it didn't last long, and we were soon reviewing again and getting paid.

One of Eudora's tasks when she worked for van Gelder in 1944 had been to assign books to outside reviewers, *Rome Hanks* to me, for example. In turn, I extended invitations to numerous friends from Mississippi in a practice Bill Hamilton called "carpetbagging in reverse," all these Mississippians drawing money from this Yankee paper. On one Sunday, five Jacksonians appeared as reviewers in the *Book Review*: Bill, Eudora, Hubert, Marjorie, and, naturally, me. The week before, George Stephenson had reviewed. George continued to review for us over the years, from the churches he served in Gulfport and Jackson and as Millsaps College faculty member. He served several summers in New York's Trinity Parish at the Chapel of the Intercession and became a familiar figure in the *Book Review* offices. Bringing good friends and talented writers into the New York paper was one way to keep Mississippi closer by.

Before my second year was out, van Gelder had had enough. He took a ten-thousand-dollar advance from Doubleday for a proposed novel (a princely sum in those days) and departed the *Times* to write *Important People*, in which an alleged Markel look-alike was pilloried. John K. Hutchens was elevated to editor, held the post for a year or two, then left for the *Herald-Tribune*, the *Times*'s great rival only two blocks away. DuBois became acting editor for about six months, during which time the *Book Review* descended to the eighth floor, and Herbert Lyons, a Markel protege, was sent in from the Sunday department as editor (the plan all along, Hutchens thought).

Lyons was a young, abrupt, explosive individual. He stirred things up, limited DuBois's role, decided Lask did not need a telephone on his desk (we all had one) and had it removed. Isaac Anderson was forced into retirement. Lyons was accompanied by a close friend, Walter Pistole, who took on much of the work I and others had been doing. I was not too concerned, did what I was asked to do and observed the drama.

For one thing, I had never dreamed I would spend the rest of my working days in New York, and though that is what happened, I always had in the back of my mind the possibility of returning to teaching or full-time writing. New York was an adventure and a change of scene, and I enjoyed it. But for thirty years I never felt myself more southern than when I was in that city. I was never naturalized.

When automobiles became available after the wartime scarcity, we made it a matter of pride never to have a New York license tag. For years, by various strategies, we drove with Virginia or North Carolina tags, and finally accepted New Jersey tags only because I argued speciously and to general amusement that the southern portion of New Jersey was below the Mason-Dixon line.

From time to time job offers elsewhere did turn up (or were investigated), from Groton (of all places) to schools and colleges in the South. But we became more and more comfortable and solvent in New York and stayed put. I did occasionally take on part-time jobs that I enjoyed. At one point I was happily writing or editing for (and receiving checks from) four different sources other than the *Times*: serving on the editorial board of a weekly magazine, editing manuscripts for a publisher, and writing a monthly book review column for a minor magazine and publicity for a church institution.

The *Times* disapproved of this sort of thing, even when there was no conflict of interest, but many staffers did it, and if the outside work was low-key and not too conspicuous, little objection was made. Van Gelder, for example, was on the editorial board of *Book Digest* magazine and once or twice even subcontracted some of his work there to me! When the *Book Review's* John Leonard began writing television criticism for *Esquire*, however, even though he used the pseudonym "Cyclops," the *Times* issued a "no, no." It was excellent criticism, I might add.

The Lyons regime at the *Book Review* was short-lived. I remember the day it ended. It was the day after Margaret Mitchell was killed in Atlanta. I heard Lyons talking on the phone (he talked loudly) to R. L. Duffus, a tenth-floor editorialist, who wanted someone from the *Book Review* to write an editorial on the passing of the author of *Gone with the Wind*. "Nash Burger here can do it. He writes well. I'll send him up to see you," said Lyons. (I was interested to hear this opinion from him on my ability. I had not heard it before.)

I went up and talked to Duffus about what he had in mind, ran through the clips in the morgue on the author and composed a few appropriate paragraphs emphasizing the southernness of Margaret Mitchell and her home town: "So far as she was able, in the face of the enormous popularity of her book, she continued to live quietly, continuing her normal life in Atlanta. And Atlanta, while it took great pride in the success of Margaret Mitchell, reacted as other Southern towns have been said to do when fame has come to one of their own: they accepted it as no more than the recognition that was due to one who was both a Southern lady and an Atlantan." The next day Lyons and Pistole were gone. Lester Markel had struck again.

It was about this time that I was talking on the phone to a publisher, asking him for a list of his upcoming books. "I'll give you a list of our upcoming books," he said, "if you'll give me a list of the *Book Review's* upcoming editors." I didn't know the answer then, but I do now: Francis Brown. He came, bringing peace and tranquility to the *Book Review*, and stayed for twenty years. I was to outlast him by only four years (he retired in 1970 for health reasons) and to serve as speech maker at his *Book Review* retirement party. I think sometimes I got along so well with Brown in part because he looked a good deal like my father, a little larger but resembling my father in the face, and with a similar calming influence.

Brown had worked at the *Times* and with Markel previously and knew what he was getting into. He returned from *Time* magazine, where he had been a senior editor. He was a Massachusetts native, a graduate of Dartmouth, who had taken a Columbia Ph.D. and had taught there. It did not hurt that his dissertation had been on Henry J. Raymond, the 1851 founder and editor of the *Times*. The paper had struggled until Adolph

Ochs came along from Chattanooga, bought it for seventy-five thousand dollars, and created the modern *Times* in 1896. The *Times* was then one of fifteen or twenty dailies in New York, none making money. Brown's hope to turn his dissertation into a biography of Raymond for general circulation got nowhere—until his appointment as *Book Review* editor. Suddenly, publishers were interested, and soon *Raymond of the Times* was in bookstores.

Brown was a historian and editor, not a litterateur. He had a certain presence and aplomb and *looked* like a *New York Times* editor, which many of the new generation did not. His values were traditional and well-informed, and he resisted the trendy lunacy that issued from many a publishing house and was often pressed upon him by his own staffers. I cheerfully supported Brown's agenda when evaluating books for review, selecting reviewers and editing the results. There was support too, from Raymond Walters, a quiet intelligent editor (like Brown, a Ph.D. and historian), who had come from the *Saturday Review* to be Brown's assistant. Ray and I were allied in backing Brown's moderate, time-tested values.

The continuing post-war publishing boom required a larger staff, and that produced an increasingly formalized division of labor. Previewing of books for review (books stacked on desks according to the person's interest) and editing the reviews when they arrived occupied about half of the staff. To preview, we would semi-read the book. Quite often if the book was a good one, we'd read the whole thing. It took a good deal of time, but we were paid the same no matter what. We filled out forms, suggesting reviewers, illustrations, and so on.

Brown made the final decision on reviewer, circling the name of the person he wanted to review it and assigning the number of words, 1500 or 750, whatever. The forms and books would go to the secretaries to be sent out with little yellow slips: typed name of the reviewer and number of words— "500 words, please"—and the date the review was expected. Reviews usually came in on time; if not, the secretary would call. Occasionally, though not often, the reviewer would return the book to say he didn't want to do it.

Brown was the first to read the resulting review, perhaps jotting a suggestion for the editing. And the review (united with the original preview and a copy of the book) was sent out to me, then turned over to the original previewer for editing. Edited reviews were returned to me for looking over, for further editing or suggestions as needed.

When Brown became editor he insisted that changes be cleared with the reviewer and that galleys be sent to the reviewer for approval. I remember sending a review with suggested changes back to Ovid Williams Pierce, a North Carolina author of historical books, and it was pleasing to have it returned after our considerable revisions with a note, "Well, you people certainly know what you are doing." Galleys of every review were also given to staff members as an aid in catching errors and possible further comment.

Once Brown was so annoyed by an error in the *Book Review* he announced that every statement of fact, every name in the review, every date had to have a little check placed over it by the copy reader, guaranteeing accuracy. I said, "You mean even if we say Shakespeare wrote *Othello* we have to check it?"

"Yes, sir, check it." Fortunately we had an extensive collection of reference books for checking most anything. In fact, the Sunday staffers who prepared the crossword puzzle for the *Times Magazine* would frequently come in to check our books to see if such and such a fact were correct.

I sent the reviews down to the composing room according to how soon they might be used, and once a week I gave the preview sheets to a secretary for payment.

Another half of the staff was engaged, in one way or the other, with the mechanical side—doing lay-out, running down illustrations and pictures, and so on. This involved searches not only of the *Times*'s own extensive picture files, but of the city's galleries, museums, and picture archives. An artist might be commissioned to do a certain picture. And permission to use illustrative material had to be obtained. Six or eight people were busy on an activity that had once occupied two or three.

Two days a week, the staff, from Brown on down, turned to and proofread the page proof for the issue that was to appear in about ten days. Typos were corrected (we hoped) and final editorial improvements made; after all this, a new and perfect set of the page proofs was turned over to some veteran staffer who had been kept out of the process so far (this staffer changed from time to time) for a "cold reading" to discover any remaining mechanical or editorial flaws. As a result, typos and obvious errors were rare, a tribute to the benign but no-nonsense reign of Francis Brown.

The *Book Review* seemed a sort of Shangri-la to many a *Times* person—all those books for reading and comment in an enclave out of life's hurly-burly (so it was thought)—and some did join us, from office boys to editors of one sort or another. Charles Simmons, a marvel at layout, whose wit and intelligence enlivened many a *Book Review* headline (and the novels he wrote) and George Woods, who became a notable children's book editor after Ellen Buell retired, both came to the *Book Review* as office boys. Grace

Glueck moved on from the *Book Review* picture desk to an expanding career as editor and writer with the daily *Times* on the third floor. Lewis Nichols moved in the reverse order, from the third floor drama department to the *Book Review*, where he urbanely composed the books-and-authors' page for many years.

For my own reviews, I would read the book beginning to end, making a few notes and queries on paper. I would write the review in longhand and then go back and do a good bit of changing, altering a word, moving a sentence around before a final typing. Because I usually wasn't rushed, I would do a considerable amount of research on the book and author. Was this work? The *Times* thought so and paid me for doing it. I thought differently—but never told anyone.

It dawned on the editors (and surprised me) that I was the only one who had an interest in religious matters, or knew anything about them, it seemed. Miss Flora Walthall, the teacher for our Saturday night group years before in Jackson, is responsible, I believe, for my original interest and such expertise as I have. More and more, the editors would happily turn the books on church history, doctrine or biography over to me. I began reviewing two or three books together, and then, starting in 1951 and continuing for the next twenty years, I often rounded up five to eight titles of a religious nature to review together under the heading "In the Field of Religion." For October 17, 1954, for example, I reviewed *Sources of Western Morality*; *Katherine, Wife of Luther*; *Truth is One*; *Holy Land*; *Like a Mighty Army*; *Cardinal Manning*; *The Church Speaks to the Modern World*; and *The World in Tune*.

In addition to the round-up reviews, I edited a number of religious supplements, several of which earned the Publisher's Merit Award (one hundred dollars). My favorite note accompanying such recognition read, "Heartiest congratulations for the Religious Supplement of March 16." It was "first rate," wrote the publisher, Arthur Ochs Sulzberger. The congratulations closed, "By the way, the necessary tax has been withheld from the amount of this check."

I argued for religious books to be treated as books, judged on their importance in an important field of publishing and on their interest to a wide circle of readers. Francis Brown supported this view. Ideally such books were sent to articulate, knowledgeable reviewers who could catch and hold the attention of the reader (who may or may not have had any special interest or competence in religion) and yet would not outrage the scholar (except as any scholar is outraged to find his perceptions, his vision of "truth" contradicted.) John Leonard, who succeeded Brown as *Book Review* editor, indulged my interest, and important religious books continued to receive up-front reviews.

In my quarter century and more at the *Book Review*, I saw a number of changes and shifts in emphasis in religious books, from postwar peace-of-mind through death-of-God to social involvement. This is partly a result of mankind's inbred desire for change and novelty and the natural result of the merchandiser's efforts to foster that desire as an aid to business. (Even religious-book publishers have to make a living.) Religious books have been around for some time; they will certainly be around a while longer in one form or another. At the *Book Review*, and this became my responsibility, we continually commented on both their form and content, as St. Peter says, "for the praise of them that do well."

Work at the *Book Review* was gratifying in other ways. When I reviewed *Knights of Christ* in a round-up of religious books, for example, Helen Walker Homan, the author, wrote, "Were I a book-editor or reviewer, and had been asked to comment on that enormous tome, I would have just rolled over and died. It would be easier." Lengthy books, if the subject was of interest and the book well-written, did not dissuade me in the least.

I had not been long at the *Book Review* when one day van Gelder asked me if I would like to make "a couple of hundred dollars." I replied that I would indeed like that. Well, he explained, the centennial of the *Times* was coming up in 1951; ace reporter Meyer Berger was already at work on his commemorative historical volume, and something should be done about book reviews in the *Times*. The *Book Review* as a separate publication had begun in 1896, and its own fiftieth anniversary would be along soon also.

The *Times* had printed reviews of important, newsworthy books in its regular columns from the very beginning. Unfortunately there was no adequate index through which to locate these early reviews, and someone would have to go through the bound volumes of the *Times*, page by page, to locate the reviews, make a list, even copy out a few interesting or notable comments, so that eventually some sort of commemorative publication could be issued. I was to be that someone, doing the work on my own time, that is, weekends, holidays, after hours, or whenever I liked.

It proved a fascinating assignment. Searching out those long-ago, first reviews of books that had become classics and of books hailed as classics that then sank into oblivion (sometimes to be rediscovered and hailed once again) was a real pleasure. It was difficult to confine my attention to book reviews. The news columns, especially of local events—the crimes, scandals, and marvels so similar yet different from our own (especially in the way they were reported)—kept catching my eye and interest. Even the advertisements were distracting and entertaining.

For weeks, months, I continued my project. Sometimes when things were quiet at the *Book Review*, I would disappear from my desk and slip away to the quiet room where the bound *Times* volumes were stored and continue my search on company time—all in a good cause.

Van Gelder left the *Book Review* before I completed my assignment. John Hutchens was appointed editor and inquired as to what it was all about. When I finished, he saw that I received my "couple of hundred dollars." I would have been glad to do it for free. I was probably the only person (and may still be) who had read, in whole or part, every book review in the *Times* from 1851 to 1896. A separate, eight-page Saturday *Book Review Supplement* was begun on October 10, 1896, after Adolph Ochs had bought the paper, but I continued my search and note-taking, which now became easier, until I caught up with the 1940s.

The Saturday *Book Review* became the Sunday *Book Review* in 1911. In 1920 it became the thirty-two-page *Book Review and Magazine*, but this was so successful in terms of advertising and editorial matter that two years later it was necessary to issue two separate publications, the situation that prevails today. I emerged with a vastly increased knowledge and appreciation of the *Times* and its book reviews.

Nothing was done with all my notes until the *Times* centennial year of 1951, by which time Francis Brown had become *Book Review* editor. In that year, the *Times* issued a promotional publication, sold for a modest sum, of forty-seven large-size pages about the dimensions of the *Book Review*, titled *A Century of Books*, consisting of one hundred reviews from the one hundred years of the *Times*. Charles Poore, assistant *Book Review* editor, wrote a characteristically wise and witty introduction.

The reviews chosen ranged chronologically from William Makepeace Thackeray's *Henry Esmond* (1852) to Winston Churchill's *The Gathering Storm* (1948) and alphabetically from James Truslow Adams to Emile Zola. Most of the reviews in the early years were unsigned, though H. L. Mencken appeared as both reviewer (very good on Dreiser) and reviewee (*The American Language*). Early on, the *Times* thought nothing of reviewing books by prominent foreign authors in the foreign edition before English translation was available.

A Century of Books offered contemporary reviews of Walt Whitman's *Leaves of Grass*, Charles Darwin's *On the Origin of Species*, Tolstoy's *War and Peace*, J. G. Fraser's *The Golden Bough*, Anton Chekov's *The Cherry Orchard*, Sigmund Freud's *The Interpretation of Dreams*, Sherwood Anderson's *Winesburg, Ohio*, Marcel Proust's *Swann's Way*, E. M. Forster's *A Passage to India*, and John Steinbeck's *Grapes of Wrath*, to name a memorable few.

Not all the reviews agree with posterity, at least not yet, as, of course, reviewers at any time never seem to agree with each other. One can only marvel. The 1877 reviewer of *Tom Sawyer* firmly stated that "In the books to be placed in children's hands, . . . we have a preference for those of a milder type." A 1915 critic objected that in Somerset Maugham's *Of Human Bondage*, "There are certain episodes . . . which seem both repulsive and superfluous." As for Virginia Woolf's *The Voyage Out* (1920), "There is little . . . to make it stand out from the mediocre novels which make far less literary pretensions," while the reviewer of Eugene O'Neill's plays (1921) lamented that "Mr. O'Neill's characters never have any fun."

Many readers will approve the comment by the reviewer of Karl Marx's *Capital* (1887) that "Amelioration of human affairs was never further from solution than by the methods Karl Marx proposes," and note the double-edged observation on Willa Cather's *O Pioneers!* (1913) that "Some might call it a feminist novel . . . but we are sure Miss Cather had nothing so inartistic in mind."

James Joyce's *Ulysses* (1922) is mysteriously pronounced both "the most important contribution to fictional literature in the twentieth century" and also a book that "the average intelligent reader will glean little or nothing from." T. S. Eliot's *The Waste Land*, which does not appear in *A Century of Books* and was not reviewed in the *Times*, might, as a poem, have received a comment similar to that given *Ulysses*. Eliot's *Ash Wednesday* is included, but in a baffled and baffling review.

The *Times* has never been stampeded by best-sellers, though Hervey Allen's *Anthony Adverse* (1933), which led the best-seller list two years running, racking up over a million copies sold, received a glowing review and appears in *A Century of Books*, while William Faulkner's *Sanctuary*, which appeared two years earlier and sold about as well, did not make the list of one hundred books (*Soldiers' Pay* did). *Sanctuary*, when reviewed in the *Times*, left reviewer John Chamberlain "in a limp state," his nerves frayed, but convinced that Faulkner "shows promise."

Other top best-sellers reviewed by the *Times* but missing from *A Century of Books* are Thomas Dixon's *The Clansman* (1905) in which "the aims and accomplishments of the Ku Klux Klan, so far as Mr. Dixon describes them, seem wholly admirable"; Edith M. Hull's *The Sheik* (1921), "a shocker written for undeveloped tastes"; Edgar Rice Burroughs's *Tarzan of the Apes* (1914), "crowded with impossibilities [but] told so well readers will look forward eagerly to the promised sequel."

Yes, indeed, as Charles Poore points out in his introduction to *A Century of Books*, the reviews included (and excluded) show "the diversity of different ages, different standards of writing and criticism," suggest how a book in one age influences the writing of books in another, and reveal "that no writing is an island, complete in itself. It's all part of the main." I learned a lot about the *Times* from reading those old reviews, as well as about books and book criticism. I should have paid the *Times* for the privilege.

My pedestrian explorations of New York City, begun my very first summer before my family came up from Mississippi, continued. Marjorie (and our sons when not otherwise engaged) often joined me on my jaunts, with a good meal at some recommended or recently discovered restaurant as a reward at the end. I certainly was not the first *Times* staffer for whom walking was a recreation and a way of getting to know a colorful and historic city.

A portion of the promenade overlooking the East River in Carl Schurz Park at 86th Street is marked with signs as "John Finley Walk" for a great *Times* editor and popularizer of this means of getting about. The German movies, restaurants, and *konditoreis* of Yorkville were nearby in my early days and often enjoyed.

On the opposite side of Manhattan, overlooking the Hudson River, at the northwest corner of Broadway and 84th Street, I discovered the marker announcing the site of the house where Edgar Allan Poe had written "The Raven" in the summer of 1844. I followed the Poes (Edgar, his childbride Virginia and mother-in-law Mrs. Clemm) to the Poe cottage in the Bronx, where Virginia died, inspiring the poet's "Annabel Lee," which Poe never saw in print. It appeared in the *New York Tribune* two days after Poe died in Baltimore while returning to New York from a trip to Richmond.

I sought out other Poe sites in New York over the years. A "Topics of the Times" (the name of the column appearing daily on the editorial page) on Poe was gestating in the back of my mind. I must have read a dozen books on Poe, as well. My walks and reading led, years later, not to a "Topics," but to a *Book Review* "Last Word," "Writer in Residence," not about

Poe in New York but about Poe and William Faulkner at the University of Virginia.

Not all of my wanderings were in Manhattan. I traveled by subway to the borough of Queens and walked to College Point, overlooking the East River and Long Island Sound, and learned that a planned nineteenth-century Episcopal College had supplied the name. Here again, I was thinking of a "Topics." There is no college at College Point; but as I write, the *New York Times* has purchased much of the land and is building a $315 million super-printing plant there to match a similar plant in Edison, New Jersey, that will take care of *Times* printing needs well into the next century.

When completed in 1997, College Point will eliminate the need for the ancient presses at West 43rd Street in Manhattan. When this great venture was first reported in the *Times* house organ, *Times Talk*, the reporter expressed puzzlement and amusement as to why this isolated spot with no college was so named. My wanderings years before enabled me to supply the answer. If everyone walked more, I assured the editor, they would be healthier, wealthier, and wiser.

My explorations once produced an even more surprising result on Staten Island (the Borough of Richmond). This island, five miles across New York harbor from Manhattan but only a stone's throw from New Jersey, should in all reason be a part of the latter state, but politics are not always reasonable. In any event, Staten Island and the ferry from Manhattan (five cents a trip in my early years) often attracted me. Edna St. Vincent Millay's famous poem about that ferry ride had long been a favorite.

Except for the northern end facing Manhattan, the island was largely rural, a few villages scattered across farming and dairy country, a little light industry, an uncrowded beach or two on the east side, some steep hilly acres in the center. I found Burger's Hill there and many Dutch and German Burgers in the large Moravian cemetery dating from colonial times. A little rapid-transit line ran the length of the island, drawing it all together. It was a welcome relief from Manhattan, and I walked many a mile there, and swam there, too.

One day in the village of Tottenville, at the island's far south end, I noticed a shop just off the village center. It bore a sign that read "Henry Burger— Cobbler—Shoe Repair." I was ever alert for clues as to the colonial history and origin of my family (about which I knew much less then than now), and here was a Burger who bore the same name as my eighteenth-century immigrant ancestor.

I approached the shop and stepped inside. A black man was cobbling away industrially over a pair of lady's shoes. I saw no one else about. "Excuse me," I said. "I'm looking for Henry Burger."

"I'm Henry Burger," he replied pleasantly. "What can I do for you?"

I hope I concealed my surprise. Then I launched into an explanation about my Mississippi and Virginia background, and perhaps my Pennsylvania and New York origins before that. What he then told me was even more surprising. Tottenville had been a stop on the antebellum Underground Railway for slaves fleeing the South, and while Henry Burger's family had not been among them, Henry's grandfather had come north after the war to join relatives.

The grandfather, former slave of a Bedford County, Virginia, farmer named Burger had, as often happened, taken the name of his owner, who, in fact, had helped him come North. Bedford County, I knew, adjoined Botetourt County, where my family had lived, and I vaguely recalled that one of my grandfather's brothers had moved to Bedford and married, where he might well have acquired slaves. The Botetourt Burgers owned no slaves, either because of objections to the practice or lack of need.

Henry and I talked for quite a while as he continued his work. Finally I thanked him and went on my way.

In later years my family and I on a weekend or holiday often drove into Manhattan from our New Jersey home via the less-crowded Staten Island route, and once I stopped by Henry Burger's Tottenville shop to see him. The shop was still there, but Henry had gone—moved to Virginia, I was told.

My mother had not come with us to New York when we moved from Mississippi. After my father's death, with small funds and no Social Security, she sought to take care of herself as well as she could. She became a companion to the well-to-do widow of one of my father's friends. During my Historical Records Survey days she found work with a New Deal program herself, something to do with state land maps. When World War II shut down both the HRS and the map program, she resumed (now in her sixties) her early occupation of secretary.

Walter B. Capers, rector of St. Andrew's, employed her to handle his correspondence, although, according to Charlotte Capers, the rector's daughter, her father and his secretary spent most of their time talking and recalling anecdotes of old-time Jackson. Some letters were certainly typed, however, because I received several of them and saw others. That was, I believe, a happy time for both, the Episcopal rector, son of a Confederate general, and my Massachusetts-born mother, who had never entirely lost her Boston accent.

After some years my mother did join us in New York, living with us or nearby as necessity dictated, well content as babysitter or companion to our sons when Marjorie and I were away. Ever reconciled to life's vagaries (she had had plenty of practice), she enjoyed New York, making friends with other old ladies on the benches of Morningside Drive and Broadway (not to mention old gentlemen), and with patrons and staff in the public library branch at Columbia University and with the canons and dean of the Cathedral of St. John the Divine, where we all worshipped regularly.

Among the Jackson colony in Manhattan were Evelyn Spickard and her mother. Evelyn had taught piano in Jackson (Lehman Engel was among her pupils and, some say, Eudora Welty also, which would perhaps make Evelyn the model for Eudora's memorable character Miss Lotte Eckhart of the famous story "June Recital"—but Eudora denies this is so. Notice the similarity, though, of the names Spickard and Eckhart).

In any event, in Jackson Evelyn had come under the influence of that tireless apostle of Anglo-Catholicism, Miss Flora Walthall, had become director of religious education at several prominent Episcopal churches (including Houston's Christ Church Cathedral) and was now at the Chapel of the Intercession, a gem of French Gothic architecture connected with the sprawling Trinity Parish cemetery at Broadway and 155th Street.

It was through Evelyn that George Stephenson was invited to spend several summers supplying at the Intercession (and, indeed, was urged to stay on permanently, a secure, well-paid, prestigious post he turned down in order to remain in Mississippi). We all, especially my mother, spent much time and shared many meals with the Spickards.

In the 1960s my mother's increasing physical weakness (but no diminution of wit or spunkiness) made a move to a nursing home imperative. Jackson was the logical place. (Evelyn had herself retired there.) After some investigation I took my mother back to Jackson, to a nursing home happily located in two adjoining houses just next door to our old Boyd Street home. It had previously been the Eyrich home, of course, and Gladys Eyrich and other friends from our early Jackson days were also in residence.

My mother had taken three books with her, and these she read over and over, as long as her eyes held out: *The Book of Common Prayer*; *Peace of Mind* by the Jewish rabbi Joshua L. Liebman (over a million copies sold; I had given her my review copy); *The Private Papers of Henry Ryecroft* by George

Gissing (she had owned it for years, she and Gissing both having known the numbing bleakness of poverty).

As usual she adapted to the new regime, which does not mean she suffered fools gladly. She did not. She would sputter and go on her own way. It was the custom at the home for the ladies in wheelchairs (as my mother was) to be wheeled into the living room daily for several hours of television. My mother was having none of that. "Boring trash," she called it and demanded on pleasant days to be wheeled outside to observe the real world of birds, trees and flowers and of her own old home next door.

On inclement days she sat by a picture window and looked out. Thinking of what? Brattleboro, Somerville, snow on the Boston Common? Early happy married days at the Crafts'? Gray depression months in Houston and Dallas? Jackson again, Virginia, New York? The bitter and the sweet. Change, the one constant.

On her bedroom dresser she kept two portraits, one of my father, one of me. In her nineties now, when she talked she was not always sure which Nash she was addressing, but we had been her life, and it didn't matter. She died on Boyd Street on May 14, 1973.

I flew down the same day, and the day after she was buried beside my father in Cedarlawn. George, who had been her favorite and most frequent visitor, read the funeral service as she had wanted. On her grave marker I included not only the date of birth and death but (as was once the custom) the place of each: Somerville, Massachusetts, and Jackson, Mississippi. She would have wanted that, too.

ELEVEN

Reading and Writing
for a Living

If my first five years at the *Book Review* were a sort of shakedown cruise for me and for the *Book Review* itself, with its five editors in as many years, the years that followed, with Francis Brown at the helm, were halcyon days, indeed. The reading, writing, and editing were increasingly congenial, with freedom to review or to write pretty much what I wanted. I was also contributing reviews to the daily *Times* and brief columns for "Topics of the Times." I wrote a few pieces for the Sunday *Magazine*, an occasional literary essay for a quarterly, and reviews for papers other than the *Times*. I wrote a number of "The Last Word" essays that the *Book Review* published weekly on such topics as I chose myself. I enjoyed this writing and the extra pay it brought in.

For obvious reasons, publishers were not slow to seek out *Book Review* editors and byline writers for special attention. Invitations to lunch were received almost daily for Sardi's, the Algonquin, the Century, University, Harvard, Princeton or other clubs. "Or where would you like to go?" the publisher or his eager young representative would ask. I preferred the nearby Blue Ribbon, a quiet, darkly paneled restaurant with marvelous German food and superb pastries, smaller and less pretentious than the better-known spots, with the cozy charm of a Bavarian ratskeller. Diarmuid Russell, Eudora's great friend and agent, had introduced me to the Blue Ribbon, and I often went there with Eudora, Frank Lyell, George Stephenson, Hubert

Creekmore, and other old friends. John Bettersworth was especially taken with the place and always demanded to be taken there. Like much of mid-town Manhattan, the restaurant has since fallen victim to the wrecking ball.

Marjorie, the boys, and I continued to live in our original apartment just off Morningside Drive. We enjoyed Morningside and Riverside parks until the boys were one day accosted by some youths who demanded, "Gimme your loot." Both arrived safely home, but we became more cautious. The boys went to the New York Cathedral Choir School of St. John the Divine. Marjorie was busy as secretary and registrar for the school.

Just as the *Book Review* began to take order under Francis Brown and we were celebrating the *Times's* centennial, a third son arrived in our family, a genuine New Yorker, born on Fifth Avenue. We gave our new son the expansive cognomen of Stephen Gilbert Christian Burger. The Stephen was for the saint of our marriage day, the Gilbert for a favorite English saint, the Christian for Marjorie's mother's family name. We had no complaint, just a great assortment of girls' names unused. Busy as she was, Marjorie continued reading new books to the boys and writing reviews full of their reactions for the *Book Review*.

The daily *Times* ran one book review each day under the heading "Books of the Times." During my early years at the *Times*, these were written by Charles Poore and Orville Prescott. Prescott did four a week, Poore two. I started doing some daily reviews as early as 1946 when Poore or Prescott went on vacation. Later when Poore was out sick for several months, I filled in during his absence. I wrote my reviews for the *Book Review* and the daily *Times* on my own time and was paid extra for them. I enjoyed doing both and enjoyed the additional income no less.

My first review for "Books of the Times" was of Gertrude Stein's GI dialogue between soldiers, *Brewsie and Willie*. It is a small book, but I had fun inventing a discussion among the characters themselves. "You know Willie, said Brewsie I have been reading, reading this book Miss Stein wrote about us and I wouldn't be surprised if some of it isn't pretty good, now just listen." I tried a similar jocular approach for a review of William Faulkner's "Spotted Horses" for the *Book Review* but didn't get away with it. The review never ran.

Nine days after *Brewsie*, in my fourth daily review I decided to cover both *The Portable Mark Twain* and *The Portable Rabelais* and began: "The 'Portable' in the title of the Viking Portable Library Series cannot be said to be a narrowly definitive adjective—since there are also portable sawmills as well as portable houses. However, the Viking 'Portables' are truly portable, a coat-pocket will contain them. . . ." I enjoyed reviewing for the daily "Books of the Times" because I had a choice in the books I would review and plenty of time. The daily reviews were expected to run 750 to 900 words.

Writing the daily reviews at my own speed outside the office, I would often do a good bit of research, stimulated by my own interest. I would read other books by the writer, get clips from the morgue and read through maybe a hundred clips and articles. This was the case, for example, in reviewing E. M. Forster's *Collected Tales*. I hadn't reviewed anything of his before, but by the time I finished my research, I was a Forster fan and wrote: "Although E. M. Forster had begun a first novel at 20—which means he has been writing now for nearly half a century— . . . Forster has been compared to, among others, Meredith and Henry James (though he writes more simply than either) and, in his distrust of civilization and progress, to D. H. Lawrence (though he is more comic and, therefore, saner than Lawrence). Yet Forster has never been read as widely as his talent would justify. His manner is not sensational enough. . . ."

That first summer of filling in for the vacationing Prescott or Poore, just at the beginning of my second year at the *Times*, was very satisfying. The highlight was a reissue of best-seller *Anthony Adverse* by Hervey Allen, a Columbia University scholar and master narrator. *Anthony Adverse* had sold a million copies and been translated into twelve languages. But the best novels don't usually become best-sellers. When they do, it is usually for the wrong reasons. Allen's novel is more than just another long, imitative, history-cum-sex novel, and the protagonist is more than one-dimensional. I welcomed Anthony back to the bookstores and wrote in the daily *Times* that he is a "Modern Man, with all the restlessness, the uncertainty, the longing for security that mark our time. He is seeking, as he says, 'something beyond us and yet in us and with us.' He encounters in the course of his travels characters who illustrate most of the classic reactions to the problems of life. And the episodes of the novel are selected to present experiences of perennial concern." At 1,240 pages, *Anthony Adverse* has been called the "first of the half-million-word and million-sale novels to appear in one volume." In my opinion, it is one of the few that improve with reading.

The daily review that gave me the most satisfaction, I think, is of *Catcher in the Rye*. The review ran the day it came out. At that time the *Herald Tribune* and the *New York Times* were the two prominent newspapers, with the *Tribune* being older and perhaps more influential locally. It was the period when the *Times* was overtaking the *Tribune*, but the papers were neck and neck, and the *Tribune* had a longtime and highly respected reviewer, Lewis Gannett. He was a veteran and the most esteemed of the New York daily reviewers, I would say. He was certainly better known than Prescott, who had recently arrived at the *Times*.

I habitually read reviews in the other paper; they didn't necessarily review the same books, but on the day *Catcher in the Rye* came out, Gannett reviewed it also. He put it down. He said it was just another book about teenage angst, so boring, about all these teenagers. Well, I was taken with the book, so my review was highly praiseworthy of the more-or-less unknown J. D. Salinger. I found his rendering of teenage speech "wonderful: the unconscious humor, the repetitions, the slang and profanity, the emphasis, all are just right. Holden's mercurial changes of mood, his stubborn refusal to admit his own sensitiveness and emotions, his cheerful disregard of what is sometimes known as reality are typically and heart breakingly adolescent."

This review caught the eye of Julius Ochs Adler, a top *Times* executive and nephew of Adolph Ochs. Adler wrote down to the daily books offices, inquiring, as Lester Markel once had, "Who is this Nash K. Burger?" Adler had evidently read the Gannett review as well as mine. Gannett was the oracle, and as far as Adler knew I was the nobody who had taken an opposite view in the *Times*. Because *Catcher in the Rye* became such a success, I thought of this little incident as something to remember. I even received a brief thank-you message from the reclusive Salinger.

Over the next nineteen years, I reviewed more than one hundred books for "Books of the Times." In the summer of 1947 and during the next spring and summer I was reviewing as many as ten books a month. It was steady work, too steady really, and I cut back to one or two a month and then to a few a year until 1956–57 when Poore was again out of the office. Many were histories: of the South and her heroes and battles, or biographies of figures such as FDR, Churchill, and Thomas Hardy. I was able to choose or refuse the books for review and to cover a book such as Hubert Creekmore's *The Fingers of Night*, which had been neglected by the daily *Times*.

Much fiction and opinion passed under my review, some eminently forgettable. But others books, such as Peter Taylor's first collection, *A Long Fourth and Other Stories* (he was just thirty-one at the time), Graham Greene's *Heart of the Matter*, and Louis Rubin and James Jackson Kilpatrick's *The Lasting South* were a great joy to read and review.

It mildly surprises and amuses me that what I wrote about some writers nearly fifty years ago can still be said today, as with my review of Taylor, for example. His stories then and now are "concerned with much more than regional idiosyncrasies." I generalized, "It is typical of Mr. Taylor's balance and perception that he can see both the virtues and the defects of the society and the individuals he is portraying. More important in these stories than the treatment of surfaces (however skillful) is the unusual degree of cultural and social understanding."

When I wrote that *The Lasting South* was not about segregation but about the South's history, traditions, and place in the American scene, Louis Rubin was so delighted that he sent a note. He had worried that the collection of essays might be "interpreted and received as an apologia for enforced segregation." He wrote, "You have pointed out the nature of the book in such a way that nobody who reads your review can mistake it." He was one of several authors who expressed pleasure (and gratitude) when I understood their books. Another thanked me for "ferreting out what the book is all about." It was good reading and extra money, but when Prescott suggested that I move permanently to write for "Books of the Times," I declined. What was highly enjoyable on occasion would have been too much for a constant deadline.

Sometimes a publisher decided a review was so fine that the reviewer should be invited to write a book on the subject. Thus when I reviewed a Hodding Carter novel in which the Mississippi River flood of 1927 figured, presto! A publisher suggested that I should write a book on the great American floods. Declined. A review of a controversial book on American education brought an invitation for a book on education. Declined. Invitations to tell what Confederate leaders did after the Civil War (*South of Appomattox* with John K. Bettersworth) and what every teenager should know about Confederate agent Rose Greenhow (*Confederate Spy*) were accepted. A frustrated writer of fiction, I would have composed a novel or two if invited, but no invitation appeared, and I was reluctant to invest the time and energy on speculation—although Diarmuid Russell encouraged me to give it a try. I was enjoying my remunerative nonfiction career too much.

When the publishers first asked for a book about the Confederate leaders and their roles in Reconstruction, thinking I didn't have time, I told them to get John Bettersworth, my old friend from Central High School days, to write it. They insisted on me, for obvious reasons, and it was settled that John and I would write it together. It was a pleasure to work with him.

We covered Alexander Stephens, the vice president of the Confederacy and conscience of the South; the quiet gentleman Robert E. Lee; Nathan Bedford Forrest; Matthew F. Maury, scientist and founder of a Confederate colony in Mexico; James Longstreet, "the reconstructed" we called him; Jefferson Davis, the unreconstructible; Wade Hampton; "Old Joe" Johnston; L. Q. C. Lamar (whose son owned the house in which I was born); and John C. Breckinridge.

We each wrote five chapters, on a total of ten people. So it would have a unified style, we sent the chapters back and forth, and we each would take out a little and put in a little, with consideration for the other. When the book came out, Orville Prescott reviewed it in "Books of the Times." Later he said, "The way I figure it, Bettersworth did the history, did the research on it, and you went through and gave it the lively style." Actually, the reverse was the case. Bettersworth could write the history without a thought. I, on the other hand, had to dig, dig, dig to feel I fully understood those men and their importance.

Bettersworth, a fine stylist, thought the manuscript needed some liveliness, which he gave it. He also put some additional history in here and there, relevant matter usually. When it wasn't on our subject, I had him take it out. At least as far as my chapters went, it was hard-won history, and I learned a lot from it. Bettersworth could probably have written his chapters out of his head. Even so, our treatment of our leaders and the Confederate viewpoint prompted the editor at Harcourt Brace to ask, "Didn't these people ever do anything wrong?" "No," we assured her, "they never did." We were well pleased with what we had written. The book did well enough with the critics and in the bookstores, selling some twenty-five thousand copies, as I recall.

On the lighter side, I was writing brief columns for the "Topics of the Times," which ran daily on the *Times* editorial page, nearly a full column, without any byline. The topic could be most anything and was usually connected in some way with New York.

My "Topics" were often eclectic at best: there was the one on oysters that began with a reference to the Sunday *Magazine* that I slyly thought would annoy Markel (it did), another regarding a *Times* news story about a man in New Jersey who had managed to raise cotton in that state and (my contribution) how that might influence the state's politics and culture if expanded, and one on the emu (why, I don't recall). My only "Topic" that was turned down was one on Philip Freneau, poet of the Revolution, who had Freehold (New Jersey) connections. Charles Merz, who was handling "Topics" at the time, thought my column rather "remote," meaning Freehold, I guess, though I, who was commuting from there every day, thought it a suburb (fifty miles away). I realized then that I should have stressed Freneau's New York City connection more (he had been a newspaper editor there). He died in a snowstorm, walking from a Freehold tavern to his home near Matewan, in a community named Freneau (still to be found on some maps). I sent my Freneau column (the date was some sort of Freneau anniversary) to Frank Adams, an editor in the news department, and he ran it as news. So my labor wasn't wasted.

I enjoyed most the columns in which I could combine history, literature, and often, the church. One such column appeared on the occasion of the investment of James A. Pike, Columbia University chaplain, as dean of the world's largest cathedral. It is only "a short walk," I wrote, "from Columbia University's handsome white-stone-red-brick buildings that cluster on Morningside Heights across Amsterdam Avenue to the great Gothic mass that is the Cathedral of St. John the Divine." I enjoyed noting in the "Topic" that King's College (later to become Columbia) had begun in the early eighteenth century adjoining Trinity Church in lower Manhattan and that, after two centuries and many changes, removals and vicissitudes, school and church once again stood side by side at the other end of Manhattan on Morningside Heights, their relationship symbolized by Dr. Pike's short walk, the metamorphosis of chaplain into dean.

I continued in the "Topic" to tell of the 1703 decision of the Vestry of Trinity to satisfy the governor of the colony's desire for an establishment of a college with "any reasonable Quantity of the Church's Farm," then thirty-two fertile acres in lower Manhattan earning a tidy rental of thirty-six pounds per annum. Fifty-one years later, when the college charter was granted, the vestry gave additionally "all the land on the West side of the Broadway . . . fronting easterly to Church street between Barclay street and Murray street 440 foot and from there running westerly between and along the said Barclay street and Murray street to the North River."

This process of digging into records to discover interesting connections reminds me today of the continuing searches I have made over the years into my ancestral Eddy, Burger and related families. And the survey of the land grant brings to mind letters to my Jackson friend of fifty years earlier, R. J. Landis, to gather details of the exact placement of Jackson's newly named Eudora Welty Library. As I had suspected from the Jackson *Clarion-Ledger*, the library occupies the space on the block where I was born, the southwest corner of North and Mississippi streets.

Another of my "Topics" concerned the renovation of St. Peter's Church, Chelsea, in West Twentieth Street. I had stayed in the seminary my first summer in New York, and, as I mentioned earlier, it was the home of poet-clergyman Clement Clarke Moore. Chelsea had changed mightily, I wrote in the column, since

> Moore lived quietly here, taught in the General Seminary built in his old apple orchard and wrote "A Visit from St. Nicholas" to entertain his children Charity, Clement, and Emily. The descendants of the Dutch and English, whose farms, homes and gardens were scattered along the Hudson above Greenwich village, became outnumbered in the nineteenth century by German, Scotch, and Irish newcomers. And now in the twentieth, the Puerto Ricans largely replace the latter. Dutch, English, German, Irish, Puerto Rican, all have made of Chelsea a microcosm of New York and of America. All have found a home in Chelsea, where St. Peter's old stone tower stands watch.

Its blue Spuytenduyvel stone, worn and gray from many years of Manhattan sun, rain, smoke and fog, restored should continue to stand for generations to come.

One day I received an envelope from the *Reader's Digest*. Sweepstakes were not quite the rage they are today, but nonetheless, I was initially inclined to toss what I perceived to be yet another advertisement and inducement to subscribe. Luckily, I did not. Inside was a check for $250 for a condensation of my "Topic" on Boston-born Samuel Francis Smith, author of the words of the patriotic school song "America." The occasion of the original column was that "The Board of Education has decided that the fourth stanza of 'America' might properly and effectively form a portion of an opening 'devotional exercise' for the city's public schools and has ordered that it be so used." Such a "devotional exercise" today, when even the legality of sixty seconds of silence for private devotion has been challenged in court, would have hard going. Forty years ago, however, "Our fathers' God, to thee, Author of liberty, To thee we sing; Long may our land be bright With freedom's holy light; Protect us by Thy might, Great God, our King" caused no such stir. At least, it offered me a topic for the daily *Times* and a small bonus from the *Reader's Digest*.

The "Topics of the Times" had been a staple of the editorial page for many years, and *Times* staffers from the office boys (anxious to display their skills and earn twenty-five dollars per column) to senior editors with a hobby to extol or an opinion to ventilate supplied the material. Tom Lask, Charles Simmons, and Nona Balakian were among *Book Review* staffers who also wrote "Topics." In 1969 Herbert Mitgang, a *Times* editor and contributor to the "Topics" column, published a collection of these little essays under the title *America at Random*, which did very well in the bookstores and in critical notices. But the "Topics" were too casual and literary to survive the brisk and trendy ideologies of subsequent managers of the *Times*, and they no longer grace the editorial page.

First to last, my self-propelled, free-lance writing for the *Times* found its way into just about every section of the paper, even including the sports section (when St. Bernard's School in New Jersey attended by our sons won a football game) and the society section (when the son of our Episcopal rector was married). I had a typewriter, and I was determined to use it. Next to "Topics" my most frequent appearances were in the Sunday *Magazine* and the "Last Words" column on the *Book Review's* final page, a weekly feature introduced in the Francis Brown years and continued for some time under John Leonard.

In these two new venues I indulged my interest in history, education, books and authors and the church. "Honors for Dr. Mudd" in the Sunday *Magazine* probably raised a few northern eyebrows. Dr. Samuel Mudd, the Maryland physician sentenced to life imprisonment as one of the conspirators in Lincoln's assassination because he had given medical aid to John Wilkes Booth, was granted a kind of useless amnesty in 1959 when Congress passed a law honoring Mudd. The bill provided for the erection of a memorial tablet commemorating Mudd's service to yellow-fever victims at Fort Jefferson, Florida (where he had been imprisoned), but did not resolve the extent of Mudd's complicity, if any, in Booth's escape.

Writing *South of Appomattox* had focused my attention on such misunderstood heroes as Mudd, and I went on to write a piece for the *National Observer* about Swiss-born and European-educated Dr. Henry Wirz, who was a doctor-planter in Louisiana when the Civil War began. Wirz was in charge of Andersonville prison when Johnston surrendered to Sherman and was arrested and tried as a war criminal. Johnston's surrender to Sherman had insured the return of all officers to their homes, but Wirz was hanged. The Wirz essay, like the "Topic" on S. F. Smith and the defense of Mudd, sparked further interest and publication. It was condensed for a junior high school reading curriculum.

My favorite pieces for the *Times* and for the *Book Review* are the "Last Word" essays. (The one following my retirement was titled "The Guest Word.") The "Last Word" pieces tended to have to do with my love of literature and books themselves. My first was about the day's many religious best-sellers and translations of the Bible. I began, "After the heady and expansive 1950's and 1960's, American religious life and American religious publishing are experiencing what Wall Street would call a 'technical correction.' Church membership gains have slowed; religious book sales and the number of titles published have declined. Why?" My answer, my title, was "Creeping Secularism."

The eightieth anniversary of the *Sewanee Review* (they've now passed their one hundredth) was a subject for a "Last Word" much to my liking. I wrote also about two of the University of Virginia's "writers-in-residence": William Faulkner in the 1950s and the nineteenth-century undergraduate, Edgar Allan Poe. Next it was the first anniversary of the Savannah Beehive Press, founded, owned, and operated by Mills B. Lane IV when he stepped back from Atlanta banking. Mills still publishes handsome, useful and interesting books about his state and region. Among the earliest of the Beehive Press titles were Henry Grady's essays *The New South*, a new edition of Mark Catesby's eighteenth-century *The Natural History of Carolina, Florida, and the Bahamas*, and Louis Milford's *My Sojourn in the Creek Nation*, a Frenchman's narrative of Indian and frontier life.

Another favorite was my essay-review of the six-volume *Religious Trends in English Poetry* by Hoxie Neale Fairchild; it covers English poetry from the eighteenth century to the twentieth (to 1965, I should add, as we approach the twenty-first). Fairchild, according to the *Times Literary Supplement* reviewer with whom I concurred, "takes these poets to pieces less that we may understand them than that we may understand ourselves."

My research into Fairchild's volumes was similar to but much simpler than my forays into the years of *Times* book reviews. I listed in "The Last Word: Beyond 'The Waste Land'" Fairchild's judgment of a dozen or more poets, Blake, Shelley, Coleridge, and so on. Of Hardy, Fairchild wrote, and I quoted, "Strangely, this resolute atheist is constantly talking about God or making God talk about himself," and of Eliot, "One might say that he became a Christian on discovering that he already was one—a very common type of conversion."

A year later one of my "Last Word" pieces was titled "A Meeting South" (the phrase was Sherwood Anderson's) describing the variety of writers having written of or from New Orleans. On the one hand, the idea of the French Quarter, Jackson Square, and the Mississippi took me back to my youthful sojourn there. My one published story was actually set in New Orleans. On the other hand, I had an interest in the writings of fellow Mississippian Elizabeth Spencer, whose latest novel at the time, *The Snare*, took place in New Orleans.

Sherwood Anderson, William Faulkner, Tennessee Williams, and Eudora Welty might be the best known of the set, but John James Audubon, William Thackeray, Mark Twain, Lafcadio Hearn, and Shirley Ann Grau (a Pulitzer winner) were included. "Anything could happen," said Oliver LaFarge (well before Tennessee Williams), "in a town where the signs of the trolleys showed that one line ran to Desire and one to Elysian Fields."

Most of the "Last Word" pieces were written in the 1970s, but I was busy too in the 1960s traveling to Jackson on several occasions to speak at one or another literary festival. Twice, these talks later appeared in print. "A Story to Tell: Agee, Wolfe, Faulkner," delivered to a college literary festival at Millsaps, was published by Bill Hamilton in *The South Atlantic Quarterly*, where my essay-review of Elizabeth Spencer's novels was also printed. Another talk delivered in the Old Capitol (a grand site), at the Mississippi Arts Festival, titled "Truth or Consequences," reviewed the nature of bestsellers and the way in which public opinion is dominated (not always for the better) by critical opinion emanating from the eastern media establishment. Bill published this talk also.

A faculty wife wrote me after my Old Capitol talk that she believed I was just telling "the ladies" (most of my audience) what they wanted to hear. I replied that I hoped she was right, since a missionary always hopes for a receptive audience. My old friend Winifred Green Cheney had been responsible for my invitation to Jackson on that occasion, and in her introductory remarks to my talk, she reminisced pleasantly of old times gone and not forgotten. Among those who stood in line to shake my hand on that day was Jackson physician Dr. Leonard Posey. He then paused and recited William Alexander Percy's "Overtones," which he had learned in my Central High classroom nearly forty years before.

The fine quarterly *Shenandoah*, published by Washington and Lee University, put together a special number on Eudora Welty in 1969. My reminiscence, "Eudora Welty's Jackson," was in company with pieces by Walker Percy, Allen Tate, Martha Graham, Robert Penn Warren, Diarmuid Russell and Reynolds Price. Eudora was delighted and wrote:

> Now here comes *Shenandoah*, and I'm more cheered to read it than I
> can say. You were extra generous about me and extra ungenerous, even
> parsimonious, about yourself when it came to telling it like it was. It
> was very gallant of you to make me out that I was all that smart. It was
> probably the case that I was a terrible prig. . . .

I've often contemplated a sequel to dispel that last notion.

Hubert Creekmore had been part of the thirties group of friends at home
in Jackson and working in New York. Hubert was one of the first that Eudora
would look up in the city; they shared a pair of nieces, for his sister was
married to Eudora's brother. He had gotten review slots for both Eudora
and me in the Creative Age Press magazine *Tomorrow*, owned by a fairly
mystical woman named Eileen Garrett. (The magazine wasn't half bad; one
reviewer wisely called Eudora the "American Isak Dinesen.")

A published poet, Hubert, educated at Ole Miss and Columbia, was also a
novelist and a translator. He had been the first to publish my work, a chapter
of my transcription of Sherwood Bonner's diary, and I started him writing
for the *Book Review* as early as 1947 with Langston Hughes's *Fields of Wonder*.
He reviewed Peter Taylor, Elizabeth Spencer, Carson McCullers, and John
Faulkner's reminiscence *My Brother Bill* in 1963. In many ways, Hubert
was the ideal—his copy was accurate and clean, his opinions distinct.
He never used a book or the subject of a book to exalt himself. The
range of books that Hubert could criticize was as great as that of any
Times reviewer.

It was startling news that, on an afternoon in May 1966, Hubert died of a
heart attack in a taxi on the way to the airport. He was leaving for a vacation
in Spain. As a reviewer he made a scholarly study of each assignment. He
read all the books by the author and the previous reviews. So many were
cut or not published (I was not involved), that Hubert stopped reviewing,
although he did not cease writing. Just before his death, he completed a
serious book with a light title, *Daffodils Are Dangerous: The Poisonous Plants
in Your Garden.*

Eudora, too, was reviewing for the *Book Review* less frequently than in
the forties and fifties. Of course, she was busy with her fiction, but she
was not paid what her finely wrought reviews deserved. And it was often
difficult to steer her literary prose away from unimaginative copy readers and
quarterbacking from the Sunday department. At one point, Brown ordered
all editing cleared with the reviewer, but with the more important writers
such as Eudora, this was a diplomatic task.

Another of our Jackson-in-New York friends was Lehman Engel. A composer, conductor, and writer, he knew everyone in the theater. Back in Jackson when Hubert had started his gallant little *Southern Review* preceding L.S.U.'s prestigious quarterly of the same name (and wherein appeared my Sherwood Bonner), Eudora had begged at the Lehman laundry for ads (and revenue). We all recall the jingle: "When clothes are dirty, Ring seven thirty." A. Lehman, as we called him, was a year behind Eudora and me at Central High, but we met now and again in New York. Eudora was at Columbia with Jackson's Rosa ("Dolly") Wells, younger sister of my longtime friend Calvin Wells, and with Frank Lyell while Lehman studied at Juilliard. Frank wrote home to Jackson regaling his family with stories from the night court melodramas he and Eudora took in on occasion. Eudora dedicated *The Golden Apples* to Frank and Dolly. Whether in New York or back in Jackson, we gathered for card playing, campy photographs, writing at anything we could get.

Eudora kept up with Lehman's career, writing in 1933 for the Jackson *State Tribune* about Lehman's compositions for Martha Graham, the Yaddo Festival of American Music, a Viennese concert, and an opera singer from Budapest. She reviewed Lehman's *Words with Music* for both the *Book Review* and the Jackson *Daily News* in 1972 and advised him on his autobiography a few years later. When we published a favorable review of Lehman's autobiography, he sent me a note: "It's hard to believe that you and I are pointing toward the other end of life."

When Francis Brown retired in 1970, we marked the end of an era, for he had reigned over the *Book Review* for nearly twenty years. During that time, we had tripled the staff, delegated duties, and expanded our readership. I often recall the long-ago Saturday (our day off) that I encountered Brown in the local history room of the New York Public Library, where he was working on his book *A Dartmouth Reader*, and I was tracking down my father's eighteenth-century Virginia and my mother's seventeenth-century Massachusetts forbears. Since I had always been the token southerner in the *Book Review*, expected to speak softly, say "you all" and defend the Lost Cause at the drop of a hat, Brown was greatly amused when I told him I was checking into my Massachusetts Bay Colony relations. As Brown's ancestors had also arrived here on the Winthrop fleet of 1630, I believe our relationship grew noticeably warmer thereafter.

The Brown-induced tranquility and continuity at the *Book Review* seemed to evaporate as subsequent editors came and went with disorienting frequency. Several men were in line and qualified for the job Brown left vacant. Ray Walters, at one time the literary editor of the *Saturday Review of Literature*, had come to the *Times* to assist Brown. But he was passed over at Brown's retirement in favor of John Leonard, a brilliant stylist who had worked for the *National Review* and then the *Book Review* and in 1970 for the daily *Times*. Ray was a bit stung by Leonard's promotion and offered to resign, but he was prevailed upon to stay.

Leonard had left the Sunday *Book Review* for the daily *Times* after a competition (a terrible idea) in which several *Book Review* staffers each were given a chance to write a few daily reviews and the "winner" (Leonard) was given the job. Maybe a few non-*Book Review* Timesmen took part, but most of those competing had already done daily reviews from time to time, and their abilities were well known. It sounds like something A. H. Rosenthal or his alter ego Arthur Gelb might have thought up. Richard Locke (later first editor, briefly, of the revived *Vanity Fair*), Roger Jellinek, Tom Lask, Charles Simmons, and Walter Clemons, as well as Christopher Lehman-Haupt, entered the fray. Later, Lehman-Haupt did move from the *Book Review* to the daily "Books of the Times."

Clemons, a published writer and former Rhodes scholar, was already a skilled editor when he came to West 43rd Street. He wrote reviews for the daily *Times* and interviews for the *Book Review* (one with Eudora) and edited reviews. Clemons was clearly the best of the lot in the competition. When he did not get the job and when Leonard came back to replace Brown, he was faced with a lifetime of previewing books and editing copy for me (he was the world's best). He departed for *Newsweek* in 1971 where he became a senior editor and writer until 1988 when he began freelance writing.

One of my early reviews was of Shelby Foote's first novel *Tournament*, published in 1949, a review that appeared under the pseudonym invented and used by Eudora, "Michael Ravenna." The last review I wrote for the *Book Review* was a long and positive report on the third and final volume of Foote's account of the Civil War. His narrative was one of the longest and best on that conflict and has been a best-seller. That review was an appropriate ending to a career at the *Times* that began with another Civil War best-seller, *The History of Rome Hanks*. That Foote was a fellow Mississippian added to my satisfaction.

I had had the pleasure of meeting Foote when I spoke at a Millsaps literary festival in Jackson. We shared a table at lunch, and I found him congenial. I mentioned a collection of William Faulkner's early New Orleans sketches I had recently reviewed for the Boston *Herald* (their book review editor, in turn, occasionally reviewed for us), and told Foote that Charles Poore, *Times* daily book critic, had said the youthful sketches "showed not a grain of talent." Foote immediately became less congenial. I might as well have questioned the infallibility of the pope to Mother Theresa. I hastily pointed out that I was just quoting. Perhaps my subsequent up-front paean of praise for Foote's Civil War work did something to redeem my faux pas.

All things must end. I had spent thirty years keeping four-letter words (and other enormities) out of the *Book Review*. The first (perhaps only) time that one of those no-no expressions was dropped casually at a staff meeting, I knew the *Book Review* would be next. Adolph Ochs, Arthur Hays Sulzberger, and Lester Markel were dead, and I was reaching retirement age. A few months after my sixty-fifth birthday, I told Leonard it was time. He politely replied, "Well, there are a number of people here I'd rather see retire than you." After some talk, it was agreed I'd stay a while longer.

When the day came, Leonard and the staff gave me an exuberant party at his home. He called me the "last Christian gentleman." Lewis Nichols offered a review of my participation in the *Book Review*:

> Nash has done his work and gone home, avoiding posh lunch places, the scrawling of graffiti on washroom walls and departmental in-fighting. If at any time he has been an office politician, he was so good at it that no one ever knew.
>
> Despite shivering through 29 northern winters, he has remained as much a Southerner as the julep and hush puppies. . . . He has been given to spending family vacation time tracking down family roots, searches which led him—this is a real prank of fate—into dour New England. Family tree watching can be a blight on the entire neighborhood, but not as practiced by this one. This one would glory in Burgers hanging from gallows, and indeed does boast of an ancestor who publicly bit someone, bitee and cause unknown here.
>
> The major preoccupation, as all know, is with words. To those who live on the sunny side of the street, the evil called Copy Reader can be summed up as jerk, meaning butcher. Nash doesn't hack away for the sake of hacking but just to upgrade the product, usually finding a clearer word or two. . . . To the apprentice devils under him, he has seemed slow to anger, soft in correction. One of the sights of the *Book Review* has been that of Nash, glasses perched on the end of his nose, strolling over to an associate to point out where a bit of just edited copy could be improved. Class work in the home room never ended.

Eudora sent a kindly tribute, and a copy of the *Concise Oxford English Dictionary* was thrown in for good measure. The *Times* generously sent salary checks flowing to my new home in Charlottesville for several months even though I had departed and my pension checks were also flowing. *Times* publisher Arthur O. (Punch) Sulzberger sent a note and a set of old-fashioned glasses from Tiffany's etched with the *Times* logo.

Francis Brown, from his retirement in Amherst, Massachusetts, sent a note written with his left hand, as he had learned to do following serious brain surgery:

> I'm sorry for the *Book Review*, but happy for you that you're retiring. Now you can do all those things you have left undone. You can even sit on a Virginia mountain top and do nothing. But you won't. But how the *Book Review* is going to miss your quiet words of wisdom, whether it be on a matter of style or on some scheme that in retrospect was horrendous.

Similar sentiments were voiced by other colleagues. All very fine.

Very early on a spring morning in 1974, I pulled out for the last time from 535 Cathedral Parkway, near the corner of Broadway, where we had been living in our later New York years. My station wagon was packed to the roof with last-minute items I couldn't bear to leave behind. My family was already in Charlottesville, Virginia, and I was headed that way.

I turned south on Broadway toward the Lincoln Tunnel, seventy blocks away, feeling both jubilation at my release from the workaday world and a bit of melancholy at leaving the scene of so many years that (despite a few pot holes here and there) had been pleasurable and satisfying. As I drove, I caught sight of St. Ignatius Church in the Eighties, where I had talked with Wystan Auden and so often worshipped, and only a few blocks farther on, the little park at 72nd Street, once pleasant enough, now so notorious as a meeting place for drug users and sellers it was known as Needle Park.

So on by Lincoln Center, that grandiose example of modern architecture, ostentatious outside and in, its opera house lacking the warmth and people-friendly welcome of the old Metropolitan it had replaced. There had been streetcars on Broadway when we arrived in New York. Now there were only buses, belching smoke and fumes, swerving unaccountably from midstreet to curbside and back again, impeding traffic, forcing pedestrians to dodge and scramble.

On to 42nd Street where the *Times*'s 1904 move from lower Manhattan had caused Longacre Square to become Times Square. The original *Times* building, with its neo-Gothic trim and upthrust tower, the traffic current flowing on each side, always had to me the appearance of a castle on the

Rhine (an appearance that must have pleased Adolph Ochs). I had a last brief glimpse of the vast Times annex on 43rd Street, where the editorial operations and much of the weekday publishing were centered. An area once vibrant with theaters, upscale hotels and fine restaurants, it was now grimy and rundown, littered with X-rated movies, hot-dog stands, drug dealers and human flotsam of all kinds.

Weaving through the early morning maze of cars, pedestrians, trucks and buses, I ruminated over events of past and present. A glimpse of the Empire State Building to my left just below 42nd Street reminded me of the humid afternoon in the summer of 1945 when I was standing on Fifth Avenue just a block or two from that building and a low-flying military plane hit the seventy-eighth floor, making the ground beneath my feet shake (so it seemed). Fragments of the plane and building fell all around, much of the plane remaining impaled inside. I knew that my Jackson friend Dolly Wells worked in the Empire State, and I was concerned until I realized that it was the weekend and she was probably safe at home.

By now I had missed the turnoff to the Lincoln Tunnel (as my subconscious had probably planned all along) and was passing the intersection where another great newspaper was memorialized (Herald Square) and where those vast, many-storied bazaars, Macy's and Gimbel's, supplied (as I well knew) anything you might desire at prices often less than you would pay in Virginia or Mississippi.

Memories welling, I detoured a bit below 14th Street for a look at Washington Square, where the Robert van Gelders had lived and entertained us (and where I delivered more than one of Marjorie's Mississippi pecan pies by subway from Morningside Heights). Henry James and Edith Wharton had known that north side of the square, and Dreiser had written *An American Tragedy* across the way, where Stephen Crane, Willa Cather and John Dos Passos had lived as well.

Maneuvering now in increasing traffic and the maze of one-way streets, I managed to see Patchin Place off West 10th, where E. E. Cummings, Eugene O'Neill, and an impecunious, future English poet laureate, John Masefield (when not scrubbing floors in a saloon on Greenwich Avenue), had lived and written. And I noted Chumley's on Bedford Street, that 1920s speakeasy now legitimate, where Hemingway, Faulkner, Salinger, and Simone de Beauvoir, among many others, had refreshed body and soul.

SoHo had become the name for the part of Manhattan below Houston Street (the name of that Texas city pronounced in a way no Texan would recognize), but Tribeca (the triangle below Canal Street) had not yet been invented. Canal Street had once been a real canal though, and Wall Street possessed a wall, built by Governor Stuyvesant in 1683 to protect the little town from invaders. And there was a British fort at the Battery on the island's southern tip to repel seaborne marauders.

More than once a *Book Review* staffer and I had spent a long lunch hour travelling from 43rd Street to Fraunces Tavern at Pearl and Broad, where a black man, Samuel Fraunces, had opened his Queen's Head Tavern in 1762 and Washington had bade farewell to his officers in 1783.

And so to the Staten Island ferry and the magnificent view of the Manhattan skyline (not to mention Brooklyn Heights across the bay, where Truman Capote, Norman Mailer, Carson McCullers, Gypsy Rose Lee and a host of others had found shelter—including that Thomas Wolfe who told us you can't go home again, which I was in the process of doing). On the ferry ride and the drive across Staten Island to the Outerbridge crossing, the New Jersey Turnpike and Virginia, memories of my thirty years continued to well into my consciousness.

I remembered an incident from my first Christmas Eve at the *Times*. The day had been a mixture of some work but mostly holiday festivities in the various departments. By afternoon the *Book Review* offices were empty except for me, the staff having departed for the Sunday department party two floors below. I was finishing up a little work in no hurry to party, wanting to be sure there were sufficient others on hand to guarantee me (still a newcomer) a few familiar and friendly faces.

As I eventually headed for the door, I noticed a pleasant-appearing, rather handsome man I did not recognize standing there, looking around at the empty office. He seemed about to turn away as I approached, but he paused, reached out his hand and said, "Happy holidays." I appreciated this gesture from a stranger and returned the greeting. As I soon discovered at the Sunday department gathering, my friendly encounter was with *Times* publisher Arthur Hays Sulzberger.

And as I learned over the years, it was characteristic of the familial, paternalistic atmosphere of the *Times* of that era. There was never any doubt whose paper it was; it was the Ochs-Sulzberger paper, but consideration for those who worked there was evident in many ways. The *Times* was frequently more generous in its financial relations with employees than the letter of the law in their Newspaper Guild contract required. The very existence of a labor contract, the occasional strike and threat of strikes distressed Sulzberger and, as Turner Catledge has recalled, "The great strike of 1962-63 nearly broke his heart."

Confrontation was not the Sulzberger style, nor the style of those old timers who got out the nation's finest newspaper in those early postwar years. "Happy holidays," the publisher had said to me, and that's what those thirty years had been. They were years of doing what I had always most enjoyed, reading and writing, and in a vibrant and colorful city, a city still a livable meld of neighborhoods, communities and cultures.

Happy holidays.

Afterword

Any memoirist worth his salt pauses at the end of his narrative, looks back over his prose and pens an afterword or summary, seeking to find meaning in his movement through time and space. Riffling through the pages of my own wandering tale, the notes, writings and recollections on which it is based, I became aware that my afterword had already been written—twenty years ago, well before my memoir. It consisted of the words Eudora had sent to New York in 1974 that were read at John Leonard's house on the occasion of my retirement from the Times*—better written, of course, than I could have managed (and more flattering than I would have dared). "Might I use this as an afterword?" I asked her. "Of course," she replied. "I would be honored." (There is no doubt who is really being honored.) So here, my afterword.*

"Nash K. Burger Jr. of Jackson, Miss."
by Eudora Welty

Nash and I grew up in the same town and in the same years; we were in the same grade and often the same room all the way through school. In those days the honor roll of the public schools in Jackson was considered news and was carried in full in both daily newspapers. Better than that, every boy and girl on the honor roll won a free summer pass to the ballgame. Nash and I would both end up in the grandstand, so we'd average just about the same—anywhere you like between 95 and 100. If he'd beat me on scholastic grades, I might beat him in deportment (prig that I was?), and of course we made the same 100 in attendance. Our set hadn't thought of dropping out. Of Davis School? You couldn't even have left the classroom without a written excuse from home, and then you'd still have to get past Miss Duling in the

178

principal's office. You couldn't. Miss Lorena Duling would freeze you, maybe kill you, with the look of her eye. She'd have stared down a dropout the way Saint Peter would if he caught one trying to get out of the gates of Heaven.

Nash's own abiding wish, of course, was just the opposite. He was hell-bent to keep on learning. I've had time to find out—I've known Nash all my life—that he may have been our class's earliest, perhaps only, real scholar. Being deft and witty, he managed to keep the rest of us, so busy laughing, from guessing his seriousness too early, say the 4th grade.

In our Davis School days, Jackson didn't spread out very far, and somehow that small size gave us more scope. Nash's house (it had once been in the family of L. Q. C. Lamar) was just a block from Capitol Street, mine only two blocks on the other side of the New Capitol, with Davis School right across the street from our front yard. We were both within a child's walking distance of everything—school, the library, the ice cream parlor, the grocery store, the two movie houses, Smith Park. On summer nights there were band concerts in Smith Park, and whole families—Nash's and mine included—would stroll there after supper and listen, and let the children dream in the swings, run up the seesaws, climb the statues, and drink lemonade while the band played selections from *William Tell*.

Without the exact approval of home, we children made free of the nearby State Capitol too—riding our bicycles down the steep terraces or the long flights of steps, flying our kites or playing ball on the lawns. We'd skate through the Capitol, skimming over the marble floors (very desirable echoes in the rotunda) and rounding a circle in the Hall of Fame, in the center of which, for an unknown reason, was exhibited an Indian mummy in a glass case. It's about the only inaccessible thing I can think of in Jackson, and it was a fake.

Nash was a movie-goer, State Fair goer, Chautauqua goer, Century Theatre goer, church goer, library goer, school goer. I never have yet received the impression that Nash would ever want to stop going to a one of these. In Jackson he grew up a part of every good crowd.

Everybody went downtown on the night of an election to watch the returns come in; these would be thrown on a screen outside the newspaper office above the street. The whole of Capitol Street below would be swarming. I remember one such night when my mother spotted Nash out in front of the crowd. There he stood, in the knee pants and long black stockings the boys wore then, and I think a baseball cap on backwards; at ease, his eye cocked on the screen, and all the while spinning a school tablet on the end of his finger—like a juggler with a platter. My mother said, "That's the boy with the brightest mind in your class." I think she must have spotted the tablet spinning for what it was—philosophical detachment.

High school gave us the chance to see what Nash could do with writing. In English class, he varied the monotony furnished by the rest of us by writing his book reports on imaginary books by imaginary authors. For the school paper, the *Jackson Hi-Life*, and the annual—he was of course on the staff of both every year—he would come out with some fine parody—of boy's books, westerns, sentimental novels of the day—the same thing Corey Ford did a little later on. He was a satirist at 16. No, 14? Both at work and play. I remember the Junior Jupiter Juvenile Detective Agency, which took up a page in our annual; Nash was its founder and the president. They even wore badges—ordered off for, Nash told me, in bulk, from the back pages of a church publication called "Kind Words."

Ours was a small class—we'd been picked to graduate a year early, for some special reason—and we all knew one another well, having been together after all since we were six years old. We all knew what each other was doing and what each other was reading. When I signed the card to take a book out of the Carnegie Library, I'd invariably see the signature of Nash K. Burger Jr. a line or two above—he'd beat me to it. And what else had he beat me to? I think now that he may have been the only one in our fairly smart class who had developed any real taste in books by the time we went off to college.

In wayward fashion, over the next four years, letters traveled back and forth between Nash and me—his from Sewanee, the University of Virginia, from Jackson or even from France, where he rode his bicycle over it one summer; mine from Mississippi State College for Women, the University of Wisconsin or Columbia. This didn't mean a letter from Nash wasn't likely to begin, "Your letter has finally reached me after being forwarded over all the islands in the South Pacific. We are on the return leg of a huge horseshoe which takes in the entire southeastern archipelago, on the good ship Uncle Ben." He could also give me gentle warnings about my false starts: "When I find a college student who does not agree with everything the *American Mercury* and James Branch Cabell have ever said, I intend to take up my bed and walk." He put me onto Sherwood Anderson, so I came to *Winesburg, Ohio*, but he also told me to read Joseph Hergesheimer, Joseph Hergesheimer, Joseph Hergesheimer, so repeatedly that I wouldn't then and haven't yet.

Nash edited something everywhere he went. It was *The Mountain Goat* at Sewanee, I recall, and back in Jackson he started, from Millsaps, a statewide college literary magazine, open to every college both white and black, called *Hoi Polloi*, which must have been a first. In the 1930's, same as now, Jackson had no good newspaper, and after graduation, which threw us all out into the Depression with no likely jobs in sight, Nash and another classmate, Ralph Hilton, saw no reason why that wasn't as good a time as any to start a paper of their own. Somehow they got hold of some space up over a store on a side street, a few rickety tables and a second-hand typewriter or two, and went at it. Nash and Ralph covered the news and wrote the editorials—sample subject: Prohibition; I was thrilled to be assigned the book reviews, and can recall turning one in written in heroic couplets. Up under that flat, hot tin roof, it was like working inside a popcorn popper. We survived briefly, even if we never put the notorious Fred Sullens and the *Daily News* out of business. (Ralph went on to the Associated Press and upwards.) Our Ole Miss-Yale graduate, Hubert Creekmore, started his own, earlier, *Southern Review* somewhere along then, too, to which Nash contributed a fine article and for which I aided Hubert in getting ads and reading proof. When we had to quit, we dumped all the copies we had left, with a short bridge-side ceremony, into the Pearl River. Hubert said they should at least be rare.

It was the unusual visitor that ever came through these parts in those days—we were a little off the beaten path. But Henry Miller was unusual. Fresh home from Paris, he was going to drive himself across the continent in an auto made entirely of glass, to see what his impressions of America might be. Along his way, Doubleday alerted their authors to take him in and help him in gathering information for the forthcoming book, which was to be called *The Air-Conditioned Nightmare*. I was now an author and Jackson was on his route, but my mother put her foot down. It wasn't that she gave a hoot what Henry Miller wrote in his books; where he'd made his mistake with her was in writing a letter to me. He offered, a little earlier, to put me in touch with an unfailing pornographic market that I could write for if I needed the money. It could have been a stranger's idea of a charitable suggestion to the author of a first book of short stories, but my mother didn't see the suggestion as charity. (I didn't either, I confess—I was ashamed of him.) "Well, he needn't expect to be invited into my house," said my mother, and of course neither would she have countenanced my begging off by saying I had to be out of town: that would be telling him a lie.

A good thing I knew whom to call on: Nash. Thereupon Nash, and Hubert Creekmore too, and I settled Henry Miller in the car and kept moving. (When he showed up, he wasn't in the glass car or any kind of car at all, so we used my family Chevrolet.) We showed him Vicksburg, Port Gibson, Natchez, the ruins of Windsor, the Mississippi River. Nash, who had in his command all the fact and history and lore Mr. Miller might have ever needed to gather, offered him tidbits now and then, while Hubert put knowledgeable questions to him about his work, and I drove. All of it, and our landscape, seemed to leave him imperturbable, though no less imperturbable than Henry Miller left Nash. I only remember that he stayed three days and never did take off his hat—even while we were having our picnic lunches. Was he really looking? We took him to the same place to eat every night—the best we could afford—and he thought it was three different steak houses.

When Robert van Gelder began editing the *Times Book Review*, he changed the old pattern of using the same reviewers over and over till they wore out, by inviting some brand new names. Nash's debut (from Jackson, where he was by then a schoolmaster, and the husband of one of his ex-pupils) was a review that delighted Mr. van Gelder so that he popped it right onto the front page. When it came under Mr. Markel's eye, it's told, he phoned Mr. van Gelder and demanded to know who in hell was Nash K. Burger Jr. "Nash K. Burger Jr.," Mr. van Gelder replied, "is the author of the book review we are using on page one."

In 1969, Nash came down to Jackson to make a speech at the Mississippi Arts Festival, which he delivered in the historic House of Representatives in the Old Capitol. It was a beauty, and here is a bit of it, which says something in the best way I know of, his own words, about Nash as the child and as the man:

> . . . It was early on a chilly morning in November, 1918, that I went out on the front porch of the house where we were living, just down the hill from the Old Capitol, to gather up the *Clarion-Ledger* and see how World War I was going; like most small boys I was excited by the war. I was elated to learn from the headlines on the paper that the war was over. Our side had won. Having taken this amazing news and the paper to my parents, I dressed quickly and scampered up the Amite Street hill to the corner of Capitol and State, where a few other early risers were also beginning to appear.
>
> On the grounds just in front of the Old Capitol . . . in a ramshackle scaffolding hung the historic antebellum Jackson fire bell that had escaped

the Federal intervention of 1861–1865. Dancing about with excitement, I noticed the old bell and decided it should peal forth the good news. I dashed across to attend to this, but found the bell lacking a rope. Somewhere I found a piece of rope, clambered up the scaffold, tied the rope to the clapper and started hanking away, sending clanging sounds far and wide and alerting any citizens not already aware of it that the war was over. I continued banging for some time, receiving stares, smiles and jocular remarks from passers-by, until my arm got a little tired, I began to think of breakfast and that it was approaching time to be at Davis School. About this time an ancient colored woman known as Aunt Nancy, who could tell fortunes and work other marvels, and was well known to almost all of Jackson's fifteen or twenty thousand inhabitants, appeared on the scene. She asked if she could ring the bell a while. I was ready to call it a day anyway, so turned over my job to her and hurried home.

Now we approach the point of this rather lengthy remembrance of things past. The next day in the *Clarion-Ledger* there was a long and glowing account of the zeal of Aunt Nancy, this fine, old-time colored woman who had patriotically appeared at the Old Capitol early on the morning of Armistice Day and despite her age and obvious infirmity had continued for several hours to sound the old fire bell in celebration of the historic event. Moreover, the article informed us, appreciative Jackson citizens had stopped to press nickels, dimes, quarters, halves, even a few dollar bills on Aunt Nancy as a reward for her enterprise. No mention of me, of my scrounging rope for the clapper, of my long hour or so of banging (my arm was still sore from the effort) and, of course, no financial reward.

So it was that I first learned—and this is the point, so long delayed, of my story—of the gap between the printed word and the facts of life, between what we call truth and the way a writer, either deliberately for a planned effect, or innocently out of ignorance, distorts reality. Having been raised to believe in the inerrancy of the King James Bible and the Book of Common Prayer, I was startled to discover at the age of 10 that this inerrancy did not extend to all that was printed. In subsequent years I have come to realize even more just how wide this gap between the facts of life and the printed word can be, whether in newspapers or books—to say nothing of reviews of books.

And so on. It's a mind both clear and wise, responsive and reflective, that has yet to be amazed for the first time at the human comedy around him. Just as always, and of course from now on too.

What will he do at this point? Teach at the University of Virginia, or just enroll—or should I have put it the other way. Grow figs? Re-read *Quiet Cities* by Joseph Hergesheimer? He won't stop living with books, whatever he does—he'll write or edit or publish. Nash used to say off and on that one day he'd have a press of his own. He even said once he might let me design the type. Well, for my part, I'd be willing to learn, if we could some day still carry that out.

Index

Cummings, E. E., 175
Curwood, James Oliver, 23

Daily Telegraph, 138
Dallas, Tx., 95, 111–12
Darwin, Charles, 153
Davidson, Grace, 40
Davis, Burke, 137
Davis, Jefferson, 164
Davis School, 5, 17–21, 18, 19, 20, 21, 32, 37, 43, 178, 179
Davis, William Stearns, 36
de Beauvoir, Simone, 175
de Lion, Richard Coeur, 83
Dickens, Byrom, 73, 74, 77
Dickson, Harris, 40
Dinesen, Isak, 170
Dixon, Thomas, 60, 154
Dos Passos, John, 175
Dreiser, Theodore, 152, 175
DuBois, William, 128, 129, 132, 133, 146
Duffus, R. L., 147
Dugan, Arthur, 45
Duling, Lorena, 19–20, 27, 32, 178–79
Durant, Will, 64

Eddy, Clara Emily Kelley, 4
Eddy, Frederick Abijah, 3, 4
Eddy, John, 3
Eddy, Mary Baker, 4
Eddy, Nell, 4
Eddy, Peter, 129
Eddy, William, 110
Edwards Hotel, 43
Edwards House, 42
Eliot, T. S., 4, 83, 107, 153, 168
Elliott, Bishop Stephen, 67
Empey, Arthur Guy, 34
Engel, Ellis, 43
Engel, Lehman, 43, 104, 124, 157, 171

Episcopal Diocese of Mississippi, 40, 120
Eyrich, Albert, 15–16, 22
Eyrich, George C., 15
Eyrich, Gladys, 15–16, 21, 102, 157

Fairbanks, George R., 67
Fairchild, Hoxie Neale, 168
Farley, Walter, 129
Farrell, James, 83
Faulkner, John, 170
Faulkner, William, 12, 59, 83, 118, 139–40, 153, 155, 160, 168, 169, 172–73, 175
Federal Writers' Project, 118, 126
Felleman, Hazel, 133
Fincastle, Va., 3, 6
Finney, Benjamin, 69–70
Fitzgerald, F. Scott, 53
Flaubert, Gustave, 82
Flecker, James Elroy, 53–54
Flye, Rev. James Harold, 62
Foote, Shelby, 172–73
Forrest, Nathan Bedford, 164
Forster, E. M., 153, 161
Fraser, J. G., 153
Freneau, Philip, 164–65
Freud, Sigmund, 153
Frost, Robert, 139
Fry, T. Penrose, 95

Gabriel, Gilbert, 129
Galsworthy, John, 99, 107
Gannett, Lewis, 162
Garrett, Eileen, 170
Gascony, France, 87
Gelb, Arthur, 172
George Peabody College for Teachers, 108
Gissing, George, 88, 157, 158
Glueck, Grace, 149–50
Gordon, Armistead, 98, 102, 110
Gordon, Caroline, 129
Grady, Henry, 168

LaFarge, Oliver, 169
Lamar Life Insurance Company, 5, 28
Lamar, L. Q. C., 63, 164
Lambert, Peter William, Jr., 70–71,
  72, 74, 75, 77, 78–79, 81, 83, 86,
  89, 101, 116, 141
Landis, Robert James, 103–04, 165
Lane, Mills B., IV, 168
Lanier, Sidney, 99
Lask, Thomas, 138, 146, 167, 172
Lawrence, D. H., 161
Le Havre, France, 81, 89
Lee, Gypsy Rose, 176
Lee, Robert E., 23, 164
Leftwich, Elgie, 6, 44, 45, 46
Leftwich, Frank, 44, 45, 46, 53
Leftwich, George J., 4, 6, 13–14, 44,
  45, 49, 53, 104
Leftwich, George, Jr., 44
Leftwich, Jabez, 4
Leftwich, William Groom, 44
Lehman-Haupt, Christopher, 172
Leonard, John, 147, 151, 172, 173,
  178
Lester, Annie, 106
Lewis, C. S., 97
Lewis, Sinclair, 60, 83, 107
Liberty, N. Y., 70
Liebman, Joshua L., 157
Lightcap, N. Pugh, 40
Locke, Richard, 172
Loire Valley, France, 86
London, Jack, 23
London *Times Literary Supplement*,
  138
Long, Tudor Seymour, 75–76
Longfellow, Henry W., 109
Longstreet, James, 164
Lyell, Frank, 29, 43, 104, 118, 121,
  124, 140–41, 159, 171
Lyons, Herbert, 146, 147

Macdonald, George, 18
Maclachlan, John, 62

Mailer, Norman, 176
Malden, Mass., 31, 32
Markel, Lester, 128, 130, 131, 135,
  138, 142, 145, 146, 164, 173, 182
Martin, Abbott, 68–69, 70, 74–76,
  77, 78, 97–98
Marx, Karl, 153
Mary Washington College, 102
Masefield, John, 99, 175
Massachusetts Bay Colony, 3
Maugham, Somerset, 139, 153
Maupassant, Guy de, 82
Maurois, André, 88
Maury, Matthew F., 164
May, E. A., 14
McBryde, John, 94
McClure, John, 101–02
McCullers, Carson, 170, 176
McDowell, Lillian, 110
McWillie, Mrs., 18
Memphis *Commercial Appeal*, 135
Mencken, H. L., 152
Meredith, George, 161
Merz, Charles, 131, 165
Milford, Louis, 168
Millay, Edna St. Vincent, 155
Miller, Henry, 139, 181–82
Miller-Smith Hosiery Company, 50,
  80
Mills, A. J., 72
Millsaps College, 58, 59–60, 62, 109,
  121, 145
Mississippi Department of Archives
  and History, 104, 120
Mississippi Historical Society, 45
Mississippi State College for Women,
  102
Mitgang, Herbert, 167
Moore, Clement Clarke, 129, 166
Moore, Ross, 59
Morgan, John, 72
Mountain Goat, 77, 79
Mudd, Samuel, 167
Mullen, Dale, 120